# PRESSURE

The Autobiography of A Real
Miami OG "Gigaveli"

## KEITH HUNTER

ISBN: 978-0-578-92795-4

Printed by Power Of Purpose Publishing
www.PopPublishing.com
Atlanta, Ga. 30326

# CONTENTS

# INTRODUCTION

I remember being told By Real "OG "Young Thug that Pressure busts pipes, but it also makes Diamonds. We all come into this world by Pressure. Our moms are told during birth to push, push, then the Pressure brings us in. But for so many of our young people growing up in the inter city, the Pressure never lets up, until it either busts the pipe or they learn a way to release it on their own. This book tells the true story of how I learned through my struggles in and out the system to release the pressures in my life.

# DEDICATION

All praise is due to Allah for blessing me with this message to all my real ones coming up under pressure of life in the ghetto we call hoods. I want to dedicate this book to my mom, Naomi Hunter my number one supporter. I'd like to honor my big brother Greg, may he rest in peace.

My big Ma Naya, who was a blessing to everyone she touched with her heavenly hands as a midwife. To my beautiful daughter Kevia, thanks for Zion.

A special honor and remembrance to my grandma Reed and my granddaddy Joe Hunter. With this book I'm hoping to send out love ,prosperity ,success, motivation, inspiration, and good energy to all my Hunters' and Parkers' family members. Breaking all generational curses of incarceration, young deaths, drug abuse and dysfunctional family units.

To all my Muslim brothers "as Salam alkum lakum".

To all my real OG's still on lock in the system state and federal this book is the beginning of the brand that represents the message that we stand on. Long live the Real "G-Code".

PEACE AND LOVE TO EVERYBODY THAT WAS APART OF THESE PAGES OF MY LIFE AND FOR THOSE THAT ARE STILL ON THIS JOURNEY WITH ME. IT GETS GREATER LATER.

CHAPTER 1

# **Fatherless Pressure**

Little Pig. November 1, 1974. The night I was born. The way my mom told me about my birth was that her labor began on Halloween night. So if you believe in omens, I guess that would've been a sign of how bad a boy I would be. If that wasn't dark enough, the way she came up with my name sure was. But first, you would have to understand my mom.

Everybody that knew my mom would tell you that she was a "real full-time Christian lady". So it was right up her alley to use a story out of the Bible to help her name me. Somebody had left a copy of the Miami Times newspaper in her room and she went to the back where the obituaries were printed. There was the name of a black baby boy. So like the story of Jesus raising the dead boy to life in the gospel of St. John, I would be her Lazarus.

I don't know if Pig had any say in the matter. But knowing my mom, it wouldn't have mattered either way. Pig being him, gave me my first nickname: "Hot Shot." Yeah, just like the name of the "roach spray". See back then my pop was strung out on that heroin, better known as *dog food* or *Boy*. And hotshot was a deadly dose of pure heroin. So even if my mom had a hard time believing it, she gave birth to a bad ass little boy. Pig knew I was the real deal. I don't know that much about my pop other than the small memories I had as a kid. I would pick up bits and pieces from others later on in life. But as far back as I could go, he seemed to have been a "real street dude". I remember the respect me and my mom would receive from everybody whenever we were in the hood. The OGs of the hood would always tell me how much I looked like Pig and some even went as far as "breaking me off with the money". I had credit in all the stores in the hood. Shout out to Willie and Clara on 46$^{th}$ and 21$^{st}$ Ave, Miss Jackie on 41$^{st,}$ and 21$^{st}$ Ave in Brown Sub aka "The Sub". Yeah, as a shorty, I had the run of the hood.

I had family up the hill and even more down the hill. My Pop's people were "the Hunters", they were all mechanics. My Granddaddy Joe Hunter had a "Mom & Pop store" that he ran with my Uncle Zek. He also had an auto shop in the hood. I used to love going around my grandparent's house because it was like a young boy's heaven [There was always something to get into]. I mean there was the big fishing boat in the yard. I always had fun playing Captain in it. There were all kinds of tools and other junk to experiment with. Not to mention the swing set and all the other toys that my cousins had left. I forgot to mention all of them. Well let's see; there's my older cousin Tasha. She was like the underboss of all the kids. She was in charge when no adult was around, sometimes even when an adult is around. I can't leave out how pretty she is; "I've always been proud to say she was my cousin." Next in line is my cousin Felicia. "That's my girl right there." Felicia and I were so much alike, neither of us could talk straight. What I mean by that is, for some reason, we both couldn't pronounce *sh* words because we were what people called tight tongue. [Whatever that meant.] I didn't care either way, just as long as you understood what the hell I was trying to say.

Then there were     my cousins Kendrick and Lil Tony by my aunt Joanna Wright. "They had money." That was the first impression I had of them. Man, I could write an entire book about them. My Aunt changed my cousin's name from Deman to Tony. His brother, on the other hand, was     my dawg. I looked up to him coming up. Cousin was cool, a real street dude. They called him Double-0-7 ... "Yeah, just like

James Bond." I thought it fit him to a tee because he was always into something trying to get money. He was like his daddy in a lot of ways.

And then we had my little cousins. My Auntie Greta's three boys worshipped me. I was their big cousin. "Man, if you thought      I was bad. Then you should've met them. Those three were something else altogether." For real it was mostly the two oldest, Ivan and Jelani. The youngest one, Philip was too much into eating to get into any trouble. All he cared about was when his next meal was coming. My aunt used to find wrappers all over the house. Last but not least, there was my brother Ace. He would show up over at my grandparent's house all mad looking like he didn't want to be around me or the rest of the Hunters. I don't know which one it was? It was cool with me either way because I was used to being by myself anyway.

As far back as I can remember, I was always hustling in one way or another. So, most of the time I spent around my grandparent's house. I was taking advantage of all the free toys and food that was always there. I used to love when all of us kids would be there. And my grandma Reed used to pull out the ice-cream maker to make ice-cream and bake a cake. You could always count on some fish being fried.

Before I go on with the story, I have to share this part with you. Growing up, I didn't have many toys. So whenever I would go around my grandparent's house, there was always plenty of toys laying around in the front yard. Most belonged to my aunt Greta's boys. So this one time I told myself I was going to steal some to take home with me. My grandparent's house had a screen in the porch and the yard was out front. So that day, everybody was sitting on the porch when I made my move to go home for the day.

I remember it just like it was yesterday. I said all my goodbyes. I had already worked all the toys I was stealing across the street. "Oh yeah!", I forgot to mention that Earlington Heights elementary school was across the street. [I went there for kindergarten.] Well, the teacher's parking lot was right in front of my grandparent's house. Of course there was literally nowhere to hide anything in the empty parking lot but you couldn't tell me that. My plan was to put everything behind the little stone parking markers. Clearly, I hadn't fully planned this caper. I remember looking back seeing my whole family staring at me. I was so embarrassed for getting caught in the act. It took a while before I had the nerve to show my face    back around there.

*　*　*

Growing up as Lil Pig in those days was a constant hustle, and I was born for it. Hustling came easy for me. No one had to show me how to get money. My Aunt Evelyn was the candy lady. She sold; frozen cups, pops, and candy, so money was always coming through there. I just had to think of a way to get me some of it. I found a weak spot in the business.

See, the porch was not connected right onto the old style house that was set up on bricks. There was a little gap between the steps that led up into the front door. It was just big enough to let change fall out of the little kid's hands. I would make it seem like an accident. Then all I had to do was crawl under the house and collect my check. A typical day for me always involved multiple money crawls. I know it sounds "low down", but what else could I do, when all my mom used to do was drop me off with couple cans of Campbell Soup. Maybe if I was lucky she would give me a dollar. You had to fend for yourself over my aunt Evelyn's house. She was the candy lady to *everybody*, even family had to pay to eat at her house. I didn't have a problem with that because I always had money. She knew all about me going under the house for those dropped coins. When she knew I was going down there, she would be waiting on her cut. She was one of the first people to tell me things about my daddy Pig. None of which was good!

She would say things like, "You not going to be nothing but a dope head, just like Pig." She always chastised me claiming that all I wanted to do was run the streets. Whenever I would be gone for too long she would have something to say. She didn't want me to hang out at the corner store. Thinking back now from this prison cell, I hate to say it, but she was right in some ways. I did come to prison and I was on drugs. The one place my daddy's reputation didn't follow me to; was school. I messed that up on my own.

To me, school was my personal stage. I was a rising star. While everybody else was learning and listening to the teacher, I was busy trying to impress girls. That's how I flunked the first grade. I was always in the Principal's office. If it wasn't for fighting, it was for talking back at my teacher, or something worse "You name it, I did it all!". My mom stayed at the school so much, that they offered her a job as a "teacher's aide". [We both knew they were     just tired of calling her to deal with me.] It was a gift and a curse. In one way, my mom was so cool and could dress her ass off. All the little girls used to compliment her on how good she looked, and in return kick it with me. But that also meant I had to start paying attention in class. The funny thing was, when I wanted to learn, I was actually smart. It just takes me a little longer to catch on to things. But with the watchful eyes of my mom.

I was able to pass through the rest of my elementary years. It was those early years that brought about my first name change. See, I was an early starter when it came to girls. I was always getting into trouble for either kissing some little girl or feeling on another one. So with me being into girls like I was, I always tried to meet a new girlfriend. I had some bad experiences introducing myself as Lil Pig. To little girls that name was a major turn off.

I could remember some of the feedback I would get when I told them my name. Most would say "Ugh!" Some would just straight up laugh in my face, and make a pig squawk, oink, oink." I knew then that I would have to come up with a cooler name. Little Pig just wouldn't do. It was alright for the hood, but in the real world of high school it wouldn't cut it. I needed a name that the girls would be attracted to. My dilemma was solved by a trip to the movies.

I went to see Purple Rain. [No, I wasn't about to start calling myself Prince.] There was another lead actor that had the right kind of swag and his name fit me well: *Mr. Gigolo*. The way I saw him handle women onscreen inspired me to want to be called Gigolo. And all I had to do was replace the "P" off Pig with a "G." So the first thing I did was make a trip to the USA Flea Market on 79th Street in Miami. I bought me a Gucci sweater and had Gigolo put on the back of it. I wore that sweater at least three days a week to school no matter how hot it was. I was becoming Gigolo and too cool to care.

With my charisma and charm, it wasn't too long before I had all the girls calling me Gigolo. My reputation started growing fast. I took pride in how I dressed and looked. Watching "Morris Day" do his thing in Purple Rain really had an effect on me. It was nice to get so much attention from the girls, but you already know it didn't sit well with the guys. It seemed like every day when I went to school, I was having to fight a different dude because his girl liked me. What a lot of guys didn't know was that I'm a real fighter.

I came up with the word "fighting", but they would find out about me the hard way. After I whooped a few of them they stopped wanting to fight me one on one. So, they started jumping me. That only made the girls want to fight harder for me. With the girls coming to my aid, it only boosted my rep! That was something big to have [a bunch of girls willing to fight on your behalf]. Man, during those days you couldn't tell me nothing. I was the shit and I knew it. "Morris Day" would've been so proud of me.

Around the time I was six, we moved out the Sub. Me and my mom left my grandparent's house. My Pop Pig was paralyzed and in a wheelchair. How he became paralyzed would remain a mystery for the rest of my life. I heard all kinds and versions of the story. Some say he robbed some guys for some money and dope. The guy that got robbed retaliated by cutting Pig's brake line on his car resulting in a bad car crash. Pig could no longer take care of his family because he now needed somebody to take care of him. Nevertheless, that's a whole other story in itself.

The move to the new hood came with a new opportunity for my hustle game. We moved right in the heart of Liberty. As a matter of fact, this bossed up dope boy from back in the day named Big Ike converted a movie theater into a night club called "The Heart of the City!". We stayed right around the corner from it. Our new address was 81st 21

Avenue. We had 7 East on the front end. 27th on the side, 22nd on the other side. That became my hustle ground. I would pump gas at the Shell station after school. If that wasn't jumping fast enough, I would cross the street to Earle Supermarket and bag groceries. When most boys my age was on their way to little league football practice. I was on my way to grind. I guess they got a thrill out of playing sports. Up to this point in my life, I was mostly a loner. It wasn't that I had a problem making friends or anything, it was just that kids my age were busy playing. Once I got into school, and needed presentable clothes, things changed.

My Mama had learned from my grandma about the second-hand store where they sold used clothes. That became her go-to store. Well, I had different plans. That's what led me to start my little hustle crew. It was Tony, Johnny, Mike, and me. They were my friends. We had a lot of fights with the winner changing by the day, but we mostly got money.

The area we lived in was made for a young hustle. We had so many ways to get money all around us. And leave it up to me to find them all. We were in to everything, except pimping and selling drugs even though that was the environment that we existed in. We stayed right around the corner from 79th Street, one of the busiest hoe strolls in Miami. Every day I would come up with a master plan to put some money in our pocket. Whether we were stealing plants and nice flowers from yards to resell or collecting cans and bottles for the recycling place in the hood we were on it. I remember pushing my buggy down to recycling next to Bojangles' already "dressed to go to the movies" at Northside Mall across the street. So before I would go to the movies, I'd eat some dirty rice and wash it down with ice tea.

My Mama would see me laying out my clothes on the bed, getting ready. She would wait good until I put them on and ask, "Where do you think you're going, Mister?"

It would always puzzle me when she asked me that because it was my every week routine. Now, I knew all she wanted was the respect of me asking her permission. She never really had a problem with me going anywhere on my own. She knew I could handle myself. I was a real man-child. Little did I know my Mama had a big surprise in store for me. It was around this time I found out I had a big brother. I wasn't an only child as I thought I was. My mom had kept him a secret all these years. Here I was all of six years old, and there was no picture of him. She never even mentioned him until I came home for school one day and there he was.

Bro was black as can be. I thought to myself, *"Man, wait until Aunt Evelyn sees him"*. She had a bad habit of talking about how black you are. I mean she would go hard on you especially when she had been drinking. And on top of bro being black, he had a deep accent when he talked. So, I felt like it was going to be my job putting bro up on game in the hood, the dos and don'ts. It would not be easy. Bro had a problem with moving to the "state" - as they called it back on the island. At first, I didn't understand why he missed the Bahamas that much. I would have to visit the Island on my own, to fall in love with it like he was. But later on in life I would long for the island myself. But right then all I knew was I would have to help him prepare for the streets of Miami. I had an up-and-coming rep to protect. After a few fights and with the help of our neighbor Cassius, who stayed in the front part of our duplex apartment, [his dad was Muhammad Ali's sparring partner]. That's how Cassius got his name.

My new brother and Cass quickly became good friends. They were both the same age. I was thankful for them being so tight because it was hard trying to school bro. He had a problem getting game for his younger brother. And Cass was a real super cool dude. He dressed fly, had a lot of girls on his line. It was a known fact that he was nice with his hands. Like I said before his Pop used to spar with Ali. [So you know, he taught Cass how to fight.]

It didn't take bro long to get with the street code of life. He dropped his island name Omar and started going by his first name Gregg. I liked that move because it started with a "G." I don't know why I was so fixed on that letter. It would define me for years to come: the "G-Code!" Me and bro had our normal brother fights which always ended up with me getting my ass beaten.

But bro would have to learn just like everybody I ever got into it with. I bar none, I don't back down from a fight. Those early days of me fighting so much would make me a damn good fighter later on in life. And the places I would end up in, I would need to know how to fight, and be good at it. And I would. Even though me and bro fought, we had each other's back all the way. My Mama made sure we understood that.

She would say, "Ya'll are brothers. I don't care who it is, if they mess with one of ya'll both of you better fight them."

And we did. We won some and lost some, but the hood knew that we were 'bout it. So, we had respect. Bro would end up being a real lady's man for some reason or another. Girls would draw to him. He would prove to be one hell of a dresser. I was more of the street guy, the "go-hard" type. Bro was the opposite of me. He was a real thinker, very smart one.

Everything had to be well planned before he made a move. I liked that about him. I began to try and be more like him. He didn't like that. He thought I was cramping his style if I wanted to hang out with him. But later on in life, he loved to be around me. Those early days around the old hood would build our brotherhood strong for each other. When my mom finally got a better job, we ended up moving again to a house in Carol City. The house was nice, but I missed the hood.

At first, after school, I would catch the bus all the way back to the old hood just to hang with my crew. That didn't last long because I was getting back home late on a school night. So I would just have to see what Carol City had to offer me. It didn't take me long to find where that happening was going down. "Cloverleaf Apartments" would be my new stomping grounds. With the change of hoods also came a change of crew. I started a new school and was already going by a new name. Lil Pig was dead and Gigolo was born.

CHAPTER 2

# **Peer Pressure**

I already told you how I had chosen the name Gigolo. Yeah, it was Mrs. Morris Day himself. Gigolo get lonely too. Well, it's one thing to give yourself a nickname, it's altogether another job, to get folks to address you by it. I had my work cut out for me. Elementary was a walk in the park compared to High School. It was easy to impress a bunch of young kids, teenagers not so easy. My first year of High School would set the stage for things to come years later in my life. Interacting with others has never been a problem for me. I had a way about myself that made you rather be down with me, or hate me altogether. I wouldn't say I was arrogant. [*Cocky* that may be the word.] Just put it like this, I wasn't shy nor was I the most handsome guy, but I wasn't bad looking either. The most attractive thing about me was my swag. The way I carried myself and make whatever I'm doing fly. To this day, that's how I live.

So let me get on with how I came to be Gigolo. I knew it was time to upgrade from Lil Pig. The name no longer represented who I wanted to be. I wanted people to like me. I wanted to meet girls and have sex. Yeah, I know what you're thinking ... "at that age, *really?*" "Yeah", I was very sexually active. I ended up getting one of my girlfriend's pregnant in High School. [We'll get to that soon.] So I had to put my Gigolo game down, and make it stick. So the first thing I know I would have to step up was "my dress code".

I would have to stay fresh and smell good at all times. And be ready to pop game at a drop of a dime because that's what Gigolos do at least that was the way "Morris Day" did in the movie. The summer before I started High School I got my first real job. [Yeah, no more running the street to hustle and steal.] My uncle Joe came through for me. He was like a fall-in dad to me. I loved him to death. Well, he had his own lawn services. He let me work the whole summer, so I could get me some clothes money. I was grateful for the job and saved every dime except for lunch money that I spent during the day. At first I didn't even want to spend that. I would drink water, and eat fruit of the trees in the yards we were cutting until one day uncle got on me.

We were at the gas station filling the truck when Uncle came out eating a hot sandwich. I was looking at it so hard. He asked me did I want one. Thinking he was buying, I said yes. So he reached into his pocket and handed me a $5.00 bill. I thought to myself that's too much. That's when he said "this is coming out your pay". So from then on out I would spend $5.00 on lunch. I liked cutting grass because it was something that I was good at. I loved the way we made a yard look after we were finished. The only thing I was scared of was somebody from my new school seeing me cutting grass and all that. I don't know why, but I just couldn't see "Morris Day" working at a lawn care service. So if it wasn't good for Mr. Gigolo himself, it wasn't good for me. But if I didn't get this money, then how else would I get my school clothes. Well, I would just have to take my chances. To help keep myself from being noticed I wore a hoody as I worked. When the summer was over, I had $1,000 saved. Just as I was keeping up with my money saved, my mom was too.

So out of the $1,000 I had to $200 went to my mom. I didn't mind. I liked helping my mom out anyway I could. So I had to make $800 work for shoes and clothes. I didn't care about school supplies like paper and other stuff I needed. I was not there for education; it was strictly a "hook up spot". You know the place to meet girls and make friends. One thing

I learned from my mom was how to get the most out of your money. I went to the flea market, the outlets, and shops around for the best deal on the name brand gear.

I bought all of my shoes for the flea market. They were cheaper there anyway. Now that I had my gear together, it was all about laying my game down right once school started. That wasn't hard at all. Once I got into mingling with a few of the girls. I let them become a mouthpiece for me. I told a couple girls my name was Gigolo and they like the way it sounded, but once they understood what it meant they really became interested in seeing if I was that type of guy. Moreover, my plan was to not let them down. Thinking back now on it, I think they liked the fact that I was trying to be a player.

I say that because they made it so easy for me, I had girls claiming me as their boyfriend before we even talked. They would have their girl come up to me at my locker or some other place in school and tell me that they liked me. The next thing I knew, people would be saying that particular girl was one of *Gigolo's girls.* Man I'm telling you, it went on like that. I was becoming popular and it seemed like girls wanted to be known anyway they could. So the quick and easier way was to be associated with me. I wanted to be a real lady's man but, "with every good thing there's always a catch".

See, all these girls liking me made a lot of dudes hate me. That's when all my early years of fighting came to use. What a lot of these dudes didn't know was, I loved to fight just as much as I loved girls. The more popular I became with the girl, the more enemies I made. I didn't care because I was used to not having many dudes as friends. I started having a lot of sex with different girls. It seemed like a lot of the girls at that age wanted to lose their virginity. They chose me because I was experienced and the word got out that I was a freak. I didn't have no hang ups in the bedroom. A lot of other guys my age had a problem with going down on girls. Well, I loved it and I guess that information had got around too. I was a bit rough at first. I didn't do a lot of foreplay. I just would push my dick in that extra tight box so hard where there were cuts on my head. I thought I had gotten burnt because of the burning when I peed.

During that time in my life, it was hard for me to take a relationship serious until I met Shawn. She was real, pretty and had a big ass on her. Even as a young boy I could appreciate a fat ass on a woman. Me and Shawn got real close. She and her friend, Angie, would catch the bus from the projects all the way to Carol City to be with me. Angie messed with my homie Donnie. We would go get something to eat or just hang out. But we always ended up having sex. Either we would be over my house or at Donnie's. His mama didn't mind us hanging out at her place. My mom, on the other hand, was something else. So the only time we chilled at my crib was when she was at work from 3 to 11 PM. She didn't get home until around midnight, and by that time, Shawn would be already gone and the house would have been cleaned. This situation would last all school year, until the night Miss Coop called.

I remember the phone rang when I was in the room with mom while she ironed her work clothes. I was watching "Yo! MTV Raps" nearby because the only TV in the house was in her room when I received the news that I had a daughter on the way. I didn't know how to take the news because I was so concerned about my mother's response. [I won't say the news was bad because my daughter is a gift from God that I am eternally grateful for. She is the best thing I ever did in my life. But at that time mom had no problem with putting me out the house.

I had stayed with my Aunt Greta on many days.]

Back to the call. The phone was ringing so my mama told me. I picked up the phone and there was my girlfriend's mother asking me who I was, and if I was the boy who had gotten her daughter pregnant. I knew it was something important, but for me to find out that I had a baby on the way like that was shocking. I didn't know why Shawn hadn't told me about her pregnancy. I guessed it was alright for us to know, but not our moms. So I did what I thought would buy me some more time before I told my mama the news.

I hung up the phone right in Miss Coop's face. She didn't take too kindly to that and called right back. My mama was already trying to find out who was on the phone and why I had hung up like that. My mind was racing trying to figure out a lie but, before I could think of something believable the phone rang again. Sensing something was up, she beat me to it. Knowing that the cat was out the bag now, I shot out the room. I could still hear my mama on the phone just giving a lot of *ok's, alrights,* and *um-hums.* The second she hung up she was yelling for me to get my ass back in front of her. To my surprise she was a little more understanding about the news that I had just learned of myself. On top of that she didn't even kick me out like I thought she would.

***

With a baby on the way, all my player games had to stop. [Shit just got real so fast.] News about me getting Shawn pregnant traveled around fast. You have to understand, we were only 14 and still in Junior High School. All I could think about around that time was money and how badly I needed it then. Before Shawn was pregnant, I used to hustle just to buy clothes and stay fly. Now I was going to need money for Pampers[diapers], milk, daycare, and all the necessities of a new life. And you already know I wanted my baby to be fresh all the time. So I started selling dope.

I got me some coke to cook up. Crackheads wanted a fast high and I wanted a fast buck: that's how I got into the game. Yeah, my gigolo days were coming to an end. No more cutting grass for my Uncle or doing small time hustles around the hood. I was in the streets for real now.

I was still hitting on all the girls at school, but it wasn't the same now because my baby-mama went to same school and she was getting bigger by the day. I don't know if it was some kind of girl code, but it seemed like my game was getting blackballed. It wasn't the same. Girls would still flirt, but that was it. No more skipping school and going around the way to get a mid-day fuck in. Luckily there were a few die hard side chicks on my roster, but I liked getting the new-new, ya dig.

So I started going to other schools to meet new girls. But my reputation would follow me. So I just stopped focusing on girls, and I focused on my hustle. In the streets there ain't no time to be hollering at girls. You're either getting money or you're in the way. Not to say you don't get none. Selling crack came with its advantages. Junkies would do anything for that rock. And 15th Avenue was full of them. Niggas was going hard, so that made me do the same. The way I got put down on the Ave was by way of one of my OG cousins. His name was Chico. They called him that because he looked like a Spanish nigga. He was a tall and real light skin nigga with good hair. Chico was a real smooth player.

When it came to hoes. Chico had real game. He had to be smooth with his talk game, even though he was getting money on the Ave slinging dope. He had a real bad cocaine habit. Couz could snort some coke. Well enough about couz, I started off as a watch-out boy. It was my job to post up on 71st and 15th Ave. I would lookout for the 17th way and the 14th Ave way. See 15th was the dope stroll. It ran from 62nd to 71st Street. It was so much dope on that little street of road to supply the whole Miami. A lot of people came there through to cope. So you already know where there's dope, there's money and guns, cars and hoes!

Back in the 80s and 90s, 15th Ave was live. I mean wide ass open! If you was a street nigga, a hustler, player, or any kind of real nigga, you got down on 15th Ave. Everybody in the city knew that. Fifteenth was so popular that a song was made about the Ave: *15th Ave nigga get paid on 15th Ave!* That was music to my ears. To me, 15th Ave was where I belonged. I was born to hustle and to be amongst real go getters. I was the son of Pig: A real nigga!

Back to my role on the Ave: Watch out was the bottom of the ranks, only one up from being a junkie that clean up the spots after the shift change over. Yeah, back in the day selling dope in Miami was ran like a real life business. There was none of that "free for all" shit you see today with everybody selling dope when and wherever they wanted to. That type of shit would get you killed so fast in Miami. That was called "short stopping" – a real violation of the street code. So being a watch-out was just my way of entering the dope game. I would be content with that role for a little while. So when the opportunity came along to make some extra money slinging rocks for the Big Homie, Lil Jit who ran Star Bowders, I took it.

Jit liked my style, how I was dedicated to the corner. See even though I worked for the other spot called "Peeping." I would always make sure I looked out for the whole corner. Jit's spot was on 71$^{st}$, the same street I used to post up on. Only it was at the corner of the Sugar Hill Projects. He would pull up and see me on my post and call me over to his car window to make a little store runs for him. Mostly cigars for his weed. When he first asked me, I told him that I was on the clock and I couldn't leave the Ave. He already knew that, it was a test. He told me to make it fast and he'd watch the block in my short absence. I got $20 for my effort.

I knew who Jit was, that he was the boss of his own spot. They called him Jit because he looked young as fuck and he was a lil short nigga too. Word in the street was he was a real go-getter. Before becoming deep in the dope game, he used to rob and whatever else for that check. I think he gravitated towards me because he saw a lot of himself in me.

It became a daily routine for Jit to pull up and fuck with me until one day Jock, his regular bomb man, didn't show up. Jock was my homie and I think he had gotten locked up behind some baby-mama drama. So Jit asked me if I wanted to make that money. Who was I to turn it down? And you already know, with me if it's about money, count me in.

Serving for Star was the easiest money I ever made up to that point in my life. Jit's brother, Hen aka Super, would bring me the bomb (5000 packs of what was known back then as Jungler). They called it that because you could take a $5.00 Jungler off the Ave and go back to the beach or out of town, like Broward County and sell them for $20 or $40. Soon as Super handed me the bomb, it was gone. It was so bad that I used to make tips just to serve a junkie first, or hold some rocks until they got there. During this time, I started seeing some good money for a young nigga back then. I started making just $50 a shift watching out, but there were always other ways to make a little more. For instance, before I went to work, I would go in the Pork Bean Projects to cope a few Blue Dot dimes of powder.

See, Blue Dot had some fat ass dime sacks that was packaged just like our Peeping $20 halves.

Only difference was Blue Dot was shake up coke and we had raw. They had a little blue dot on the pack and we had a bumble bee on ours. So here the game is! I would collect some of our stickers off of the empty bags. Sometimes I would invest like $40 on four dimes of Blue Dot. All I had to do was put our sticker on them. So now I would have 4 half sacks for sale which doubled my $40 to $80, plus my $50 for watching out. So I'm $130 to the good. I was cool with that for a while, but I had to be careful with that game because that was another form of short stopping the spot. And if word got back to the niggas I was working for they sure would try to make an example out of me.

Shit was real in them streets, but like I was telling ya'll before I got into that side hustle to run my money up. When I started serving Star and watching out for Peeping, I was making a fat knot. Jit was breaking me off $250 for serving the bomb, plus the extra I was getting from the hustle with the bomb. For a while I was seeing $400-$500 a day on the Ave. That was a lot of money for 14-year-old young nigga back in them days. And just think about it for a minute, I was at the bottom of the food chains on the Ave. So think about all the money the older niggas were making like the LTs, gunmen, and the niggas at the tables. Just thinking back on them days, 15th Ave was the shit for real. Nothing but foreign whips, Cadillac Bromes, Benzes, Jaguars, and BMWs. So many big time dope dealers, celebrities, and sports figures were coming through 15th Ave.

During this time in my life, I was really coming of age. I was about to turn 15 at the end of the year. A lot could happen in a few months in the streets living the fast life of a young hustler. I would learn firsthand as my life was making a turn for the worse. Yeah, I was getting money for a young nigga but being in the streets and seeing things I was seeing in the unfolding crack cocaine era the game was changing. It was more and more young niggas being let in to play. In school I was used to standing out more because of my style and the fondness that the girls gave my game. But it was different in the streets.

On the Ave, nobody cared about how good you dressed or your style. It was all about money, power, and respect. It was mainly two ways to gain those three goals: violence or hustle. Earlier on I saw how dudes sought to be either the most violent nigga in the streets or the nigga with the most money. To most, it was easy to be violent. That made niggas respect you. If a nigga knows you quick to do something to them, or even kill them then they gave you the utmost respect. Once you had the respect of the street, and you was smart enough, the money would follow in most cases. That is, if you don't get locked up or killed first. With all these cutthroats, killers, and dope dealers making up the immediate world I lived in, I guess you could say that I'm a product of my environment.

As I began to hang out more on the Ave instead of school, it became more about making a name in the streets. So instead of trying to be a gigolo for the girls in school, now I wanted to be a gangster young nigga, that had respect on my name. But what I didn't quite understand was that lots of other young niggas had the same ideas and was coming up in the game just like me. A lot of them dudes will cross paths with me and some will be cool. Others will be envious. That's just how it played out in the streets. It's funny now that I think back on a lot of those. But because we were so young, playing in a grown man's game, we all called ourselves "Lil" this or that. I knew of Lil Bo, Lil Willie, Lil Ced, Lil Fred, Lil Burt and Lil Gig.

I stopped introducing myself as Gigolo because it didn't fit no more. I was all about being respected in the streets, so called myself Gig for short. And like all the other young niggas that was in the streets, the Lil was added.

Things went from sugar to shit real fast. My homie Jock got out of jail. Normally that would've been a good thing. Of course it was for him, but his return mark stopped me from serving Star's bomb because he got his job back. Now I was left with barely holding on to the watch-out spot with Peeping. Things were hitting up for me. The word was out about Blue Dot dimes being worked into the bomb. It wasn't just me who was "short stopping" now, just about everybody around the corner was doing the flip game on Peeping sacks. It got so bad that the head nigga - World - had put the word out to the niggas in the Porking Bean that if any of his workers went through there to cope from Blue Dots to let him know. That didn't stop us because all we did was have somebody else grab for us. For real, I was about tired of working for a nigga anyway.

One night when I was working with the homie Jap Bo, I noticed that he was hitting the bomb pretty hard. What I mean by that is he was getting on the books for Coke. At first I didn't think much of it. Everybody hit the books for advancement on their pay. I didn't make it a habit because I wasn't making enough to be going on the books. Jap Bo didn't care one way or the other. He was busting half sacks like Tic Tacs. I even asked him about it one time after about his fifth half.

I said, "Damn, Jap Bo who that one on?"

He just laughed and said, "This on World."

That's when I started to think that something wasn't right. My gut feeling was right because about 2:00 AM. Jap Bo called me down to the hole aka the spot. And put me up on his plan. He knew that for it to have a chance to work he would need me to be down with it. The plan was to say Nine rushed the spot and we had to run and they got the bomb. It would have to work, but there's one thing you have to understand about all the moving parts of running a drug hole. There were people in play that you may not even know exist, and they may be in plain sight. They were the eyes and ears for the boss niggas. The crazy part about it is we all knew about them and who they were.

One of World's snitches was this crack head nigga named Cheer. He mostly just cleaned up the spot, sweeping the store, clearing out the dope wrappers and shit like that. On this night Cheer tried to clean up early so he could get his $5 pay to go get high. Well, Jap Bo didn't pay Cheer. So the smoker set across the street and looked at Jap Bo for the rest of the night. We forgot all about him while we was setting the stage to make it look like the jump out boys [aka Nine] had rushed. We turned over rocks, pushed down the garbage-cans and flipped the place up. Jap Bo had convinced me to go along with him because he was going to bust down the bomb and what little money he made for the night. A bomb of Peeping $20 halves was made up of 25 sacks which equals $500. Jap Bo had two bombs out on the block. So we bust it down; Half money, half sacks. The second part of the plan was to meet back up on the Ave the next morning so we could tell our story together. Well, I kept it real and showed up because I didn't feel worried about nobody being mad with me about losing the bomb because, for real, I was only a look-out. But I was in for a rough awakening.

When I walked up on the Ave the next morning, the whole team was up there waiting. It kind of reminded me of the scene out of New Jack City with Nino Brown confronting his crew after the raid on the Carter. It was World's little brother, Dee, who had a Rottweiler with him. I knew of Dee. He drove the hooked up Jeep Cherokee. Our Lieutenant over the spot was by his side, his name was Speedy, from the Porking Beans. This other nigga that was riding the wave was named Narod. There was another fat nigga I never seen before. I can tell they had talked about me because as soon as I walked up it got quiet.

The first one to say something was Speedy. "There goes Lil Gig right there!"

Hearing my name made me know shit was real. I stepped right up and said, "What's up, my nigga?"

That's when Dee said, "I don't know, I'm waiting on you to tell me."

It was no sense in playing around. I knew what he meant. They wanted to know why nobody was up here serving the dope. And where the dope was? So I gave it to them exactly the way me and Jap Bo planned it. I could tell they weren't buying it. It seemed like they already knew what I was going to say. The look Speedy was giving me should have warned me.

See, Speedy was cool. Out of everybody, Speedy really rocked with me. But there was nothing he could do for me. If I was a dirty nigga, I should've just changed up the story and looked out for myself, because, for one, where was Jap Bo? He was supposed to be here. This had been his plan anyway. Little did I know Jap Bo had never planned to show up. And to make matters worse, the dirty ass nigga had gone and grabbed another bomb after we bust down the first two. So what I was trying to convince these niggas to believe didn't make any sense. Because why would anybody go get another pack after Nine was done rushing the spot? I didn't know about that fact. So all I could do was stick to the lie.

Dee wasn't having none of it, but he was too soft to do his own work. It took his do boy Narod to make the first move on me. He called me a liar, and said I better get that dope up! I told him fuck him and we started fighting. Before I knew what was happening, I was being choked out on the hood of the Jeep by the fat nigga. He slammed me on the ground and that's when Dee walked over and let the dog start barking in my ear. I thank God he didn't put him on me. I got to give thanks to Speedy because he pulled me up.

Speedy acted like he was put down on me by telling me to go find that nigga Jap Bo and tell him they were looking for him. I took that as my pass to leave. But before I left I gave all them niggas that look as though payback is a mother fucker! I didn't notice, but there was a lot more people out now than when I first walked up. And it seemed like they were all looking at me. I can't lie, I felt ashamed. Even though I got jumped, I wasn't used to letting nobody handle me any kind of way. As I walked off, I made a promise to myself that I would never work for a nigga in the dope game again. And I wasn't going up on the Ave until I was getting my own money!

This would be a turning point in street life. This was the Summer of 1989. I had $200 and 10 Peeping sacks in my pocket. I was still going to school whenever I felt like it. I was going to Miami Center at that time. It was still early and I knew I could get some of the sack off at school. So that's where I went. Those days were kind of different to me. I wasn't even trying to learn nothing. It was more of a meet-up place. Whether I was setting up a date for some pussy or meeting up with some of the other hustling young niggas I called my dawgs. It seemed like every young nigga that was about anything had something for sale or an idea on a lick we could pull off. You could get a plug-in on anything at school from cars, rims, guns, dope, jewels, and clothes; whatever you wanted. So for me, high school was just an opportunity to make more connections to the streets. I was not worried about being a gigolo no more. I wanted money, power, and respect in whatever order it came. Lil Gig was on the come up!

# CHAPTER 3

# **Juvenile Pressure**

The Summer of '89 would be a turning point in my young life. I was just 14 when I started working and I had a baby on the way. I was getting a little money working the Ave, but that came to a screeching halt after getting jumped for running of with Jap Bo. After a while I got back in the game dealing dope for myself. There was this Arab store in the hood called Lucille's on 94<sup>th</sup> Street and 17<sup>th</sup> Avenue right down the street from my high school. I used to wait on the bus right in front of it. We nicknamed the area "Robbin Hood" because most of all us young niggas around there would rob a motherfucker quick. Nevertheless, I noticed that a lot of crackheads [aka "basers"] would come in the store to buy lose cigarettes. They would always ask me if I was "holding" as in; did I have crack for sale?

I got rid of all the Peeping sacks I had and now had my bank roll up to $400. So being the hustler that I was, I took $80 and got me an eight ball of crack rock. I chopped the 3 gram-cookie into $5 bags. I flipped that eight ball so fast that I knew I was on to something there. It was sweet up there because back around this time nobody had work in this area but me. So I kept it to myself and that spot for a week until I found out why nobody was working the spot. The fuck ass Arab or somebody else nearby was snitching because an undercover cop came through in a van.

I didn't know no better. Serving up there on my own was way different from being on the Ave where everybody looked out for each other. I made two mistakes; One, serving a white boy I didn't know, and keeping the money and dope on me. It did cost me the rest of my summer and being out when my daughter was born. That would be the beginning of my cycle throughout the criminal justice system. Going to Juvenile Hall wasn't my first time being there, but this time I would have to stay awhile because of the felony charge. I was arrested for Possession with intent to sale, within 1,000 feet of a school zone.

I remember walking in the Hall [what we called Juvenile Hall]. They put me in Unit 2 to be processed. Inmates would stay no longer than a week before being transferred to permanent housing depending on your age and how many times you had been locked up. If you had beef with someone else in the Hall, it was a lot of little shit to be considered before being placed in open population. The main thing to be considered was who was a known informant. Snitches couldn't be placed on the rougher units. There was a separate unit for girls. Unit 6 was for the mental health niggas. Them motherfuckers were all on meds and crazy as fuck.

Mr. Davis was the old dude who ran Unit 2, where I had been placed, and he took a liking to me right off. Came to find out, he knew my dad. Pig's rep was still following me, but it always helped me in some kind of way. Mr. Davis was a real player. Just ask any nigga that ever came through that Hall … I could tell he wasn't only a Juvenile Hall staff member; he had a hustle on the side. He kept a big bank roll in his pocket that he claimed came from gambling. He was too smart to be just a dope dealer. Matter of fact, he used to give us speeches about selling dope. But because he dug me, and on the strength of Pig, he used to look out for me. He let me hang on Unit 2 longer than what I was supposed to stay. I did a month instead of a week.

Being on Unit 2 had its advantages. For one, I didn't have to go to school. I could stay out of the cell longer and watch more TV. Mr. Davis always brought me something out the vending machine. Since I was the orderly, I was able to stay out the cell longer while everybody was locked down. But I had to clean up and that meant the bathroom too. That's the only part I didn't like but, the job made sure that I had extra trays to eat which all contributed to my smooth stay in the Hall.

While I was on Unit 2, I used to see everybody who came in first because I would have to dress them out and get their mat to sleep on. Dong this gave me the opportunity to feel a new nigga out because when a nigga first comes into the Hall, you could tell if they was scared, fake or if they were a real street nigga. Most of the time I would just let them tell on themselves. If they started asking a lot of scared nigga questions: *Do I get a cell to myself?, Do it be a lot of fights?, Where the staff be?* – I would know they were fuckboys. Some of these same niggas get on the yard around a few of their homies and all of a sudden they hard. I used to laugh to myself when I see that happen.

Niggas would come in asking if I knew this nigga or that nigga or if I knew what unit they was on? Sometimes it would be a family member or a co-defendant. A lot of times it was somebody they were trying to duck so they could let staff know they couldn't be in the same unit with that person. With my job, I was plugged in with some real niggas and chicos too! I didn't care about plugging in with no white boys, besides their family came and got them pretty quick. You had to be a wild, crazy ass white boy to make it in the Hall. There was one crazy white boy in Unit 6 I'll never forget because he blinked really fast all the time. His name was Billy and he would fight too.

I ended up becoming close to a dude who came to Unit 2. Mr. Davis came to my cell and opened the door around 11:00 PM, so I knew somebody was coming in late. I had to get out the bed so I could dress him out and get a mat. But this one was different. Mr. Davis said he was coming from Ward D, the hospital unit. My first thought was, "he done got whooped by Nine, or they put the dogs on him". I was done seeing all kinds of young niggas go in fucked up by the cops. So when I saw Shawnta Ward who was also called Burt or De Bo being pushed in a wheelchair with his head wrapped in a white Ace band and arm in a sling I thought *"Damn, this nigga been in a real battle."*

Burt was still wearing paper thin hospital clothes and shivering from being cold. The band was turning as his head was continuing to bleed. I asked him what size he wore. Most niggas always want a bigger size, so I gave him 3X everything except for the 2X boxers. I didn't know if he was real or not yet. But I had a good feeling about him. I had been doing it for so long to the point where I could pick a nigga out just by looking at him. Mr. Davis told me to give Burt two mats and to set them outside the cell. That meant he would be in the cell by himself. Mr. Davis only did that when he felt like somebody couldn't defend himself and that was the best call because my nigga wasn't in no fighting condition but, for some reason, I had a feeling this young nigga still could get down if he had to. He looked like the type that didn't "duck no rec"! I gave him an extra blanket too so he could use it as a pillow. He wouldn't be able to get a real one until somebody left. I used to hustle pillows because they were limited and in high demand. In jail, that meant "luxury" items.

The first night, me and Burt didn't talk at all other than him asking about whether the food was good and when they fed us? That was cool with me because I wasn't a real talker, and I knew the rules on asking too many questions. The number one, biggest No-No was asking a nigga what he was in for? If a dude wanted to share that information, he would. The reason why cats didn't talk about their charge, or their case was because it was still going on. And jail house rats were real, even in juvenile. There were a lot of other reasons incarcerated people didn't just openly discuss what their charge(s) were, in some cases, some niggas had a fucked up case. Man, young niggas in Miami was wilding out for real. I knew niggas that had rape, kidnapping, and murder charges all in one case. Some didn't have any trouble talking about that shit because they did it and the victims were white.

There were guys in there for shit they done to a family member, even their mom. The most common charges were auto theft, burglary, robbery, and shoplifting. There were starting to be a lot more young niggas getting their hands on guns around the way. But, back to me and Burt.

The next morning when it was chow time, I decided to help Burt out by pushing him in the wheelchair not because I was a friendly ass nigga but because nobody wanted that label on them. But by pushing him, I would be able to skip to the front of the line, that was my spot anyway because I was the Number One in the unit. The line was a big deal in the Hall for inmates and staff. The staff always wanted the line to be straight and stay tight. I guess it made them look like they had their unit under control. The line had a different meaning for us. When we moved through the compound we could make a move on an enemy in another unit. So when we're in the chow line everybody is on high alert. It never failed that when two or three units were moving through the chow hall something always jumped off.

There was a fight every day all day in the chow hall for some reason or another. That was just juvenile life in the Hall. When Unit 2 came out all the other units paid real close attention for a lot of reasons. Niggas be checking out who was moving through, checking for enemies or if any of their homeboys had arrived. Sometimes a local star was in the bunch: That nigga that made the news with their case. I did do it two times in the future landing in the Hall. "I will tell you about that later."

That morning when I was pushing Burt, a real nigga bond was made. I guess Burt had seen how wild the Hall was because before we even sat down to eat, staff had broken up two fights. Niggas were yelling threats back and forth to each other. But nobody fucked with us or said nothing our way. Yeah, I had big respect already in the Hall. Niggas knew all I did was work out and stay ready for whatever. Burt picked up on that vibe right away. He saw how niggas that worked in the kitchen had thrown me extra shit to eat. In the chow hall, you had to pay real close attention. It would be like three units in the small space and staff would be off to the side at both ends of the room, but there were only 6 adults present. Each unit had about 30 inmates, sometimes more; that's about 90 wild ass young niggas in one area. The staff had their work cut out for them. To keep order was a 24-hour job. They had to stay on top of who was at war with who. I did learn later while growing up in prison, all the way to the Feds, that gang beef made up a lot of the violence on the inside.

There was the South Miami vs. North Miami beef. Then you had hood rivalries from time to time. There was a small beef with the Spanish niggas: Latin Kings against the I.N.P. They got into it from time to time. Mostly they would put their street differences to the side and band together on the inside. It all depended on the make-up of the unit. If the niggas were getting along with each other, then it would be a race split in the unit.

Me and Burt wasn't concerned with all the chaos surrounding us as I broke him off with the extra shit I had taken from the chow hall. We got back on the unit that day and started what would become a lifelong brotherhood. Me and him had a lot in common. He was a real street dude who came from a family of hustlers just like mine. We were born into this lifestyle. He finally got around to telling me what had happened to him and why he was in the Hall. He got into a fight with his cousin and ended up stabbing him. His cousin broke a bottle across Burt's head resulting in the head injury. The way he was looking, it had to have been a hell of a fight. We talked about a lot of stuff, different people we knew and all the females we had fucked or were trying to. He lived on 60th Street not far from me on 69th. That might not sound that far apart, but those streets were different ends of the Ave.

My time on Unit 2 was coming to an end. I had already been there for a month. That is a long time. The average stay on the unit was a week, but they normally have you gone the next day. Mr. Davis hated to let me go, but he was getting heat because I wasn't going to school. That's the only part that I didn't like about Unit 2. You didn't get no rec time or go to school. So I was kind of ready to move around.

They assigned me to Unit 1 right next door. The head staff was a Spanish dude named Lorenzo. He was a cool dude. All he asked for us to do, was respect each other and the staff. He liked to work out, so when we were let out the cells, we would get straight into sets of pushups, sit-ups, curls, and anything else we could do. There were fights here and there, but for the most part, it was one of the more laid back units. I ended up doing sixty days on Unit 1 before they shipped me to the drug program down in South Miami. The court had gone for my story that I was using the drugs. They still gave me the sale and distribution charges but, I had to do a 6-month residential program. I didn't care. All I wanted was my freedom again. I was going to get out of the program, that was my plan.

It was still '89, but the Summer was over, and everybody was getting ready to go back to school.

I was broke. My baby was coming any day. I used to call my baby-mama Shawn to see how she was holding up. Those conversations were always filled with tension. She jumped down on me for not stepping up to provide for our baby. I had no job, no hustle. At that time I felt like shit. I had to come up with some money, and all I knew how to do was hustle. I wasn't even thinking about no job. My mom was another issue altogether.

She was tired of my shit. She had already washed her hands off me; giving her son back to God, is how she put it. My brother Greg was in the Army. He would look out from time to time, and send me clothes and money when he could. And with my baby on the way, they both had decided that whatever they had for me was now going to be passed down to the newest addition to our family whenever she got here. I had already picked my baby's name once I found out I was having a girl: Lakevia Hunter. I made sure she had my name in it!

During this time, my young mind was working overtime trying to come up with a new way to get paid. I needed money, and I needed it fast. There was no way I was going to get some being stuck in this drug program, so my first priority was getting out. And I wasn't waiting 6 months either. But I didn't have anywhere to stay. My mama knew that I had to finish the program before I could come home and she wasn't going to let me hide there.

The program was some real bullshit with all its fake ass NA meetings and dudes snitching on each other as the rules required. I stayed for three weeks, on the last week of the month it was a Saturday, I packed up all my stuff, walk out the back door. There was a bus stop down the street. I took the bus to Over Town where one of my homeboy's grandmamma stayed. I knew I could lay there, at least for the weekend, because Big Ma was used to me spending the night over there on the weekends. My dawg's name was Donnie and we were real tight. We went all the way back to the 6th grade and were inseparable. We hung out, chased girls, smoked weed, even dated best friends. His baby-mama and Shawn were best friends even to this day. I got mine pregnant before Donnie followed me with his girl, so our babies are only a year apart.

I was now on the run. Though walking away from the program wouldn't alert the dogs to come chasing me through the woods or anything dramatic, the police would simply be notified that I had absconded and a warrant would be out for my arrest. My boy came through for me when I pulled up at his mother's house. His family always treated me like family and we've always maintained that relationship. I had a lot of pressure on me to get myself together. The only get-money quick hustle I knew was armed robbery. Yeah, it was time to step into the gun play.

I knew this young nigga that stayed around the way from the old girl's house. KK was 13 but if you knew dawg, you would say he was real mature for his age. Bro had to be, because his mom was very young when she had him. She couldn't have been no older than 25 at the time. And he had a younger brother, who was like 10, so bro was really the man of the house and he stepped up. KK was getting money for his family. When I met him, he was on these Jamaican niggas line, as one of their gunmen. Yeah, bro was packing steel at a young age. The first time I met KK he had a "nine" hanging out his pocket. Little dude was cool as fuck and carried himself like a real player. We plugged in right off and we started hanging out getting at hoes together. His mama used to let us get her car to go

out to the club or wherever else we needed to go. Since I was the one to think about getting into the robbery game, I would need a banger and I knew KK kept them. So I jumped on the bus and went to his end to tell him what I had in mind. Just like I thought, he was down. He gave me a 38 that same night. He had the same "nine" he loved so much. Our first lick came about unexpectedly.

His mom wanted us to go to the store for some cigarettes, so we jumped in the car and went down the street. We were thinking the same thing: *"Why not see how we work together on this robbery?"* It was my idea and I needed the money the most, so I would set it off. The farm store was really just a small little two-way drive-through where people could walk up to the shop. So that's what I did...

Bro parked around the corner. I jumped the fence and walked up to the drive-through and asked the Arab dude to get me a milk. When he turned around to get it, I pulled the 38 out and pointed it at his head. He was surprised but wasn't dumb. He could see it in my eyes: I wanted the money. He gave me everything he had stuffed in a bag. I grabbed a pack of Newport longs as well, jumped back over the gate and was back in the car in seconds.

"Drive!" I ordered KK. I didn't want his mother's car to be seen. Since the farm store was so close, we were back at his crib in no time. I gave his mother the cigarettes. I <u>didn't</u> know if it was the adrenaline, but it seemed like she knew what I had just done. Maybe she had heard us talking before we left. Either way, I had the feeling she didn't give a fuck as long as we didn't get hurt or caught.

I went to their balcony where KK was rolling a joint. We hadn't said anything to each other since the robbery. I sat down and put the bag of money on the table with no idea of how much I hit for. I hit the weed and passed it back to KK before getting down to business. There was $642 inside the bag. I gave him $200. He was cool with that. He knew all the shit I had on my plate with a baby on the way and no place to stay.

After that sweet lick, my little homie was ready to put in some work of his own. He suggested we go down to the Jamaican weed spot and lay on some sucker down there. He told me that niggas from out of town were going through there looking to buy some pounds of weed. That was music to my ears. We strapped up and walked down to the spot.

No real action came through that night. But it was definitely on the hit list.

I ended up catching the floor at KK's house for the night. His mama didn't care. She went out to the club and stayed all night. The next morning, when she came in, we jumped on the bus and went to Over Town to Donnie's Big Mama's house. We got there just in time to catch Donnie and his cousin Pat getting ready to go to the mall for school clothes. I now had money, but I wasn't thinking about no back to school shopping. Me and KK were on the come up. We went along to kill some time and see if we would see another lick on the way. We didn't but, that changed on the way back from the mall.

Donnie and Pat had big shopping bags of shit, so as we turned the corner from the mall and stood at the red light, we spotted a white couple. The first thing I noticed was the Benz they were in. Then I saw the Rolex on the man's wrist. I had seen enough. I looked over at KK. We didn't even have to speak. In the next second both of our guns were out.

I went to the driver side and KK shot over to the passenger side. I snatched the car door open and pointed the gun at the old white guy's head and told him to take off the watch and give me his wallet. He didn't hesitate and quickly handed me the goods. On the other side, KK took the lady's pocketbook and watch as well. It didn't take no more than a minute. Other cars at the light sped around the situation. I could see Donnie and Pat standing across the street with their eyes open wide in disbelief. As I got ready to turn around and run, all hell broke loose.

I remember hearing someone yell, "Freeze!" It sounded like a cop, but I hadn't seen any police cars nowhere. Now I was frenetically searching to find who the fuck was on the set. Suddenly a shot rang out. To my right, KK was busting at this black car behind us. I turned back to the Benz and for no other reason than to say I got off, I shot a few rounds into the car not really trying to hit nobody. After that, I just ran. Then a bullet whizzed by me. I went into self-preservation mode. KK would have to be smart and get the fuck out of there like me.

I made it to Over Town, but there was an undercover cop named Curly Perm waiting to jump out and arrest me. They had already got KK near the robbery scene. We were charged with two counts of First Degree armed robbery, 3 counts of First Degree attempted murder and I had an added charge of possession of cocaine with intent to sell which came from me leaving the drug program. I was back in the Hall within 30 days of my most recent release.

Mr. Davis was mad to see me back so fast. He didn't even let me hang out in Unit 2 like I did before. They sent me to the hard core unit: Unit 3. All the boys on that unit were headed to prison soon. They even made our uniforms match the prison blues. Thinking back to that period, it was the beginning of my institutionalization. Unit 3 was made up of some of the hard core juveniles. Every one of us were facing adult time but, before they can charge juveniles as adults a waiver hearing had to be conducted where a judge decides if there was enough evidence to file charges in the county. The waiver hearing took a long ass time because there were four different proceedings. This delayed process backed up the courts and overcrowded the Hall. To make matters worse, they usually put all the first-timers and easy cases on the front list. Niggas like me, who were looking at a lot of time, they kept on the back burner. It didn't matter because I became connected to Juvenile Hall, I didn't feel out of place.

It didn't take me long to become selected as an orderly. Ms. Margaret, from day watch, became my Juvenile Mama and took me in as one of her favorites. She would let me stay out of my cell to clean up while everyone else were locked down. The special treatment I received was bittersweet due to all the hate I was getting from other juveniles for my status. One thing about Unit 3 was if you had a problem with somebody, second shift officers would allow us to fade each other if we agreed that the beef wouldn't go beyond the fight. I had my share of fades, and I won every one of them. Being nice with my knuckle game made life easier for me. Word spread throughout the Hall that I was a knock-out artist because I put two niggas down that I had faded. Even the staff were impressed with my fight skills.

I was put in charge of the line whenever we went out the unit. The staff always wanted the line to stay tight. So it was my job to make sure that it did. I didn't have any problems with the real niggas on the unit because they knew whenever I got broke off I would I always look out. Staff would give me and the other orderlies all kinds of shit life food from the streets, extra snacks, and even shit to smoke. Being the line man, I ended up whooping this nigga named Zay. This nigga would become a real enemy for life.

Zay had been in the Hall on a murder case with two co-defendants, Joavelli (Lil Joe) and Bopee. Lil Joe would become an area close friend - my dawg. Bopee was the cousin of my dawg Burt. This nigga Zay was trying to be super hard and wouldn't listen to me when I tried to tell him that if he couldn't keep up with the line, he needed to fall back so we wouldn't get locked down early that night. If I couldn't get those dumb ass niggas together, then staff would view me like I wasn't doing my job. Zay tried to pop-off slick, telling me to let staff tell him what to do. I tried my best to reason with the fool, but the more I tried the bigger the gap became in the line. That's when I decided to get hands on.

I went up to Zay and grabbed him by his collar vest. When I pulled him towards the back of the line, he took me by surprise by resisting. That's when it turned into a fight. Zay had to find out the hard way that the talk of my fight game was no urban legend, I was like that for real. That fight would not be the end of that situation but the beginning of a serious beef. I would have run-ins with Zay in the streets and in the county jail. [That's a story for another time.]

I made a lot of enemies during this time in the Hall. Dudes who I smashed or even their homeboys had vendettas against me for the ass whoopings I gave out on the regular. But there was also a lot of clout chasing, juveniles trying to make a name for themselves. My reputation made me a target for dudes trying to use me to make a name for themselves. I was receiving threats from niggas who were already in the county jail on the notorious Tenth Floor.

I can't lie, I was worried whenever I got word through a kite from niggas I knew saying that some dude or another couldn't wait to see me up there. The only thing that really stressed me was knowing that I probably wouldn't get a one on one fade. Shit was crazy on the Tenth Floor because niggas were clicked up by hoods. They had down south cells and city cells. I was getting threats from the cells that I would be put in to. The Tenth Floor was so bad that every day there would be a line of

mothers outside the jail complaining about not hearing from their sons after being transferred to the jail from juvenile. Some of them would end up coming back to the Hall because they couldn't survive up there which was a real embarrassment. Everybody would look at the returned person like he was soft and couldn't hold his own. I wouldn't dwell on the threats for a long time because there was nothing I could do about it anyway. I would just cross that bridge when I got to it.

As I was waiting for the outcome of my case, life was still going on in the outside world. My baby-mama was getting bigger by the day. Thank God for my mama and my brother. They were already stepping up, preparing for my daughter to be born. I couldn't let the outside bother me while I was locked up because I had to be on point. Juvenile is a real serious place. Just as I was making enemies, I was also gaining respect from some real key young niggas out of different hoods in Miami. I learned early that it wasn't what you did, it's how you did it. Yeah, I was doing hits for staff, running the units and checking the lines. But I always kept it 100% with the code.

Number 1: Never snitch on one.

And I had rules that I always stood on like, never jump nobody ["latching"]. I always gave a nigga a fair fight meaning I never "stole" nobody. When you steal a nigga, that means "you sneak attack him". You had niggas that lived by that motto and they were masters at sneaking niggas. I wouldn't even let one of them niggas stand behind me or sleep in my cell. I was building a reputation and making alliances that would open doors for me in hoods all over the city.

Niggas like Sunshine, Out the Grove, Sugar Bear, Bushwick, Lil Willie, Cheese, Lil Pimp were all from Over Town. Mace and his brother Kea were from Edison Projects. I was making moves that would follow me for the rest of my life in the streets, jails, and prison. During that time in the Hall a pack of skittles and extra snack at night could get you fucked up real quick. It normally went like this: Some dumb ass young nigga would piss off a staff member, like jacking his dick on a female staff member. In return, one of the staff would come holler at me or one of the other hitters in the unit, slip us a pack of skittles and we would go to work. I'd pull up on you and say, "I need to see you." Those words put whoever on notice that he had fucked up. Once the work was done, I would eat my skittles with a few of my dawgs. I was doing all my time on Unit 3.

My co-defendant, KK, was on the first offender unit, Unit 12. I would see him from time to time in passing through the yard. I remember when I knew that niggas were really rocking with me. It had to do when I stepped up for Lil Willie who niggas were already talking about doing something to, the moment he walked in the Hall. Although bro was in Unit 1, we ended up in the same class in school so we got down like that. He knew niggas were trying to get at him because we had already talked about it. The nigga who he was locked up for killing had a cousin in the Hall. I gave him some real advice and told him how to file a toothbrush down into a banger that he should keep on him at all times.

A few days later, we were in the chow hall eating lunch when buddy tried to make his move on Lil Will. I was sitting in a different row from bro, but like always you could feel the tension in the room. But if you was plugged into the politics of the Hall you knew what was in the wind way before it happened. So I already knew what buddy had planned. He was going to jump on Willie in the chow hall. I hadn't planned on getting in it because I really didn't have anything to do with it. But it didn't seem fair to me. Dude was bigger than bro. So when I saw him start to walk over to Willie's table, I got up and made my way over there as well.

This made the whole chow hall became quiet in anticipation of something popping off. Staff became alerted because there were three different units inside at the same time. Niggas started standing up and slyly reaching for bangers concealed in their pants. Staff were now going up and down the rows telling us to chill out. Everybody was looking at me waiting to see if I was going to set off the drama. I looked at dude letting him know that I was ready for war. He read my silent demeanor correctly and just sat back down at his table. So I did the same.

Lil Willie looked at me and gave me a head nod. I returned it.

Time was going by fast in the Hall. But the holidays slowed things all the way down when it came to the courts. The New Year came around and I had missed the birth of my daughter. But during one of my court appearances they let me hold her at recess. I was nervous when my waiver hearing came. I just didn't know what to expect. This was the first time that I was going to be in the court room with the victims in my case. From what I was told, the State of Florida would have to prove my guilty. That meant that the victims would have to point me out as one of the people who robbed and shot at them.

The court room was real small to the point where we were all packed inside with the Judge sitting up higher than all of us. Me and KK were sitting right next to each other. This was the first time that we had been this close. KK had on a dark blue uniform and I wore a light color blue that state prisoners wore. I had shaved off all my hair as everyone in my unit had done together. I don't remember why we did it, but it just happened that I would wear my bald head in court. You never knew when you would be called for an appearance. Even though things were looking bad, I had a secret weapon.

My grandmamma had sent me this prayer written in a letter folded in a triangle. She had told my mama to tell me to put it in my right shoe, and whenever they said my name to press down hard on it. I did as I was told as soon as my name was called and stepped down hard with my right foot where the prayer was at.

The judge asked the first victim, which was the white man I had robbed. I don't know if it was the prayer working or my head being bald, but I really believe he was still traumatized from being robbed and shot at. Whatever the reason he could not identify me as one of the robbers. Likewise, the other two victims could not identify me. It wasn't the same for KK, however. The white woman and the wanna be hero both identified KK. So what ended up happening was KK got direct filed as an adult to the tenth floor at the County Jail.

If I had a clear understanding of the law then, I would have had my lawyer ask the judge to have the case against me dismissed. The drug charge was still pending, but that was nothing they would send me back to the program for. But I was dumb to the law. I allowed my mama's pressure and the fast talking, fake public defender to talk me into taking a deal that would send me off to state school for juvenile boys. To me and my mom it was better than going to prison. I felt bad for KK, especially since I went and got him to start robbing. His mom looked at me in the courtroom, and if looks could kill I would have been one dead ass nigga. So when we got back from court, I went back to my unit and KK went back to his. They took him to the County Jail the same night. I had to wait a few weeks before state school would pick me up. That gave me time to get the rundown on where I was heading.

The name of the school was Okeechobee Youth Development Center which we nicknamed "Chobee" because that's where it was located. If I thought the Tenth Floor was wild, the shit I was hearing about Chobee sounded like the Tenth Floor x 10. I wasn't scared of going. I just wanted to know all I could about the place. I always felt like if you made it there, then so can I. Regardless of what I was hearing about Chobee I would have to deal with whatever came my way. So as I prepared my mind I kept working out, doing my deck of cards push-ups every day. I shadow boxed in my cell during lock down. I had quick hands and I was fast on my feet. But I was small, weighing 144 pounds. My only advantage was I knew how to throw a punch and where to hit you at. What I didn't know yet, was that in Chobee all my skills would be put to the test. Before I knew it, that morning was upon me.

CHAPTER 4

# **Still Juvenile Pressure**

I heard the key turn and my cell door was unlocked. It was the night shift staff informing me that I would be rolling out at 7:00 AM. So I had to get my shit together. I didn't have nothing but a few letters, and a couple of pictures. I ran around the unit hitting all my guys' doors letting them know I was gone up the road to Chobee. There was a few other niggas waiting to go up there too. I could see they were wondering why they weren't making the ride with me.

I was taken up front to a holding cell where they gave me breakfast. I had mixed feelings about leaving that morning. I was used to having my way in the Hall, I was going to miss those weekly visits from my mom. She would bring my baby girl to see me at least once a month. But on the other hand, I was excited about getting out and going up the road since I had never been out of Miami at that point.

A cool, old ass white guy came to pick me up in a beige box Chevy. It had a cage just like the one in police cars. I was cuffed to a waist chain and my ankles were shackled. I was happy when the old guy loosened the cuffs and shackles for the four-hour drive. We only stopped once in West Palm Beach to pick up another prisoner.

It was a hot Miami morning and the driver was smoking with the window down which was cool with me. I needed some fresh air in my face. I was tired of the A/C all day in the Hall. We were on the road for about an hour not talking much at all. I wasn't a big talker anyway. My mind was on the task ahead of me wondering who was running the yard at this time. From my homework about Chobee, I learned that the two biggest "cars" [homeboy clicks] were Miami and West Palm Beach. The yard was made up of South Florida then it was broken down by how close your city was to the next city. The only thing about the politics of the yard was who could get up the most numbers to ride together. Little did I know that was about to change. And I would be plugged in with the new power nigga on the yard. As all of this was running through my mind we were pulling up at Palm Beach Juvenile Center.

When the car came to a stop, I was thinking that it was cleaner than the Hall. The old guy told me that we had to go inside. I slid out as best as I could in shackles and followed him inside. Just like I thought, it was clean and cold as hell inside. A couple of black men were on staff and they just looked at the old man like he was out of place transporting hard core juveniles. I knew that was what they were thinking because they said as much. They told him that they would help him get the new dude in the car. I didn't know why they were making such a big deal about helping him until the door behind me popped open and in walked this big ass young nigga. When I say "big" I'm not exaggerating.

Bro was at least six-feet tall and over 225 pounds at 15 years old. After I let that sink in, I quickly let it pass. I was not going to show no fear, but I was thinking how many more niggas up there were his size? I Knew I had to get me a banger asap! Even the old guy's eyes widened when he saw this nigga. Dude just wasn't big, he had these huge ass arms. He should've been playing football. One of the black officers leading the juvenile was talking shit to him. I couldn't tell if they were joking or for real. He stopped just long enough to introduce "Dusty" to the old man.

I took note of his name. Nobody was really paying me any attention for real. I was getting the feeling that this was some kind of important day or something for West Palm Beach Juvenile Center. After listening to the staff talk about how glad they were that Dusty was leaving. Now I know why. It seemed that Dusty had shook up the staff and inmate population. After the paperwork was finished, about five of them escorted us out to the car. I don't think they were there for me. As soon as we were in the car and pulling off, Dusty finally said something to me.

"You smoke?"

I did, but I wouldn't say I was hooked on them. I smoked just to be doing something. Hell, everybody was, so I just followed suit since I couldn't get weed like that. As if the old man knew what we were talking about, right on cue, he fired up a cigarette. Dusty didn't waste no time. He leaned into the cage and said, "Hey, Pop, how about you bless us with one them cigarettes?"

To my surprise, he pulled out his pack and slid one through the cage. But then we had another problem. Our hands were cuffed to waist chains. I had just enough slack to reach my chest. Dusty wasn't that lucky. Everything was super tight on him. He never complained once about the tightness of his shackles. Dusty had the lit cigarette stuck in his mouth since he had accepted it with his lips through the cage. I just waited for Dusty to pass the cigarette when he was ready since he had made the move. He was smoking it without removing it from his mouth. I guess you can say he was hot boxing it. When he nodded his head, I waited until he leaned his head over toward me that I reached as far as my hand would go and got the cigarette out of his mouth. I smoked the rest of it.

We repeated this like four or five more times before pulling up to the Chobee. Over conversation was kept to a minimum. Dusty asked what they called me. I told him my name was Lil Gig, and that I was from Miami. He said that he had already figured that out from the way I looked. I had started growing my hair back, and like most Miami niggas, I was wicking out my hair (growing wild dreads) and had gold teeth in the front. I wasn't sure yet, but I think we were bonding a little bit. It's hard to tell just by telling each other our names and where we were from. But time would tell. Just because we were coming to Chobee together didn't mean shit once we hit the yard. I had witness this same thing over again with other niggas that had come together. But when their homeboys were at war with another city or click, they had to be enemies.

As we turned onto Highway 441 and into the compound of Chobee my first impression was that it was nothing more than a poor looking gated community with some trailer homes around it but, when you looked hard you would see the razor wire fence. Basketball courts were in front of every dorm and also a football field was in the middle of the compound. It had an inside gym for basketball games. Chobee could have been a college for all anybody that did know any better could have seen from the outside. It had a building for medical and one for the mess hall where we go eat our meals. There was a chapel, school area, with vocational trades and staff had to drive cars and trucks around the compound because it was so big. All together there were nine dormitories names; Alpha, Robison, Johnson, Campmallo, Lee, Jefferson, Eagle, D.C., and Washington. There had been more dorms when girls were accepted and now the empty dorms just sat like a ghost town behind another fence.

It was midday when me and Dusty pulled up to our new home. I was ready to get those restraints off my body. After the long ride, I needed to stretch my legs. I knew Dusty felt the same way because his restraints were on tighter than mine, and he was turned sideways the whole ride because there wasn't any leg space with the cage. We pulled up to what looked like a gate house where they opened this big sliding gate first, then we drove into the area in between another big sliding gate that led to the compound.

The old man stepped out the car and handed paperwork to the guard in the gatehouse. The guard looked into the car and asked us our full names and date of birth. After that, he hit a button and the inside gate opened. The old man got back inside the car and just like that we were inside Chobee. He pulled up a little way then made a right hand turn to Washington dorm which was for orientation similar to Dorm 2 back in the Hall. We would end up staying in that dorm for a week.

The treatment was just like prison. We were placed in quarantine which was used to prevent the spread of disease. I didn't mind at all. They gave us new clothes and shoes. I liked the Converse sneakers that they gave us, especially since we wore them in the city anyway.

Since I'm talking about the shoes, let me tell you, "they played a big part in me and Dusty becoming dawgs." Well, me and Dusty made up a unit of 15 new inmates to Chobee. The other guys were just getting there the same day as us or just before. Others had been there a couple of days. Nevertheless, we all were fairly new. There was this other dude named "Dude." Yeah, that was what he said they call him back where he was from in Pock County, Florida. He was just as big as Dusty except he was short as me. He looked as though he could be a running back in the NFL. I mention him because he played a part in this story about our shoes coming up missing and how we got them back.

Our first night in Chobee, we had night gym with more dorm. When we got back to the dorm we were told to take of our shoes and leave them on the back porch. I guess this was a rule of the dorm to try to keep us from fighting. That was dumb because if it's going down, no shoes ain't going to stop it. The next morning when we got up to line up for chow all of our new shoes were gone. Everybody was looking at each other at first. It didn't make sense for one of us to rob our own shit. We were all mad, but Dusty was "38 hot." I could tell he wanted to fight somebody. I was down for whatever, but I was thinking that they would give us some more shoes. To Dusty it was personal and after listening to his reasoning I began to see his point. This was disrespectful. These niggas were trying to punk us on the low. We had to walk to the chow hall in our shower slides. Now I really felt the disrespect that Dusty was so mad about. So when we got into the chow hall and niggas were looking at us with smirks on their faces like it was a game, Dusty got right to it.

He didn't even sit down nor touch his food. He spoke up. "When I find out which one of you fuck nigga took our shoes, I'm gonna break his jaw! If you know what's good for you, the best thing for you to do is put them back on the porch where you got them."

I took this opportunity to let all these niggas know that I wasn't a joke and was about that life for real. As soon as Dusty stopped talking I took the floor. Since I was standing right by him and had dudes on the other side, I said, "To the nigga that want my brand new shoes: They size 7 and a half, we can get a fade asap."

Dude followed up my statement saying he was rocking with the team. The staff didn't stop nothing we had to say. Even they could see the change in power happening on the yard. Dusty was sending a challenge to all the shot callers on the yard. And saying whoever wanted to step up could get a fade was a strong statement. I didn't know enough about the spot yet, but I did feel like those two niggas were about it. So for now I'm rocking with the cause.

The first sign that niggas respected Dusty was our shoes finding their way back on the porch. Not only did we get our shoes back, but niggas were sending us cigarettes, and weed snacks. Word got around the yard about the new dudes in Washington dorm. The rest of our stay in that dorm went by without further incident. The day came when we were assigned to new dorms.

Me and Dude went to Robinson. Dusty went to Johnson. They walked us around the compound, and when you reached the one you were going to then your name was called. They gave us an index card with our picture on it to give to the staff on duty. When we got to the dorm, they were all outside, some dudes were sitting on the bleachers watching the basketball game. Me and Dude walked up to the staff. You couldn't miss him. He was this big, black, loud mouth man.

He introduced himself as Boss. He asked us where we were from. I told him Miami, Dude said he was from Polk County. The guys that were sitting around were looking us up and down. I knew that they were really sizing us up. Boss told us that he would give us our bunks and lockers when we go inside. I took this time to look everybody over. My survivor instinct was kicking in. I did a head count: 36, including me and Dude. I caught a few unfriendly stares. I noticed them when I told Boss where I was from. I did find out that Miami was either loved or hated. Right away I was able to tell who was the shot caller in the unit and he was one of the ones that gave me a mean look. He was tall and kind of big. Not really muscular, just big. His name was Chris. I did find out he was from Fort Pierce which wasn't that far from the compound. His second-in-command was a nigga named Bass from Orlando. He was short and stocky, kind of like Dude but not as big. Me and him did get into a few fights. The first one, I gave it to him. {I'm going to get to that a little later.} Our first night in the new unit went by okay. I didn't do no talking because there was no homeboy in my unit. Dude was being low key himself just like me getting the feel of things. The next morning after we came back from chow, they called me to the Case Manager's office.

She was an overweight white woman. When I stepped into her office it was a complete mess. There were papers and folders everywhere. You could tell she was overworked or lazy. The reason she was seeing me was for my Progress Report. She told me how much time I was projected to do there. That was how they determined our time. It's based on your charges. The plans were B-Plan, BI-Plan, and BI-Special Plan. The B-Plan was 4-6 months, the BI-Plan was 6-12 months, and BI-Special Plan was 12-18 MONTHS. But they had the power to keep us up to your 19th birthday. What plan you got was determined by what type of felony you had [first, second, or third degree]. Because my felony was 1st degree charges, I received a BI-Special meaning I had to do less than 12 months. With that she gave me a few programs. I had to take drug programs and anger management and I couldn't refuse. She also encouraged me to take the GED and enrolled me into trade classes. Those were my goals before the next Progress Report meeting. That was all secondary because my primary concern was surviving because Chobee was off the chain for real.

The shit I had seen there would set the stage for my incarceration life. My first fight in Chobee came later on that night. We were leaving the gym heading back to the dorm. [I blame that one on me.] I broke one of the codes, don't be friendly. We were in line and the nigga Bass was complaining about getting a write up for being out of bounds. He wasn't talking to me, and I just jumped in and said that was fucked up. He turned around so fast I didn't even know what was happening.

The nigga stole me with a wooden hair brush. The kind niggas used to get waves. It dazed me for a minute, but before I could regroup, the nigga scooped me up by my legs and slammed me. I was mad as hell at myself for slipping like that. He got off for real. The only thing that saved me was Boss being right there to break it up. I guess it's a first time for everything. I count this one as a loss. Even though he stole me off guard, when you look up, a slipper does count.

Everybody that knew me, knew I wasn't going to let that go unanswered. I knew I had to get back at him fast or I was inviting problems for myself. See when you doing time in any jail or prison. Your respect is all you got, so you have to protect it at all cost. There was nothing wrong with losing a fight. That didn't matter. What mattered was doing something to stand your ground. So I acted like it was over, but soon as I had my chance I took off on him.

He was going into the back door of the unit. I ran up behind him and put all I had into a right hook. I didn't get the spot I was aiming for, but I got him in the face. I kept striking him in his jaw and both eyes and didn't stop until he fell. Then I jumped on top of him and kept working him over. That's when I felt somebody pulling me off him. It was Boss again. He snatched me up like I didn't weigh nothing at all. HE radioed security to come get us.

They picked me up first and took me to DC Unit. I was put into a cell to be all to myself. About five minutes later I heard them bring Bass in. There were a few niggas in there that I could hear, but I couldn't see them from my cell.

The next day, the head security guy came by my cell and asked me if I had cooled down yet? I told him "Yeah." He said he was going to talk to Bass and if everything was over, he was going to cut us loose. Before he let us leave we had to shake hands. It was the first time I seen Bass since the fight. His eyes were swollen. My head hurt and I had a little knot on my forehead. He opened the door and we walked back to our unit on our own. We didn't talk. That was cool with me. I didn't have no problem, he did. That wasn't the last time me and Bass fought. I gained respect from everybody because I was a fighter. I soon built me a solid team around me: We called ourselves the Four Horsemen.

We were new to Chobee and from different cities. I had big boy named Z, he was from Sarasota,

Florida. Then there was Frank for Belle Glade, C-Moe from Palm Beach and then me. All these niggas looked up to me for some reason or another. They were ready to ride with me on whatever situation arose with some of my homies from Miami with some little wild niggas from Fort Myers [the same city Plies was from]. They had a pretty big car in Chobee at that time. So when my homies came to me with the beef I took over the leadership role.

I sat everybody down and strategized how we would go at the opposition, what niggas on my team would go against who on their side when it was time for war. This was a first test, to see if my team really had my back. This was not their beef it was my homies. But just like I thought, they were all in for me. It jumped off just like I had planned it. Right after lunch, we were fighting all over the school area.

I had my man, beating the shit out of him. Staff was coming from all over trying to stop it. When I saw them rolling in, I faded into the crowd. After my role in that battle, and the win on Fort Myers, I became the shot caller for Miami with my own hitters. Also my alliance with Dusty put Miami and Palm Beach on top at Chobee.

The rest of my time was easy. My hustle was cutting hair. I didn't realize at the time but things were becoming smoother because I was getting institutionalized. Things I was witnessing and experiencing in Chobee was preparing me for all the years I would spend in and out of the prison system. It wasn't nothing to hear someone scream for help when the lights went out in Boys School. Fools would throw boiling hot water on people to "welcome" them to Chobee just for laughs. We could be eating in the chow hall when some dude would just stick his hand in someone's food just to see what would happen. You learn to mind your own business and grow numb to all the dumb senseless impetuous acts of violence. I stayed focused on getting out. The thing about doing time was that it took me some time to understand how everybody seemed to go home for the most part. I say it like that because you did have that percentage that could care less. I use me for an example. I always kept going home as my objective but, the number one thing was staying alive and healthy. I remember seeing guys get out and come right back. I always thought *not me.* But it was becoming my reality as well. It had just happened to me on that case. But I told myself that was a dumb ass mistake. Not really seeing that I was on my way to becoming institutionalized. I would learn this lesson years later after spending over half my adult life behind bars.

But for right now, I had to pass the test of boy school and I was ready to get back to the streets of Miami. I made it out the gate to the work unit. They helped me get a real job. Yeah, I was going into town and working at this restaurant. I was a dishwasher. It didn't bother me. I was happy to go to work away for the boy's school loved making money for my release. I was cool with that. I would much rather go home with some money than stay broke. I had a daughter to think about. I did four months at the work unit. They went by pretty fast. I didn't get my GED like I was hoping for. So that meant I was going back to high school when I got out. I was almost 17 then, but I felt like a full grown man.

Being locked up and seeing the shit I had in my childhood was over far as I was concerned. So going back to school was really a waste of time in my book. But like the adult system, boy's school gave us probation and a case worker that was going to check if we were enrolled and attending school.

The day came when it was my time to leave Chobee. I was ready to get back home and see my baby girl and spend time with her. She was the light of my day. She was so pretty and everybody said so. I was used to work by now, so I had all the right intentions on doing right and staying out of trouble. My plan was to finish school so I wouldn't mess up my probation. I wanted to find a job working in a warehouse or something cool so I wasn't embarrassed doing it. I still had my reputation in the streets to worry about, and added to the fact that I felt like was still some kind of shot-caller. The only problem was I didn't have no real skills at doing nothing that could get me a job and I may have been important in the Hall, and in boy's school, but back on the streets the shit you did in jail didn't matter one bit. Like always it was money, power, respect; and without money you only got respect with violence. And in the 18 months that I was gone a lot had changed.

***

It was 1991. Shit was different from the 80's. It seemed like everybody was getting money in Miami. The clothes were more expensive, new designers were popping. Everybody was rocking Tommy Hilfiger, Nautica, Polo, and Jordans had the shoe game on another level. When I left, you still could've got fresh and clean for like $150 to $300 for a whole outfit. Now that shoes cost $150-$200, with $100 shirts and another $100 or better for your pants it was a whole other level. Not to include that all the young niggas my age and younger were pushing whips on rims. I had a lot of catching up to do.

Thinking the way I did, put a lot stress on me. I felt like I should be balling and rolling around just like the rest of the niggas out there on the streets. Besides, I been hustling before a lot of them. Most of these young niggas would be the same niggas running to me in the Hall or up the road in Chobee. But I owed it to my mother and daughter to try and do it the right way. I found a job washing dishes. It was wide out the way of the hood. So I wasn't too worried about nobody seeing me work there. Though I was trying to be legit, I still had a rep to think about. I was back in school at Miami Central High.

It was lit out there. Shit, the school was where everybody showed off their fruits of hustling. All the young niggas that were getting money in the streets came to school to gamble. Yeah, there were big dice games every day. Niggas would be selling dope, guns, cars, or whatever you were looking for. I was always in the mix of it all trying to straddle the fence between good and bad. The good was losing. I started missing class, then skipping school all together. I was smoking weed, hanging with other young niggas that just got out. Instead of advancing I started robbing again. This time I found a new way to rob so I wouldn't be facing so much time after seeing how much time they gave KK for the shit me and him had done. I was like Naw, no guns. This new way of robbery was jumping off in the hood.

It was called Smash and Grab. All you needed was a spark plug, really just little pieces of it would shatter a car window. When I started seeing the type of bread young niggas were hitting for by smashing and grabbing, I was down for the lick. The game went like this: We would ride four-deep in a car [because the more grabbers, the more niggas could jump out] looking for tourists, we called them the *funk.* It was a known fact that when people went on vacation, they went with a lot of cash. So that's what made them our targets. When we saw a parked car that obviously belonged to a tourist [visible maps were a giveaway] we would jump out, run up to the car and look in for bags like pocketbooks. That's when we would throw the piece of spark plug and smash the window and grab the bag. It would only take a minute when done right.

I turned out to be pretty good at this for the most part. I hit a few good licks. So many niggas out the hood were robbing tourists that we changed the name to Robbing Hood. We all looked alike and dropped more gold teeth in our mouth. All of us were growing dreads that we called "wicks." Polo and Jordans were the dress code in the hood. Everybody was dropping Chevys and I got me a Box Chevy with some 30-inch Low Lows.

I quit my job washing dishes. I was back in the streets full time. I was buying my baby girl new toys and clothes. So I was feeling like what I was doing would take care of us. It's true what they say: Robbing money come fast and it goes faster. Smash and grab became my new job. I kept a spark plug on me. I was ready anytime I saw people slipping. I went back to the Hall for a robbery, but the people didn't come to court so I beat the case. I been out of Chobee for only three months and already been back to jail. I couldn't realize it then, but this was becoming a pattern. "My motto became, I would rather be in jail than out here broke." That was really what all the young dudes I ran with was saying. With that kind of mindset, nothing mattered but getting money. Beating the robbery case made me think I would keep getting away. I kept smashing and grabbing. We were going hard in the city. It wasn't nothing to see broken glass everywhere at every red light and gas station. You could see some poor tourist being robbed, but like every great money-getting game everybody thinks they can play... "The grab game was no different." Motherfuckers started hearing about the type of money we were hitting for and they wanted in. Even rap niggas were feeling our wave. Yeah, JT Money came out with a song that put the whole game on wax. In Robbing Hood we had mixed feelings about it. At first we rocked with it for motivation, until one day we were shooting Cee-lo on Alcoa Park when robbery detectives rolled up. Louis and Nelson were playing a live version of Smash and Grab. That's when we knew the song fucked up the game. To make matters worse, some rookie in the game shot and killed a tourist. Then another rookie crew ran over a tourist lady.

Now back to me, I robbed some tourist and got away but I got snitched on by this security guard from my school. So they were looking for me on that one. When I did another one the same week, I didn't care because I knew I was already wanted. I was 17 years old. This time I was on my way to adult prison.

The thought of going to prison didn't scare me anymore. Deep down I knew I would end up there. What I didn't know then was that I would spend more than half my life in prison. When you're in the streets, life goes by fast. Six months goes by so fast, but you would have done enough wrong to seem like years passed. We were shooting dice at the car wash right by my high school Miami Central when this rental car pulled up and made a U-turn right in front of us. We all couldn't believe what we were seeing, but there it was a white tourist lady.

I sprung into action before she could complete the full turn. I had bust her passenger side window. And I reached for her pocketbook. She grabbed ahold to it and punched the gas. My legs were hanging out dragging on the road. I had to let go or be dragged. I was so mad that I let her get away. And to top of that, my arm was cut and bleeding bad. So I took off my shirt and wrapped it around my arm to stop the bleeding.

If I was thinking straight I would have gotten out of there, but I just walked back to the car wash and went back to gambling. It couldn't have been no more than 10 minutes later when the police had circled the car wash. I grabbed a spray bottle and bent down near the tire of this car that was being washed. They were looking over everybody, checking for fresh wounds on our arms. So finally one of the police officers ask to look at my arms. When he had seen the fresh cut, he asked me how I got that. I told him I cut it washing the car rims. He was not buying my story. He pulled me up and told me to put my hands behind my back and took me to his car. I was put in the back seat.

All the guys were standing around shaking their heads like they knew I was on my way to prison this time. When you been on the run and living like I was for lick to lick there was a strange feeling of relief that came over you. The best way for me to explain it is like a big burden been lifted. And all you want to do is get to the jail and get a bed to sleep in. I guess that apart of being institutionalized. They drove me to where they had the victim waiting to ID me. After that my next stop was to the robbery unit. I was put in a cold ass cell for hours. Until two detectives showed up to interrogate me for nothing as far as I was concerned. They were mad at me when I had nothing to say or to confess to them. They kept telling me how much time they were going to make sure the judge give me in prison. After what seemed like 24 hours or more. They took me to the Hall. Yeah, here I go again ... my second home.

Mr. Davis didn't even get mad no more when he saw me there again but, he didn't let me stay as long as I used to in Unit 2. They always sent me back to Unit 3 where my second mom Ms. Margaret worked. My stay this time was real quick because I was turning 18 years old. And I was what they called "County bound." I was ready to go to the county anyway. Shit was more live over there. Free phone time if you were down with the house man in the cell. Cable TV and you could wear your own street clothes. The big homies had a lot of weed to smoke. Don't get me wrong it still went down on the adult floors of the County Jail. The only difference is on the 10th floor [Juvenile floor], there were more standards on the adult floor. That too changed as years passed. I experience the changes as the O.G. niggas left and went to prison, and young niggas like myself began to run the county.

CHAPTER 5

# Prison Pressure

I was place on the 5$^{th}$ Floor, Cell 5B3. The house man was a nigga named Celo. He was from Opa Locka. He was cool. There were 15 of us in the cell that was made to hold 20. So we had room to work out. The cell was laid back for the most part. I was facing two robbery charges and had no bond. So I was going to have to ride this case to the door. Most of all the other niggas in the cell had been riding for a minute. After being on the 5$^{th}$ floor for a month they moved me to the Stockade, B-Block.

It was going down in the blocks. These cells were bigger and held up to 40 people at a time, and they stayed full. I got into more fights than I can count. The house man was Big Bud from out my hood, Brown Sub. Bud didn't care about us fighting as long as we were fading. He was old school, real nigga who was riding on a body [murder case].

One of my dawgs from Robbin Hood was in the cell. [R.I.P. O.J.] We used to be at odds with each other because every time I spark a nigga, O.J. would want to jump in. But that wasn't my style. So I would have to tell him to stay out of my fights. My time in the Stockade was a new experience for me. Adult jail had different rules than Juvenile Hall. In the Hall we were locked down in two-man cells. In the Blocks we ran the cell however we wanted. Most of us would stay up all night and sleep in the day time. There was always some way to get high. There was any kind of dope you could get on the streets. All I did was smoke weed and work out. Niggas even had their way of making homemade wine. I didn't care for the stuff. They wanted you to contribute your fruit to make the drink. Months went by like weeks. Before I knew, the new year was here: 1992. And I was on my way to do my first prison sentence.

The two robbery cases I had was dropped to one. They had a stronger case on me with the snitching ass lady that worked at my school. And they were trying to use my juvenile record against me so I would get more time if I took it to trial. They offered me a plea deal for 6 years and 2 years on paper. I didn't want to take that much time because I had seen other niggas with the same kind of robbery charges get deals for less time. My nigga O.J. got a better deal. But for whatever reason they weren't going down no more. So I got tired of waiting around in the jail and was just ready to get it over with. Besides all my homies were already going up the road. So, I wasn't worried about not knowing nobody up there.

The thing that bothered me the most about being locked up for so long was I missed seeing my little girl grow up. I was missing "all her firsts." Her first steps and now I was going to miss her first days of schools. I made up my mind then that I wasn't never going to have another kid, until I was sure I wasn't going back and forth to jail and prisons. What I didn't know then was; it was going to be over half my adult years spent in prisons. So she would be my only child.

The day came when they woke me up to go to prison. It was a lot of us going that morning. They put us on three buses and drove us to South Florida Reception Center. Even though this was not Boys School intake, it was basically the same thing. They lined us all up, stripped down naked to see how many tattoos we had. They wanted to know if were in gangs, did we have any enemies we couldn't be housed around? They also checked to see if had any contagious diseases. They made me cut my dreads off and also shave. I was designated a youth offender. They had two dorms with a fence around it designated for us to keep us separate from the adult inmates. Just my luck, the group of young niggas I was in with tested positive for chicken pox. So they put us in a dorm on the adult side of the fences. We stayed inside for 2 weeks. Then we were all cleared for open population.

They just mixed us with the older dudes. So, instead of going to one of the youth offender prisons, I was designated to one of the oldest and toughest prisons in Florida. Belle Glade Prison aka the "Muk." Because of the rise in juvenile crime, the state added dorms for juveniles in adult prisons. To me it was stupid, because we did everything with the adult inmates from work to sports, and even walked the same yard/compound. The only difference was, we slept in a dorm by ourselves and they let us eat lunch first, and gave us milk with fruits.

I liked the Muk. It was easy time for me. There were old timers from the hood that ran with my daddy. They helped me adjust and learn the rules of prison. The basic rules were the same as the Hall and Boys School. The Top 3: Mind your business, Never snitch, and Always stand your ground. Give respect and demand your respect back. Belle Glades was just like the streets. There was everything. The only things that were missing were cars and females. But some niggas were still getting pussy. They were fucking on visits and some niggas had C.O.s giving them some. It wasn't long before I was running the Y.O. unit. My O.G. homies put me up on the dope game in prison.

I was making a stack ($1,000) of an ounce of weed. I was making a stack off an 8 ball of crack, and the same off a gram of cocaine. Anybody that ever did time in prison would tell you that there is a lot of money to be made behind the wall. Some of my homies from the Juvenile Hall were up there with me. My niggas Burt, Joe, Mad, Joe Joe, Hen. There were a few of the niggas I met in the County Jail like my nigga Celo. Burt had two uncles, Big Mike Ward and Baldy Ward, who both had been down for like 20 years already. Baldy was on the O.G.s who was giving me the game. So when Burt and Joe came to the Muk, he turned them onto me, not knowing me and them were already tight but, with his co-sign we got tighter. Us clicking up then would be a big gain once we all got out. I had it made there. I was getting money, working out, eating good. I didn't have to put hands on nobody but one nigga.

That came about because I sold one of his white boys, some weak ass weed. But I told the nigga that it wasn't all that before they got it. He let the cracker buy it anyway. See this is how things work in prison. White boys that wasn't running with the ABs or the Dirty White Boys car were fair game for the wolves, booty bandits and any other predators. Well, the homie Twin called himself being War Daddy for three white boys in the Y.O. dorm. So when the cracker came to me to buy some weed, I played the game how it went and ran it by Twin first. I put him up on the weed being garbage. He told me it was cool with him and he was going to make sure the white boy payed up. So when it came time for the white boy to go to the line to get my order from the window, Twin came over and told me that he and the white boy smoked the weed and was still waiting to get high. So in a round-about way he was trying to be funny with how he was telling me he wasn't letting the white boy pay me for the weed. I wasn't about to let him buck me because that would be a sign of weakness and disrespect and if I let that ride, the next man would feel like they could do the same to me. I would never make no money like that nor be respected in the dorm.

I told Twin to shoot me a fade. He thought because he trained in boxing with this old head from the crib that he could whoop me. Needless to say, I beat the shit out of Twin. All that boxing shit went out the door when I took off on him first. We both ended up going to the box because this supposed-to-be-boxer wanted to grab and hold me because he couldn't handle the blows I was throwing at him. So when homies yelled that the C.O. was coming I couldn't run. They gave us 30 days in the box. We both agreed that was it and the beef was over-with, so they let us back out after our DC time was up.

Some of the niggas that I was in the Boys School with were at the Muk with me. One of my old enemies for Chobee was there too. I'm talking about that nigga Bass from Orlando. We were in South Florida around all my homies. If I wanted to I could have had him done up real quick, but that wasn't my style. The beef we had in Chobee was fair game and I felt like we were even. After all I had the upper hand because I got the best of him the last time we fought. In the Y.O. dorm, my homies had pressure on the dorm. When you do time in jail or prison, you fall into different categories. Either you was pressure or under pressure. Then you have what I call "Finna niggas." They the niggas that always talk about how they were finna whoop this nigga, or finna get a pack in, finna do this or finna do that. Far as I was concerned, I was pressure.

I had some real homies that loved to apply pressure for no other reason than because they could. I understood that pressure could bust a pipe. So why apply it when it wasn't needed? We were close to home, like 45 minutes away. We were getting money, *I was* at least. So I was in chill mode. If it didn't have nothing to do with my money I didn't care what happened, but it wasn't that way with the rest of my homies. They were putting down hard on the niggas we call O.B. [Off Brands]. All good things come to an end when you getting it the wrong way.

To this day, I don't know what started the little riot in the Y.O. dorm, but it was my homies against the O.B. niggas from North Florida. When I got word of what was happening it was already going down in the TV room. So not really thinking it through, I jumped out my rack and ran to the TV room. There were fights going on all over. The niggas from up top were getting backed into the corner while some of their guys were getting stomped out in groups.

I ran into a few of my Cuban homies beating an O.B. in the head with locks in socks. Blood was everywhere so I started kicking the shit out of the O.B. that fell down in front of me trying to run out the TV room. Somebody yelled that the C.O. was coming with the doom squad. I was so caught up in the fight that I got roped off with the majority of the O.B.s. My nigga Burt got caught too. So we ended up going to the box. Then everybody got transferred to other prisons.

I was so mad at myself for getting into that dumb ass riot in the first place. There was no good reason for me to be involved with this mess. After that transfer I did end up moving from prison to prison before I finished my sentence. I ended up at Baker C.I. where I would run in to my nigga Bo aka Bo-Aveli. We became dawgs for life. I knew of

Bo. He had a name in the streets for being a hitter, a real gun slinger. He was doing 7 years for attempted murder.

Baker was wide open just like the Muk. I didn't have my connect with the dope game. So, that made me turn back to the robbery game. Me and a few of the homies started robbing white boys for their wedding rings. We would take them to this old head that had the weed game on lock. I remember we were coming back so fast with rings that he had to stop us by saying his wife had enough of them. It got so bad that the Captain called us to his office demanding we return the rings. We played like we didn't know what he was talking about but, we knew that we would have to find another lick. That's when we heard about this punk who was selling weed on the weight pile.

So we got the bangers and headed right over there. We set out there and watched the punk work out on his legs until a dude walked up and we saw the punk dig down into his shoes and pull out a plastic bag with some sacks of weed in it. That's when I set the plan into play. We would wait until he got back under the weight to squat. That's when we would make our move.

My homie Guja was like, "Damn, Gig, you trying to kill the nigga."

Naw, that wasn't true. I just wanted him focused on that weight when we moved. So we ran up on him just when he was putting the weight back into the rack. Guja grabbed him around his neck in a chokehold. I pulled the banger out and put it right into his face so he could see it. He was kicking his legs up trying to buck, so I stuck the banger into his legs and told my other homie to take off the nigga's shoes so we could go. He kicked again, so I stuck the banger back into him. He went still then started crying and shit. You should have seen these big muscle bound ass niggas running off the weight pile. They drawed heat on us because the C.O working the rec yard seen them and hit the alarm ["deuces"]. At the same time that happened we got the shoes off and the bag of weed. We threw the punk down and joined the rest of the niggas running off the rec yard. We split up and went to our dorms because we knew they was going to lock down until they found out what went down.

An hour went by and I thought we were in the clear, but then I looked up in to the officer's station and saw a group of C.Os in there and it looked like they were looking my way. So I wasn't surprised when they came out walking my way. I found out the hard way that Baker C.I was tired of the pressure me and my crew was putting down. So they shipped me and the homies off the pound. The only good thing that came about from my stay at Baker C.I was I did get my GED.

They put us in the box and then transferred us to different prisons. I went to Century C.I which was up the panhandle to North Florida. It was the northernmost prison in the state, so I went from being close to home to being as far as I could get. Century C.I was wild for real. Nobody worked. Everybody just got high and gambled. It was cool with me because all the moving from prison to prison was making my time go by faster. By the time I did whole time and got transferred it was my year to go home.

Yeah, I had a 6 year bid. I came in 1992, and now it was 1996. I just got word that Bo was out. Burt had been home for like six months now. Joe was out too. My nigga Lil Willie was out. 1996 was the year a lot the homies were getting released. It was pressure in the city for real. So many niggas trying to regain the respect on their name. Then you had young niggas trying to make a name in the streets, and I was on my way back out. All I truly wanted was to get some money. I didn't have no real plan. I heard my older brother on my dad's side was getting money up the road in Tennessee. My brother Gregg was getting money up the road in Panama City. See, shit was crazy now. He had just go grabbed by the Feds for trafficking a brick of hard. That was hurting my family because bro was holding the family down, pa the bills and looking out for my little girl. He dropped me m Now all that responsibility was waiting on me and I had no knew no job would be waiting on me. So though I had 2 ye I didn't care, I was ready to go hard.

My day came, and I was ready to go. They gave me ticket. When I got home there was nobody there. I h one of my brother's homies that had the keys to the staying on the Island. She didn't know when I was getting out. She had been holding it down with the bills. So I called up one of my niggas to through [it was my nigga Bone]. He came through asap. We smoked a few Js and he did his best to run down; what was going on in the streets, who was running what spots and who was down with who. What prices was on the dope, and who had work. We both agreed that it made sense to reopen the spot my brother had in Panama. I had my phone book with a few numbers of his people up there. I still hadn't got around to holla at my other bro, Ace, yet. What I needed now was some pussy.

CHAPTER 6

# Major Pressure

Baba-mama wasn't fucking with me and I was cool with that. So, the next best thing was the strip club. My nigga Mac from Robbin Hood had this club called Foxy Lady on 79th on lock. After tricking off with this badass stripper I was ready to bust a few blocks and see who I would run in to when I was on 15th Avenue to see what was up on the Ave. Niggas were still getting money up there, but it wasn't the old Ave in the glory days. I was seeing more out of town tags on cars. The game was changing out here. Everybody was getting money out of town. All the homies were showing me love; my niggas, Dirt, Red, Spider Man, Lil Cal, Fat Toney, and Big Nate [just to name a few]. I told Bone to take me on 60th Street, 14th Ave. That was where my nigga Burt stayed. His big bro was Fred. As soon as I pulled up, the block was already full of niggas I knew from the joint and more niggas from the 61st. My niggas were really happy to see me. Burt introduced me to Fred aka Black-aveli. He told him a few prison stories and how we got transferred in the riot. Bo, Joe, and Lil Willie were there too. Before I knew it we were all loading up in the cars that had pulled up everywhere on the block. Bone had already left. He wasn't really into crowds. We made plans to hook up the next day. So we could put a trip together to go up the road. In the meantime, I was hanging out with my niggas from the joint. I was riding with Fred [I didn't mention Fred was in a wheelchair but that didn't stop nothing]. Bro was a boss and a real G in those streets with big respect on his name.

We pulled up to Miami Nights in Carol City. The club was packed. This rap group called Mr. Mike and a female rapper called Note were performing. Fred hollered at the nigga at the door and our whole crew got in. I was pushing Fred, so I wasn't doing no drinking. As soon as we got in, me and Fred and a few young niggas who were rolling with us headed back to the pool tables and the bar. I looked around to see where Bo, Burt, Joe and the other homies were rushing the stage. I was having a good time. All my senses were on high alert. You got to understand being locked up for so long makes a person institutionalized. So I was feeling a little uncomfortable. I didn't know if Fred was picking up on my vibe but, he passed me the weed, I guess to help me chill. Then this sexy ass female walked up and stopped right in front of us. I did learn that when you're hanging with Fred all kinds of hoes will be trying to holla at you. I was used to the teenage club where you just grab and feel on females if they looked good. Fred had seen me looking at Little Mama and gave me the head nod, *go get her!*

So I walked up behind her and grabbed a handful of her ass. She wasn't having none of that. She turned around looking mad as hell, yelling something but I couldn't hear her over the music. I just stood there looking at her like, "Bitch, chill out. What, you a dyke or something?" I looked over at Fred for some help since it was his idea in the first place!

He was dying laughing at the bitch going off. So when she turned and walked off I was glad but, that didn't last long because she came back with these two linebacker looking niggas. My prison instinct kicked in, so before either one of them could make a move on me, I set it off by punching the one closest to me. I knocked him down right next to Fred's chair. The other nigga was caught off guard when I caught his homeboy. I didn't give him time to react. I grabbed a pool stick and hit him across the head. Out of nowhere, all my niggas rushed over and we beat the shit out of these two niggas. I don't know what happened to the female that started all this. She got missing in the crowd.

The security guards came over in full force to break us up and threw us out. I was thinking about getting to the guns in the cars. I didn't want them other niggas to beat us to the straps. There was no need to worry about them because they were going to the hospital.

Burt was the first one to ask me what that was about. I told everybody what went down on our way back to the hood. The homies weren't mad at me but they did say I could've waited until after Mr. Mike had performed. I wasn't the only one of the homies that got into it with somebody. Lil Willie had words with this nigga from down south. The nigga was a OG from down south and a known killer. But so was my nigga Lil Willie. I didn't give a fuck; I'm riding with my dawgs. That's how you're trained to go in the joint, it could be right or wrong. When we got back around the way, we were all sitting on 60th Street in front of Burt's crib just smoking and drinking telling war stories about the joint. When I asked about how niggas were beating the piss test on paper, Burt spoke up first with his advice for me. He told me that he never checks in with the probation officer. His logic was if you didn't check in, they wouldn't come looking for you. Yeah, he was right in part. They didn't come looking, but they do put a warrant out for your arrest. His reason with that was if I did get caught for a violation all they could give me is the 2 years that I had on paper. It didn't take much effort to convince me not to check in. "So there you have it. I was fresh out of prison and already a wanted man."

We stayed into the next morning. I ended up jumping into the car with Lil Bo. I found out that he was staying right around the corner from me out in C.C. One of the homies E-Double had a few whips, so he threw Bo the keys to a candy red Donk 73 sitting on some Wus. Yeah, everybody was showing us love, now that we were home. Bo wanted to stop by the liquor store to get a bottle of Hen. So we drove to one on 47th and 22nd Avenue in the Sub, then rode around the block to Tyger Stop a dope spot some of our homies out in the Sub ran but, as soon as we pulled up at the Stop Sign there was this car just sitting there, not moving.

Bo pulled up next to it and there was a nigga slumped over in the driver seat with a hole in his head. I looked over at Bo and didn't say a word, we were thinking the same thing. Let's get out of here! We drove away in silence. When we got to Carol City, Bo dropped me over my brother's house and he went to the crib. The next day Bone came through as planned. I called one of my brother's Greg homies. His name was Dee, and well, he owed my brother a few stacks so he broke me off two ounces of white. Bone was grabbing a 9 piece of white for the trip. He had a spot in North Carolina where his cousin was from. This would be my first time going out of town to flip some work. Bone would put me up on a lot of game on how to act on the road. Everything from speed limit to when we stop to get gas or at a rest stop. There was no smoking or drinking on the road. We had a flip cellphone that we used as a burnout [meaning it was somebody else's line] and a beeper. We had a long drive ahead of us. I think it was like a 22-hour ride to Fayetteville, North Carolina. I didn't have a clue where that was and didn't care. I was just ready to learn the whip game. Bone said once we got there he was going to show me how to cook up the powder into crack rock. Whipping the work would increase my two ounces into 3 and a half of rock. I asked him, "Why not four ounces?"

He said that was pushing it and would make the dope too weak. Shit, I didn't care. I just wanted to get paid. He said we could make a $1,000 off an ounce if we sold it whole. But if we chilled, and broke them down to 8 balls and $20 rocks, we would make $1,600 to $2,000 off each one. I wasn't in no rush to get back to Miami. All this was new to me so that made it exciting to me. So we stayed up there for a week. Bone jumped a few of his ounces whole for that stack. I cooked up my 2 and a half with the whip game and stretched it to 3 and a half.

We rented a trailer home from the trailer park. It was booming with crackheads. It didn't take me long to find me a white trick to keep me entertained when things slowed down during the day time. When we were done trapping all the work we gassed up and hit the highway back home. I was feeling good about the trip. I had $4,500 in my pocket. Bone was good. He was already talking about copping a half a block and fucking with my brother's spot in North Florida. He was on my case about not spending all my money on dumb shit, but making sure I had my re-up money.

All I wanted to do was pay a few of the bills at the crib and break my daughter off a few dollars but, I needed to talk to my mom first to see how she was taking care of the bills first. If it was some kind of direct deposit out of her account. I knew it was set up something like that. Man, when I tell you I had some big shoes to fill taking my brother's place. The difference between us was my brother was more organized to be all the way real with you. He was smarter when it came to books and with moving around in what I considered the white man's game: the legal stuff. I was just a go-getter, a street hustler, hood nigga. We were just about home when the cellphone rang, only family and Dee had this number. It was Dee, my brother's homeboy, the one that gave me the work. He got word from my mom that she was coming in town to day from the island so he wanted to know who would be there in time to pick her up.

Her flight didn't land until later that night, so yeah, we could get there in time. I asked Bone to drop me off at the house first. Then he could go pick my mom up. Bone was a real nigga, and I considered him a close friend. Anybody that knew me, knew that I wouldn't use that term *friend* much. To this day, Bone has kept it real with me. Nevertheless, I had to get my mom's house cleaned up the best I could before she walked through the door. It really didn't make no difference because she was going to clean it up again anyhow. But I was trying not to hear her go off on me about how messy I had it. So after an hour, Bone pulled up with the old girl.

I was happy to see mom. It had been almost five years since I'd seen her. She still looked the same for the most part. She was putting on weight. I guess that was all that island food. We hugged and both turned and thanked Bone for the lift. I walked Bone to the car and told him to swing by in the morning to scoop me. He agreed, then pulled off.

I helped mom bring her bags inside then we sat down for the talk I knew we would have.

She wanted to know wanted to know about my plans. And if I wanted to move to the island with her? Have I been to see my daughter Kevia yet? As I was trying to lie my way through all those questions, I couldn't keep a straight face for nothing in the world. It didn't help that I was high as hell. I smoked two joints before they got there and the weed was kicking in right now. Mom could always tell when I was lying. So I don't know why I even tried. She wasn't having none of it. She told me right then and there that I needed to get my act together or she was leaving and locking her doors and going back to the island. So I needed to make up my mind about getting a job and raising my daughter, or getting back in the streets where I would die or return to prison. So there it was: Decision time. I already made up my mind. To me there was never a choice, I was born to hustle. All I had ever known was the streets. I couldn't understand why she was even asking me that.

Her, out of all people should know how I came up. She had me, but the streets raised me. "Facts!" She knew that ain't nobody ever gave me nothing. Hell, I ain't never even had a birthday party in my name. Let alone a gift present. We didn't have Christmas celebrations like other families. Our Christmas was going shopping for family members that were less fortunate than us, and that wasn't saying much because we didn't have much, but my mom would save up a little something to buy the kids on the Island gifts. Me and bro would spend our Christmas delivering them gifts. I didn't mind because I got to spend time with my grandma so that was enough of a Christmas gift for me. But still, she knew I had been in the streets from Day One. As far back as I could remember it's been a hustle for me while other kids were doing kid shit like playing school sports.

I remember running into my other big brother on my daddy's side one afternoon. He was on his bike riding to football practice when we crossed paths. I was on my way to my side hustle. Yeah, pumping gas at the Shell station on 79th and 22nd Avenue, I then walked across the street to Earl's Supermarket and bagged groceries. On top of that I used to save soda bottles for extra cash. So to answer mom's question, my plan was to get it out the streets, "why not?!"

The streets owned me, it chose me! See, a lot of niggas chose the Thug Life in the streets. That just ain't my case. My daddy was a thug and he ran the streets, so I guess what they say is true about the apple: "it don't fall far from the tree." I broke my mom off a stack telling her to use $700 on the bills and use $300 for Kevia. Then I called Bo to come pick me up. I was ready to see what was going down on 60th Street. When Bo pulled up, he was fatigued out in camo gear. He was banging 2Pac so you already know I was "Bout it, Bout it!" We went to the flea market so I could get fatigued out too. I had the gloves and Hi-Tec boots to go with it.

When we got to the city, Bo was telling me about all that I had missed while I was out of town. He told me that him and Joe came up with a few pounds of weed and Burt had the white. So they started a spot on 60th Street that they were calling Macaveli. Yeah, everybody in the city was feeling Pac's wave.

CHAPTER 7

# County Pressure

In 1996 damn near every dope spot was named after one of 2Pac's hit songs. It's a known fact that we always put names on our dope packages; it's a Miami thing going back as far as I could remember. It would inevitably work against us. Once the Feds started using the names to R.I.C.O. as in drug conspiracy charges.

There was a click of niggas in the city that I was hearing about way before I got out the joint called J.D. aka John Doe. They were putting down hard all over Miami. The name of the game was "Get down or Lay down." If you ain't serving J.D.'s shit don't be here when we come back! For the most part they had Liberty City sewn up. There was a J.D. spot everywhere in the city. Since there are still open cases going through the court system, I will not mention key nigga's names. I'm just going to call them by initials. I'm also not going to go into real details about serious criminal activities.

The nigga that was running J.D. was B, he was a real nigga far as I could tell. I didn't know him before then but, he was down with all my niggas so eventually we could be down. I had respect for my nigga "B". He was one of the type of Captains that led from the front not the back and he was making sure everybody on his line ate! He had a lot of young hitters on his line. I was kind of concerned with that part of the game. Just didn't know if they were really ready for both sides of the game yet.

Yeah, it's so easy to thug in the streets with the money, cars, guns, and everything else that came with the Thug Life, but can you pass the test of the G-Code inside jails and behind prison walls? Or even before that, the interrogation room when them crackers talking about life and football numbers? I just didn't see all them young niggas being ready. When they ain't never even been to the Hall, or the 10th Floor yet. B had enough of them young niggas that was down to ride for the cause. All up and down 61st you could hear them young niggas screaming "John Doe, No Fear! Green bag, we open!" And they were definitely wide open with everything: One stop shop on weed, coco, and base.

At that time there were all kind of major clicks throughout Miami's inner city. You had a click in Over Town doing the booster shit with the stores. They were called the Burdines Bandits [That was a fat girl and her crew]. My cousin Corn Flake was putting his foot on niggas' necks Over Town. [I will tell you about him later on.] You had niggas like Fame, Bam, and RaRa going hard in the streets. Black Girl was still the queen of Over Town. I can't leave out them niggas on 2nd Avenue and 19th Street. Cash, T.O., Gator, R.I.P. Al – I fucked with a lot of niggas out of town. My nigga Cheese, Hen, Cheeda, my nigga Lil Willie's brother Dre. Man, it's so many of them niggas that got love for me Over Town. Then you had my homies out the Sub. My nigga Juki, Phil, Wemp, Scoobo, Myshawn, Pritt and his brother Kenny Ken.

My nigga Vee and Pazo, my cuz had 44th and 17th on lock. They called that the 40s. Mike and G-shorty. Moony Boy was Flake's brother. That's the Parker side of my family on my brother Ace's side. They were all real street niggas, well respected in the streets. A lot of niggas in the streets didn't even know that they were my family. That's because I made my own name out here in these streets but, later on in the story you will see how the family became closer with me! Back to all these different clicks out here.

See, back then, Miami wasn't known for being gang related with Bloods, Crips, and GDs banging that way. But I guess you could say we was kind of like neighborhood gangs holding down spots. There was the Zoe Pound which were Haitians who clicked up to hold down Little Haiti. You had the chico niggas out of Hialeah calling themselves the Yolos. There were the niggas out of Scott Projects, Home Team, Dog Pound, the Cannon niggas on the wall in the Pork Beans getting money. So no matter where you were from, you just repped that hood or project and that was your click, gang, or whatever you labeled yourself. There were so many groups or clicks all over the city. You had Cloud 9 on 15th Ave. Niggas out of Opa Locka ["the Locks"]. It's just too many to name them all but you get the picture. This was the street culture of Miami back then.

What you see now is young niggas out of Miami following whatever the wave was on social media. I say that because coming up in my era we was given the game like this: You don't follow a nigga unless he helping you get money or teaching you how to get money. Basically, if he helped put food in your mouth, and on your table that meant he is a boss. A Real O.G or "G." Not some nigga that been put down before you in a gang, or just because he been to prison or whatever lame ass reason these young niggas letting these self-proclaimed O.Gs and Gs run down on them to send them out on dumb shit like no reason drive-bys for the hood or set. "But not to get too far away from my story, that's a topic for another book."

It was 1996, and I was fresh off the road from my first out of town flip. I was mobbing hard on 60th Street with my Veli-boys. Yeah, that's what we were calling ourselves. Just like J.D. we were screaming, "Macaveli, Macaveli, weed base, and laces! Veli-life, living out of prison, pistols in the air!!" J.D. was screaming "No Fear." We were screaming "Whatever! Whatever! However!"

Niggas Over Town was screaming "Towner 4 Life. Young nigga, Thug Out!"

Zoe Pound was riding 10-15 cars deep through the city waving their Haitian flag screaming "Zoe Pound, Zoe Pound, get down niggas!"

Black Boy, Chico, and that nigga E4 were holding Carol City down. My little brother Jay on 181st and 32nd Ave had a little crew. With all these crews running around Miami, it was bound to be wars and an escalating body count. 1996 was the beginning of some major conflicts between different parts of Miami. "I will get into some of them later on in the story."

Me and my niggas were enjoying our freedom, trying to play catch up in a lot of different ways but, at the same time making sure we stayed ready for whatever. We used to greet each other with our pistols drawn, not handshakes of daps. I watched Burt slap the shit out of one of the homies. He wasn't even a Veli but, he used to be on the block. We were all standing on 61$^{st}$ in Thug Life spot. For some reason everybody was pulling out fire [guns] and showing them off. This nigga Kojack didn't have no fire. Burt asked him why he wasn't strapped and he said some dumb shit. "Why?" I can't remember what he said, but the next thing I knew was his head was bouncing off the homie Flum's van. I kind of felt bad for the nigga because I knew Jack for a long time but, if you let a nigga slap you, then what can I say but, "fuck you!" There was no place for weakness in these streets and that's what Burt was trying to get into his head. If you ain't strapped, then that meant you ain't going to bust when the time came to clap back.

I knew another reason why Burt was pressing Kojack. He really wanted Jack on the team, working the bomb for Mackaveli. It was a known fact that when Jack post up in front of any spot it goes to booming, work moving so fast Jack could easily turn a $500 a night spot into a $10,000 a night spot. He did for Flum, with Thug Life, he did too on the Ave with Lil Sweet's spot. Burt knew if we could get Kojack to work the bomb it would help Mackaveli move more work. But he was going about it the wrong way. Actually we were having a real problem with keeping niggas that would work the bomb for Mackaveli. For one it was a new spot, so we wasn't paying a nigga much, just $100 a shift but, if a nigga hung with us they make more as the spot picked up which we all knew it would do with time. Niggas like Kojack was used to making $250-$400 a shift, if not more. Another reason why we could keep workers was because it was constant pressure being around a bunch of wild ass niggas that was used to applying pressure with violence.

Every day Joe or Bo would show up with some off brand nigga to work the bomb. No matter what their name was, everybody called them "Black" so there was a constant rotation of Blacks. One morning when Bo and me were riding to the city, he ran the problem down to me saying how the spot was picking up but they couldn't keep a bomb man. That was hurting the spot. At the time, I was still waiting on Bone so we could hit the road again. I started putting a little work down in Robbin Hood, and I had some weed pushing, on my little brother's spot in Carol City on 181st. I had money flipping, but it was a small spot, only a couple hundred dollars a day. Then I was breaking off the niggas I had pushing it, but it was a little flip. At least something was better than nothing. I was really waiting on that out of town money. I was spoiled on that! My older brother Ace was eating for real. He was putting a lot of the family down. I was hearing and seeing a lot of the cousins were shining because of bro.

He came in town a few times and broke me off a stack here and there. Promising next time he would take me with him. I believed him every time and I felt like he was going to fuck with me sooner or later. He was big bro and I knew he had love for me. I think he was trying to do too much for too many people at once. So I never really took it personally when he would come to town and do his thing. I always depended on myself anyway. So I was used to getting it however. When me and Bo pulled up on 61st Street that day, Joe came out the house and we all walked over to Burt's crib. He stayed with his mom ["Aunt Blanche"].

She was my girl. She loved me just like I was one of her sons. She was like that with all us Veli-boys. Blanche was a real OG. She could look at you and tell if you were real or fake in a few minutes and she let you know right then and there to your face. You got to understand she had been around real street niggas her whole life. All her brothers and sons were real niggas. That morning when we walked through the door, she was doing her thing in the kitchen cooking Fred some breakfast. But she always made enough for the whole crew.

There was nobody on the corner when we pulled up. I did notice that, so did Bo. So that was the first thing Bo mentioned. Everybody was looking the same way. Like what the fuck to do? I spoke up, "Where the work?" Joe had a brown paper bag, so he put it on the table. There was the bomb. I said, "What's the count?"

"$5,000," Joe answered, "on everything?" he nodded. That made it $15,000.

I put it all back in the bag and started for the door. Aunt B called my name, so I stopped. She gave me a plate. "Good looking." I thought.

Then I went outside to the spot, put the bomb up and started eating. And that's how I started serving Mackaveli bomb. With me on the corner, shit started being a lot more live because all the guys would stand out there with me. I started meeting all the other young niggas that was down with the crew like Kenwa [RIP], Ken, and Red Dog. He stayed right across the street. He had two fine ass sisters. Burt was fucking the oldest one. We all were trying to fuck the young one. There was Shard, Burt's cousin, a real wild young nigga. He was one of the reasons we couldn't keep a bomb man. Shard would fuck with them so hard they would quit.

The first time I met Shard was that day. He came up on the corner talking loud, screaming "Mackaveli! We open!"

I said, "Yeah, we wide ass open!"

So he said, "Black, you working?"

It was me, Red Dawg, and a few other dudes that was copping. I didn't answer him right away, but when I did say something it was after I served the two niggas. So he could see I working the bomb. He was looking at me like I should know who he was. That's when I spoke up.

"Dig this, my nigga. My name is Gig. What's happening with you?"

First he said, "Shit, whatever."

I knew he was strapped. I could see the banger sticking out the side of his waist. I wasn't worried about that because I was holding fire too. Just as shit was getting awkward, Fred pulled up and Bo and Joe jumped out the car and came over and handed me a joint. I pulled on it and handed it to Shard and just like that the tension was over. [Later on, in the story you'll see that me and Shard would become real tight.] From then on I would work the bomb. Once I started, we all kind of pitched in to keep the spot jumping.

If you worked a whole shift, when it was time to turn over with Joe, you just took $100 out the pot. If you worked two shifts, you took $200. We all had the same goal: Get the spot booming so we all could see some real money. I started walking around the block on 61<sup>st</sup> because of a nigga named Jeff. "Let me run that story by you so you have a clear understanding of why I was letting Jeff break me off every morning."

I met Jeff in Century C.I He was a little older than me and we had got cool after I stepped up and helped him get his poker pot back. I didn't know who Jeff was when a couple of the homies came to me about how these OB ass niggas had just chumped off the old school homie out the Pork Bean for his poker pot. They was talking about it as if it was funny. I was trained different. I saw what had happened as a disrespect to the whole Miami car. Those niggas didn't check with us first to see if we were riding with Jeff or not. So I took it upon myself to get Jeff's pot back. Me and a few of the homies pulled up in the OB niggas. Once they'd seen that either they had to hand over the pot or they were going to get fucked up over it, they chose right and gave the pot back. I went to the homie Jeff and explained to him that if he was going to be running anymore poker games he needed to have to cut the homies in so we could have his back.

From that point me and Jeff was cool. Whenever he won big he would come through and break me off. Also he took my advice and put the poker game down with the homies so they would have his back. For this reason on, this played a part with the rest of my story. [I'm also going to let you know that one of the reasons the homies didn't really fuck with Jeff was because he fucked with boys.] Yeah, the OG homie fell weak on his bid and gave into ass. Normally I don't put a nigga in prison business out there unless they get out and try to holla at a female in my family or one I care about. I did have to pull a card on my sister's baby daddy. [I'll tell you about that later on.] Back to Jeff; him being gay would come back to the hood anyway. Like it always did, but for right now, Jeff was offering me free money for doing nothing. When I fought out, who his nephew was, and they were getting money as far as I could see. His nephew was a nigga name Murrph. He liked to race cars. [Yeah, he had some real runners.] I didn't know bro personally other than seeing him in the hood but, Fred and all the other homies were cool with him. Nevertheless, my business was with his Uncle Jeff. All Jeff wanted me to do was really post up in the morning and smoke weed with him I guess, because that's all I did. Just before I pulled up to leave, he always asked me if I was straight. Of course I wasn't! So he pulled out some bread and would hand me $100.

We did this routine for a few months at least until I figured out why I think Jeff really wanted me around there with him. It was for the same reason he fucked with me in the joint. Jeff and his nephew's spot was right across the street for one of J.D.'s spots. So for real, it was like they were in competition for the money. Both spots was eating and doing well as far as I could tell, "but like I told you earlier about B" the nigga that ran J.D. If B saw weakness in you, or in crew then he would put down. It came to a head on July 4th that year. Everybody liked to show off their firepower, so the guns came out. So all the young niggas from all the different crews were out in full force. The J.D. boys all called themselves "Loso" because it had a mob feel to it. So you know Veli-boys was out and about. Thug Life young niggas was out screaming "Thug Life." Together this was the 61st Street Lynch Mob. Everybody was shouting up in the air, "Knock Down Power Boys and just flex real hard!!!"

Here came Jeff. He upped the stick [AK 47] and let off a clip. After he was done, B yelled something. I couldn't hear it from where I was standing. B said something and everybody started laughing. Jeff said something back to him before going back into his mother's apartment. Bo was standing closer to B, so I knew he heard what went down. I made a note to ask him later because if there was some kind of beef in the air, I needed to know so I didn't get caught in the middle of it.

1996 was real wild on 61st. Shit got real crazy when the city sent crews out to drop big ass lamp posts down as blockades. It was one way in and one way out. It began at 62$^{nd}$ and 15 Ave. That was the only way in or out. It went to 62$^{nd}$ - 57$^{th}$ from 17$^{th}$ Ave – 12$^{th}$ Ave. We took it as a pass to do us. It made us even bolder with our guns, now we brought out the sticks. That's what we started calling our AK-47s, AR rifles, and mini 14s because we had a lot of the wooden stock AKs. When the rest of the hoods in the world was stuck on calling them "choppers" down in the bottom, in the city of Miami we knew them as sticks. So I guess you could say they dubbed us Stick City because it was like the Wild West.

It wasn't nothing to see niggas walk through allies standing on the corner with sticks stuck down their legs, with taped up clips in their back pockets. We weren't worried about the police. We knew once they came in the hood and through the blockade they never stopped or got out of their cars. I think they were coming out of curiosity more than anything. I remember feeling kind of funny when one drove by on 60$^{th}$ Street and we were all standing over there on the corner in Mackaveli strapped. I know he saw the wood stocks coming out the side of our pants. With that many niggas walking around the same area, strapped up, ready for whatever, it was just a matter of time before we would be at each other. It was like gas and heat, there's going to be a fire.

For the most part niggas were giving us our due respect but, we did have some wild ass young niggas on our line. There was B-Love aka Boosie-Veli. He was Bo's little cousin for the Sub. Then I already told ya'll about about Shard-aveli, Red Dog, and Kenwa were laid back chilling, so was Ken-avleli. The peace for us wouldn't last long.

The day that Shard and Joe got shot, I was standing on the corner. Shit happened so fast and too far down the block for me to bust back at the nigga that jumped out and did it but, I got a good look at him, and I knew exactly who he was. I would never forget his face that had a deep scar on it. Besides he was already an enemy. Our beef goes way back to our time in Juvenile Hall. He was the same nigga I told you about, the one I had to whoop for leaving a gap in the line. His name was Zay. Back then, he and my nigga Joe were co-defendants on a robbery and body charge and now he was jumping out of van trying to kill Joe. He hit Joe in the leg but, hit Shard in the back and arm, and his ass. "We'll get to find out later that Shard was the intended target." Joe just happened to get hit in the cross fire. It didn't matter why he did it. All we had in our mind was it was a V-go [that meant a Veli-green light on his head].

Just as fast the shooting started it was over. The van sped away. The way the van was heading was one of the giveaways to who was involved with the hit. They were going in the direction of 58th, and that was where Zay was from. The 1240 building, the JaJa hole. {You've got to remember we were on the block within the blockade.} They didn't head out, they stayed in the hood. As I was running, gun still out, I made it to Shard. There were a few niggas already holding him up, carrying him down to Aunt Blanche's house. So I went to Joe. He was limping with his gun out. The head was cocked back, clip empty; that's my nigga Joe for you. Bet he going to get off. Come to think about it, as I replay the scene in my head that's why the nigga jumped back in the van so fast. He wasn't expecting to get shot back at. Joe and Shard returned fire. That's why Veli niggas always stayed strapped.

When the EMT showed up, Shard was fighting with them while they were cutting off his clothes. They treated Joe right on the spot. He just had a flesh wound. But they had to take Shard to the hospital. As soon as they EMT left, we went inside to plan the next move. It was still daytime, cars were everywhere in front of the house.

B, from JD had just pulled up. Herb, Eddie Bo, Kooda Hound and all the Veli boys were on deck. Fred wanted to know who it was. Joe wasn't even sure, he said it had jumped off so fast that his first response was to pop off. Shard wasn't there to speak up on who it was either, so I said what I saw and told everybody who it was. I said it was that nigga Zay off 58th. B spoke up and challenged me. First, on how I was sure it was Zay and why I didn't bust back. Like I told you before, B really didn't know me yet. So I didn't take offense to him coming at me like that. I told him and everybody that I know Zay real good, and the only reason I didn't just start shooting back was because Shard and Joe was between me and the van. Even before I could say all that. Bo, Burt, and Joe had already checked B on my behalf. Bo was first to say I was a real one.

Joe was like, "Oh, if Gig could have bust, he would have!"

Burt just smiled and said, "that's my dawg right there!"

B got the message, but I guess he wanted to see for himself because he was like, "Good. Because we going to put that work in tonight."

My response was, "It's whatever with me. Veli for life, nigga."

We knew the hood was watching. This was the first real attack on our squad and niggas were waiting to see how we would respond. Bo was itching to get live! He really lived for this gun play that was in his bag. Joe was laid back, like always but I could tell he was ready for action. Joe never liked no niggas to try him in no kind of way. So for a nigga to even shoot at him, and hit him ... my nigga was out for blood. Burt was always concerned with niggas respecting the squad, the hood, and most importantly, his name.

It was always hard to tell what Fred was thinking or how he felt. Big bro was always poker faced. Fred was a real chess player. He would never let you know his moves beforehand and never spoke Veli business with outsiders around. Me, I'm a soldier at heart. It wasn't no question if I was riding. For one, Zay was a personal enemy of mine. Two, I knew my dawgs would ride for me. Three, I knew niggas were trying to see if I was bout it or not. So my rep was at stake. Just like my dawg Burt, my name matters to me.

We pulled out the sticks. I didn't want one. I was cool with my 9mm. I had 17 in the clip and was planning on making my shots count. I was focused on one man. Bo had to have a stick, and still have his baby Nine. Joe was the same way. Burt had two 40s. I think B had two 40s too. The young nigga Eddie Bo, even though he was JD, was always around us. I think he dug Bo and Joe's vibe because I used to check how he used to be up under them a lot. Either way, he was down tonight. Last was Herb. Because of incriminating factors I wouldn't go in to full details on what he did but, put it like this; 58th knew it was war and they were being closed down, there would be no money made until we had Zay.

We didn't find out what started the beef until three days later after Shard came home from the hospital. His injuries weren't life threatening, but he did have to wear a shit bag for a while. Fred called a meeting when Shard showed up. I could tell he was mad about the whole thing. Fred asked Shard why the nigga Zay was busting at him? At first Shard was trying to play dumb but, Fred wasn't having it. So he told all us that he was shooting celo on 58$^{th}$ the night before and had a few word with this young nigga he guessed was Zay's little brother [but it had to be more than just a few words]. None of us were buying the story, so Fred pressed him some more. Then the rest of the story came out. Shard had pistol-whipped the young nigga. Now that made sense to us because we all knew Shard wasn't going to talk long with no nigga before he upped that fire. We didn't care, one way or another, it was war time.

Fred being the brain was the one who always saw the bigger picture. I guess that's because he's been doing it longer than us and had seen more bread than all of us. He knew war was costly and brought unwanted heat. Don't get me wrong, Fred would have your ass dealt with if you had to be. He just understood there was a time and a place for everything. He knew most of us were loose cannons and always looking to put work in. Bo, for one, had a hard time listening to reason. Once he had his mind made up there was no talking him out. I could talk sense into him from time to time, but not always, nor could Fred.

Now Joe on the one hand, he had a way with us all. Joe could make anybody see it his way. Burt would listen as long as it didn't make him look soft or lose money. That's all Burt cared about: Respect and money. He was big on family too and if you were his dawg, you was family. Me, I was a real thinker myself. I paid attention to everybody and everything. I wasn't big on talking. I would rather watch and listen. I would listen to the game Fred would lay on us. Some nights I just sat out in front with Aunt Blanche and drank some Mad Dog 20/20 or Wild Irish Rose, and listen to her tell me how much she missed her baby boy Tony [R.I.P.]. Now, back to the problem at hand.

Shard was getting into too much unnecessary shit. And Fred told him that. He said, "You got niggas over here dumping at us. Now niggas over there dumping at us too!"

We weren't the only crew going through gun play. Looking at it now, we thought the blockade would make us stronger, but it was the total opposite. Before the blockade all the crews in the hood were steady mobbing in peace. For whatever reason I'm not sure because it wasn't Veli's business but J.D. was beefing with Thug Life. B and Flum were on-to it. My nigga C.B. got out and wanted his old spot back on 60th and 15th Avenue. Him, B, and Fat Boy K jumped on some bikes and rode down on the young niggas posted by the Arab store. They told them the "Get down or lay down" speech. If they wanted to keep hustling up there, they better have J.D. packs. They were working for the old school homie off the Ave named Lemon Lime. He had a pack called *Public Enemy.* He had it up on 15th Ave and 64th Street, but fell out with the niggas up there so he moved it down to 60th Street. Now he was getting money again. C.B. told me how they put them red beams from the 40s on Lime's car shield while he was sitting out in front of the Arab store on 60th Street.

Lime got the message real quick. The young niggas had already put him on what C.B. and B had said. So when the beams hit his car window, he just crunk up and pulled off. C.B. had me laughing my ass off because I knew the homie Lime. He be on that blow. So, he probably was snorting a little blow when he looked up and saw them beams. I fucked with C.B. for real. He would always give me his keys if I needed to use the dunk. During this time I wasn't staying home with the old girl because I was on the run from my P.O. Yeah, listening to Burt, I had violated and on top of that I was still pulling little robberies on the side.

On one of them side robberies I jumped out and abandoned my car. The other nigga that was with me, the little homie Nat, got jammed up on the case. They gave my old girl the car back but, wanted to talk to me. I wasn't going. I already knew they wasn't going to let me go. So I was staying with my second mom, Emma. She was my brother, Ace's mama, but always treated me like one of hers.

I didn't have a father coming up, but I had two mothers. I loved Emma. She was a lady that we all could count on! If I wasn't there, I was laying low over Bo's house. Then there were those days I would get a motel room for about a week. I was still getting money from my spot in Robbin Hood. My little brother Jay had a weed spot down the street from the crib even as he was off playing college ball. So me and the homie Russ was holding it down but none of that really mattered. What I really wanted was that out of town money. My brother was getting it on full, so until bro decided to fuck with me I was going to thug it out with my homies.

Mackaveli was starting to pick up. I think it was because we were on high alert with the ongoing wars. Everybody was hugging the block. So with that, more people were coming through to holla at this nigga or that nigga. With more people coming through, more weed was sold. One particular day that "stands-out" was when this big event called "How Can I Be Down?".7 It was a bunch of New York rap groups coming to Miami Beach to perform for the weekend.

Everybody was hyper to go kick it on South Beach. The word was that, P. Diddy was hosting an event: A New York/Miami thing. That's why they were calling it How Can I Be Down. The word was, also Uncle Luke was calling on the hood to come out. He wanted the Lynch Mob to represent the city. So already know, niggas were looking for them Veli Boys to come through. We were all standing out on the block on 60th Street in front of the crib smoking and shooting dice just talking shit. B pulled up to see if the crew was riding out to the beach. Fred pulled the vert out, it was one of the hardest dunks in the city that year but, that was nothing for the big homie. Fred ain't never missed a beat when it came to the whip game. Burt aka Debo put on all the chunks. He loved to be chunked down. [Nowadays, they call it *drip.*]

I love to see my dawgs get fresh and jump in the dunks and head out to rep this Veli life. I never really liked to hang out if my money wasn't right. All the homies already knew if my pockets weren't right, I wasn't with it. They damn near had to make me go to the club or anywhere if my pocket wasn't fat. I'd rather stay in the hole and run the spot. Getting money was my thing, that excited me. That's how I had fun. Bo was different. He loved being in the mix of shit; South Beach, music, hoes…You couldn't pay him to miss that. Me, I was cool. Shit was already jumping. Anytime there was something major going on in the city, you can bet niggas would get high and fall through.

Joe, being the hustler he was, took a couple bombs of Mackaveli out to the Beach with him. He told me he was going to bust they heads out there. I didn't doubt him because shit automatically doubled, sometimes tripled, once you crossed that bridge to the Beach. It was like going up the road without even leaving Miami. Shit, when he said that, I hated that I had volunteered to stay back to keep the spot open. "But fuck it!" They were pulling off about ten cars deep. It was still packed on the block because everybody wasn't going all at once. We still had a celo game going on. Some niggas was down bad and trying to get back. I was shaking my head, and laughing to myself because the real money was leaving with Fred and B. For some reason Fred damn near always hit big when it came to gambling. I guess long money was hard to beat.

My cousin Charlie Parker aka Bubba came through, he hit the celo game up for a little spot. He was pushing this dark 98, I couldn't help but to notice the Tennessee tags on it. It was just another reminder that everybody but me was eating with my big brother up the road. I was just really getting to know this side of my family. The Parkers side was big and we were spread all over Miami and thugging hard in these streets. Bubba was the big OG in his hood, the 40s. We exchanged some words about the fam and he told me he would be going through more often now that he knew that I was around there. As soon as cuz pulled off, Little Willie came through. He seen cuz and knew who he was, and told me he wished he could have hollered at him for a minute. It was about my other cousin. Corn Flake in Over Town. It seemed that cuz was tripping again. He does that whenever he be on that blow.

Lil Willie said that Flake kissed his mama at a block party the other night. He said niggas told him that Flake was drunk and high and acting crazy and that his mama was pushing him off her. I could tell Willie was mad as fuck, but I had a feeling he wasn't telling me everything because we all know cuz only do that shit when he drunk. He didn't mean no disrespect. Willie knew this was fam, so I'm going to try squash the shit but for whatever reason, he still told me he was going to fuck cuz up when he saw him. All I could say was "alright." Now you already know how cuz is. But in the back of my mind, I knew I was going to let fam know, asap.

Lil Willie stayed and chilled with me. The spot was jumping just like I thought it would be. I knew something was wrong when I saw Fred's vert hit the corner followed by the rest of the homies. I wasn't keep up with the time but it couldn't been no more than two or three hours that they had left. I wouldn't have to wonder too long about why they were back so fast. Bo jumped out the vert talking a mile a minute. He do that when he was hype about something. I guess that's the Jamaican part of him coming out. From what I was hearing, some kind of fight had broken out on stage after Luke called all the Lynch Mob to the stage when the rap group Wu Tang were on stage. It seemed like them New York niggas were slam dancing on some wild ass shit where it looked like they fighting but, all they were doing were bumping up against each other and some kind of way the two groups clashed. I wasn't there so I didn't know what really happened to set it off but, what I do know was what I was hearing about it at that moment. What started off as a dance ended up with Bo and a few of the homies showing their ass out there on them white folk's Beach. They were all bragging about what they did. Burt knocked out a rap nigga. I'm not going to drop his name because he is no longer with us. [R.I.P. buddy].

They said the homie Flum was still out there on the Beach playing peace maker like he could speak for the whole hood. But R.I.P. to my nigga Flum. That's just how he was. I was shocked to hear Lil Willie trying to drop some real advice on not wilding out every time we go out. He was trying to tell Bo and I guess the rest of us that we need to chill out here if we wanted to last long. This was the only time I knew Willie not to be on blow. He was just smoking plain weed, no lace. He became a Hebrew on his last bid. He was an expert on how to stay out of jail or prison. Me, Bo, and the rest of the homies were just looking at him while he talked this *do right* shit. I guess because he had been out prison longer than the rest of us and was dead set against going back that's why he could talk to us like that. Even though I didn't think Lil Willie was the right one to give anybody advice about not wilding out, he was telling the truth on this one. Everybody was still laughing at how Burt was dropping niggas with one-hitter quitters. The whole time these niggas were talking about what went down on the Beach, I was ready to turnover packs, and do the books with Joe.

I had some plans to get with the fine Spanish female Over Town. She came through with her sister and this other female. They were following my nigga Cooda in this vert. We smoked a few jays and they were telling me about this Arab dude that had a lot of money and how he was always trying to fuck with them on some trick shit. They were planning on robbing him but needed a gun. They were following him around. He was having fun with them on the low, but when they pulled up in Mackaveli and told me about the lick I was on board. I just needed to hear a little more about the dude. I wanted to make sure this dude wasn't plugged in with nobody I was down with. This lick would make us a team. I wasn't counting on getting involved with none of them but, I ended up doing just that. I'm not going to say her name in this book but, she was fine as hell and loved getting money like me.

The plan was getting dude drunk and making him think he was going to have a good time with all three of them. They were going to do everything. I was around just in case something went wrong. The gun was with them for protection. Dude usually kept a fat wad of money and always wore expensive jewelry. They went to the liquor store and got that Thug Passion hookup [Alize and Hennessy]. He should have known something was up because Miami Inn was known for niggas getting their heads split. Even the staff there were down for the lick, you just break them off to their mouths closed and turn their head.

I was laying low in the dark, deep in the back of the parking lot. They were taking forever to pull this off. I figured it would take a while since they were drugging his drink. I didn't hear no gunshots, so they didn't have to use the gun. I had already told them if they needed me blink the lights on and off twice and I would come see what's up. I could see the room from where I was parked. I ended up falling asleep. When

I woke up, it was one in the morning. *Damn* this shit was taking longer than I thought. Just when I had made up my mind to walk in there and knock on the door, here they came running and laughing.

They jumped in talking in Spanish. I couldn't understand shit they were saying. I just cut the car on and pulled out of there. I had my eye on Little Sexy who was in front of me. She was the leader anyway. The other one acted like a dude, I knew she was gay, or at least went both ways. She's the one I gave the gun to so I asked her for it back asap. I would feel a lot more comfortable and in control with it. I didn't want them to start to think cross action with me. I drove us back to the city. We needed somewhere to break down at. I went to Biscayne Bay so I could get us a room at the Star Dust Motel.

Little Sexy jumped out and got a room with two beds. I just waited to see how much we hit for since they said the Arab dude liked to carry large sums of money on him. As soon as we got into the room, Sexy dumped her bag on the bed. Two big wads of hundred dollar bills flopped open. My eyes were glued on bracelets full of diamonds. The matching Cuban link chains was fat to death. They even took buddy's rings off his fingers. Now I was wondering was he dead or alive? So I asked them. They both agreed that he was still breathing when they left. Sexy started counting the bread. It came to $4,200 on the head. Damn this turned out to be a hell of a lick.

Now it was time to break down the take. We each got a stack and all agreed to use the extra $200 on the room. At first we disagreed on what to do with the jewelry. They wanted to go Over Town to hit up one of their baby-daddy's who was getting money to see if he wanted to buy the jewelry. I wasn't having none of that. I didn't trust none of them cats from Town and I wanted to keep as much niggas out of our business as possible. I had a feeling that this dude was connected to the streets in some kind of way. I knew a lot of Arabs that was fucking with niggas in the game by selling guns, work, fake clothes, even the food stamp game. Shit, I had my Arab connect on the travel check that I used to get from robbing tourists. Them Arabs were heavy in the game out there in those streets and one wearing that much jewelry and carrying that much cash

around had to be doing something in the hood. I knew he would put a reward out for information on the girls. So I told them all this and why I think we should go to this jeweler I knew downtown. He bought all my hot jewelry. I got them to see it my way. So we kicked back and smoked a few jays.

Sexy Sister and her girlfriends were lying in the bed together. I was chilling in the chair by the other bed. I needed to take a shower, but didn't want to leave them out there with the jewelry. I convinced Sexy to come take a shower with me. Yeah, she was digging me the same way I was feeling her. We ended freaking and fucking all night. Sister and her girl was deep into each other to say the least. The next day we didn't get up until around noon.

We wouldn't sleep good at all if we woke up earlier. The room next door was filled with junkies getting high and arguing all night about dope and who smoked the last of it. Shit, they were hitting the walls and all kinds of shit. We got up and showered again. After we were ready, I took them with me to get off the jewelry. My guy downtown was always glad to see me. I met him through Bone. The only reason he loved to see me was because he knew he could beat me out of what my jewelry was really worth. He would have to come better today because I knew this shit we had was worth its weight.

I took Sexy in with me. The other two waited in the car for us. He was trying to pull his fast talk game on us at first. He knew the shit was hot but, Sexy had her number set already so she asked for a higher price just like a true negotiator. I let her do the talking because she was doing a good job. She gave him a story about her boyfriend cheating on her, so she was selling his shit. She knew how much he paid for it. With that said she wasn't going too far under it. They finally settled on a price even higher than what she originally wanted. We walked out of there with $12,000 for the whole set. Shit, I wasn't expecting that much. I was thinking about $8,000 but, I was glad I let her do the talking. That meant the jewelry was most likely to be worth at least twice that much. Knowing how trusting my guys were all I could think about was getting with Bone.

Once we got back in the car, Sister and her sidekick couldn't wait to hear what we got. They were just as happy as me to hear what we came up with. We wasted no time splitting three geez apiece. I didn't have to worry about getting rid of them. They were ready to see their kids and break their mom off because she was the one keeping the kids. So I dropped them off Over Town with a promise to hook back up once I got back in town.

My first stop was to see my mom so I could break her off. I also needed to see my daughter. My mom kept her a lot to give my baby-mama a break. I also needed to pack some clothes to go up the road with. Mom wasn't really talking to me at those days. She was still upset by me being back in the streets. She knew I was out there doing wrong but there wasn't nothing she could do but, pray for me. Her favorite words to me was; "she was done. She had washed her hands off me and *gave me back to the Lord." I* can't lie, it used to hurt seeing my mom disappointed with me. Yet I didn't know what else I could do but hustle in the streets. I always told myself that I was hustling to get my own business. What the business going to be, I didn't know.

I always wanted a successful lawn care service. Not the little, residential kind, but commercial businesses. Nevertheless, all that would have to wait. Now all I wanted to do was get some weight of blow so I could flip up the road. I had to get back to the city so I could drop off my nigga his car and hook up with Bone.

After dropping off my dawg, his donk, I had to go back on 60th Street to see what was popping in Mackaveli. All the Veli boys were on the block. Boosie was starting to spend more time on 60th. Came to find out that the Veli whole in the Sub wasn't turning over enough to keep paying a team to work around there. I always felt like B-Love [that's what we were calling Boosie; I think Fred started that] couldn't really run the spot. He gambled too much and was more focused on chasing hoes. So Fred took him under his wing. Bro was the big homie to all of us, but the young niggas that listened to him out the crew he took them under the wing. Red Dawg, Kenwa, and now Boosie. I told Joe and Bo that I was shooting up the road to get this money.

I went inside to holla at Burt before I left. He was in the back room with Red Dawg's fine ass sister. "Damn, little mama had a fat ass." I didn't get to really chop it up with Burt like I wanted. That nigga is one of the hardest niggas I knew in the that street but, when it came to a redbone female, he gets soft as hell. I got on the phone and called Bone to come pick me up. We were going to Bone's plug to get some clean [blow]. The plan was to go to my brother's spot in Panama City.

I kept in contact with his people up there. Her name is Tee and she was a money-getting female. Bro had already put me up on game with how to work her. He told me to give her a zip at a time and let her work it. "Don't go out there in their hood trying to move my own work." [He didn't have to tell me twice.] I knew how dangerous it could be out of town in somebody's else's hood. Me and Bone would lay low at her crib and smoke whilst she did her thing.

I went back outside to wait on Bone. He pulled up an hour later. We both agreed to only grab a 9 piece of clean. We didn't want to take too much work because we didn't know how shit moved up there and we also didn't have a place to stay other than girl's crib. Also, I told him I didn't want to overstep my welcome. She didn't even know I was bringing him with me. Bone was ready to get on the road that night. So we took care of the business with plug and went to the Flea Market U.S.A. to grab a few things for the trip.

After stopping by my mom's house to grab my bags, she fixed us something to eat. I was glad because I smoked too many jays already. Bone was against smoking on the road which really made sense to me. We got on the road at 12:00 AM. It was a 9-hour drive, so we would get there in the morning. Bone did all the driving, that was cool with me. The weed had me sleep but, Bone wanted to keep talking about his baby-mama drama. I didn't have any female problems since I didn't have any main lady in my life, I was feeling the Spanish chick, but just couldn't trust her yet. Her sex game was all that and some more. She had me gone with that Spanish accent all them *papis* she was calling me the night before. That shit made me smile just thinking about it. I was nodding off and on trying to stay up with Bone. I opened up my eyes to the sun coming up in Panama City.

We pulled lover to this gas station and I called Tee. She was waiting on my call and gave me directions from the station to this laundromat. She was already there. *Damn* was the first word that came to my mind when I laid eyes on Tee. She wasn't a beauty queen or nothing like that, but she was pretty and had a banging ass body. Yeah, she was fine as hell with a small waist and tight little sexy ass on her. Them jeans were hugging that fat ass the right way. She knew who I was, as soon as she saw me.

"You look just like Runt," she said referring to bro's Panama City handle. Almost every nigga I knew that hustled out of town changed their name. It's a practice that I wound up doing myself.

We jumped back in our car and followed Tee back to her spot, which was not far from the laundromat. She stayed on the second floor of some "projects" that looked more like townhouses. Her place was clean and neat. I was paying attention to every little detail. I wanted to know as much about her as I could since I would be doing business in the future. It was early and she offered us something to drink. Bone gave me a look. He didn't mean nothing by it. He was just trying to keep me focused and on point. So I just asked for some water.

Well, I can say this, Tee was all business because after giving me a glass of water she asked where the work was? Bone spoke up first, even though it was clear she talking to me. I could tell she was still trying to figure out why Bone was even here. I never mentioned bringing nobody to her on the phone. So it was understandable if she was feeling uncomfortable about him being there. Bone dropped the backpack he had on the floor and said, "The blow in here."

She told him to bring it to the kitchen table. I could tell she was expecting to see more work. What she said next confirmed what I was thinking … "This all y'all got?"

I felt kind of embarrassed that we didn't have enough work to match her expectations. So I told her that I was just testing the trip, seeing how everything would go on this first go around. She would have laughed if she knew that only half the work was mine. I told her I only brought 9 ounces because I couldn't stay long and didn't know how long it would take to move it. She checked me straight up and said Runt never came without a whole one [kilo of blow]. Then she told me that she could grab all 9 zips on her own, but she had other people waiting on her. She told us that she was going to save us some time and money and just pay for the work out her pocket because since it was only 9 zips she kept 4 and a half for herself and let her sister get the other half. That way we could get back on the road today. I could tell she knew her shit when it came to work by the way she handled the blow.

When she went to the back to her bedroom, I found out we weren't alone in the spot. I heard her talking to what sounded like a dude. But I wasn't sure. It could've been her sister. She came back out with the money in her hand. All nine stacks. When she gave me the money, she told me that she had been holding my brother down. She told me that they talked every day and how much she cared about him. Though they wasn't in no kind of relationship, Runt was like a brother to her. He helped her and her whole family out when they needed him and for that she would always be grateful to him. That's why she was willing to help me move whatever work I got up there to her. I looked over at Bone. He had one of them rare smiles on his face. He was listening to every word she was telling me. I knew he was happy as hell about the trip. I gave Tee my word that I would stay in touch. As a matter of fact, I was planning to go back and grab some more work and come right back. I asked her could we chill for a little bit before getting back on the road. I knew Bone needed a little rest. With him doing all the driving there I knew I would have to help going back. Long distance driving wasn't my strong suit and we had too much risk.

The person in the other room finally came out and it was a dude. He was young, so I didn't know if this was her son or what? She didn't let me wonder too long and introduced him as her cousin. He had a joint in his mouth about to fire up. That's what I cared about at the moment. We all smoked and talked while Tee dropped some of the work. I could tell she liked how it worked with the soda because she talked about how much she got back. I was happy that she was satisfied with the blow. As long as the work was clean she said we were in business. She left to make a run. I could tell she was ready to make her money back.

The weed had Bone knocked out. So that meant I had to stay awake. Can't never let your guard down when you're out of town. Though her supposed-to-be cousin was young, I remember myself at his age. He could still call up a few of his boys to hit us up. Well, none of that happened. I guess Tee was telling me the truth. Her whole family loved my brother. She came back just as we were getting ready to leave. She gave me a hug and told me to drive safe and told my brother that everything had gone smoothly. I told her I would be back and have a lot more work.

Bone pulled off and just like that, we were back on our way to the city. We stopped two times to get gas and got back with no problem later that night. I had $4,500 to the good. I had Bone drop me off over my second mom's house [Emma]. Then I called Bo to come pick me up. He came through about an hour later. I told him to swing around my mother's house. I needed to grab my gun, but really needed to get this money off me. I never let none of my homies know that I left my money at mom's house. Not that I felt they would try something. It was just a rule to the game. I broke mom off like always and put the rest up. I needed to save all the bread I could if I wanted to keep my word to Tee about having more work when I came back.

As me and Bo rode to the hood, I filled him in on my trip. He heard what I was saying but, Bo really wasn't interested in going out of town to get money. Bo was focused on running Miami. See, Bo's family is Jamaican, so when his uncles and cousins and them came to Miami they put down in the 80s. B sqqo was used to having his way right here in the city. He was on a mission to make niggas in the streets remember who the fuck he was. I remember sitting on his mama's porch smoking weed and him telling me how he was going to get niggas to respect his gangster. I'm not going to go into details, but I will say this nigga was for real about his shit! I tried to reason with him telling him, "Bo, niggas respect us already. So let's get this money!"

But naw, Bo's way of thinking was more pressure, more respect, then money would come. I was like, *"Shit why can't we do both?* All I know was I needed money."* Bills, Pampers[daipers], milk and real life shit couldn't wait until niggas respect me! So while my homie looked for war, I would be looking for more ways to get paid. We pulled up on 60th Street and like always it was a block party. Niggas and hoes, dope, money, and guns were all out. Mackaveli was jumping. Weed, base, and motherfucking lace! We were wide open. As soon as Bo stopped the car, I jumped out screaming, "Mackaveli, Mackaveli, We wide open!"

All my homies showed me love. That's how it be when niggas ain't seen you in a day or two. Back then everybody didn't have cellphones, so if you pull up on the block and a nigga didn't know what was up with you, until word came around they would be clueless. I hadn't missed anything important while I was gone. Yeah, we were still at war with a few different crews just like Fred said we would be and now I was hearing that Bo and Joe ran up on 15th and 64th looking for a nigga named Speedy out the Beans.

It sounded like the nigga was talking shit about Joe over his baby-mama, Black Girl. I knew the nigga Speedy from back in the day when I used to work on the Ave. He ain't a bad nigga. He thought he was a playboy or some kind of mac with the females but, I know he ain't about that gunplay. My niggas are, so I don't know how he was going to get out of that. One thing I knew about my niggas was they didn't play about their hoes. I never really understood that but almost every nigga I know that's a real killer always had a soft spot for them hoes. My cousin Flake was like that: Don't fuck with that nigga's baby-mama. Me, personally, I'm going to really have to see what it's all about before I just jump out there for a female because I did too much time already at a young age and seen how these hoes run south on a nigga as soon as he get locked up. Yeah, I was only gone off the block for three days and from what I was hearing it seemed like we were adding to the hit list. We weren't the only crew that was in conflict.

The Loso Boys [aka JD] was aggressively taking mosre spots. I didn't know if I was the only one thinking that way but, it seemed like B wanted

61$^{st}$ to himself. The beef he was having with Flum was heating up. Some shit between Thug Life and JD had spilled over at the Burger King on 54$^{th}$ Street with a little gunplay. Then it was said that B or one of them Loso dudes had sprayed up Flum's 98 that was parked on 61$^{st}$. I guessed that was a warning that shit had got real. I think Flum got the message because I started to see less of him. B also pressed down on another crew that had a pack running out the building on 61$^{st}$ and Fat Boy's team. Word was that Zoe Pound came through ten cars deep waving the Haitian flag with sticks in the air. They made it out on Fat Boy's end, so B felt some kind of way.

Now, I don't know how true this part was but, that's how it was passed to me. Shit like that, when it wasn't Veli business I took it as useless street talk. Over Town niggas was into it with my hood Sub. Some Towner killed my big homie "Rick the Rule." I was in my body about that because Ruler was a real nigga and I grew up knowing my nigga to be a real hustler. Town was also into it with Carol City niggas. That shit was really heating up. They were giving it to each other both ways. Them niggas out of C.C. was my big brother Ace's homies. You even had my nigga O.J. out of Robbin Hood into shootouts with niggas out of Lager Mott. Shit was really off the chain in the city in '96 and all I wanted to do was get my weight up so I could get back up the road.

I had missed out on so many opportunities the previous years. My brother was up, eating real good in P.C. I helped put my dawg Donnie down with him from the joint just because I didn't want Big Bro going up the road by himself. Then my cuz Frank and my homies off 69$^{th}$ were getting major money with the weed game. I missed that run. It seems like I could never have it easy where a nigga just put me on because I was real and they were my niggas. My own brother was looking over me for whatever reason. Only thing I could tell myself was it was meant for me to get it the hard way, out the mud. I been doing it my whole life, so I was used to it. What I needed was 10 stacks.

My plan was to get me a half block so I could get back up to P.C. Yeah, Tee would see me making progress and would feel more comfortable working with me. I knew me and Bone together could have that much work, but I really preferred to depend on myself. Part of me wanted to step to Fred or my cousin Hepburn to see if they would put me on. But that wasn't my style. I don't know why, but I always hated to ask anybody for anything. What I really needed was another lick, just like the one with the Spanish girls. With that on my mind, I hollered at my dawg C.B. so he let me get his dunk.

I rode through Town looking for Sexy and her crew. No luck. But I did run into Corn Flake. He jumped in and told me to drop him off in the swamp on 8th Street. I told him watch out for Willie. He just laughed it off like Willie wasn't going to do nothing to him. As far as I was concerned my hands were now clean, I did my part as fam goes. I dropped cuz off and kept it moving. I never felt right in the swamp because niggas Over Town stay at it. Shit crazy because they feel the same way about us in the city. I jumped on the expressway 95, northbound to the city.

I slid onto 15th Avenue to see what was popping on the Ave. These days 15th was still pumping, but most of the real action was on 18th Ave now. My nigga Fat Toney and Lil Cal had open C.D.'s and Radio Shop on 69th Street across from the Cloud 9 weed spot, that shit was smoking on 68th. The big homie Clint, Prett, and Jaki had put down in the Sub and was getting money. I stopped to see what they had going on, and like always I ended up running into somebody I was locked up with. That's how it was on the Ave. You pull up and niggas start pulling up from everywhere. Everybody came through 15th Ave. I hadn't seen this nigga Kenny from Opa Locka behind the "P" [that was the name of his hood]. Since he and I got jumped on by some C.O.s in the stockade. They gave us an assault on an officer charge, and we got our ass kicked. But that made us co-defendants and dawgs for life. Ken was fighting a body case, and I my robbery cases. I ended up coping out to everything, Ken didn't take shit and walked. Now all these years later he was looking like fresh money on the Ave.

He pulled up in this powder blue vert, it was a '73 dunk sitting on Wu's. He gave me dap and we chopped it up for a minute. I could tell he was getting money out of town just because of the niggas he was kicking it with. Everybody knew that Lil Cal and Fat Toney hit that road on the regular. Ken was acting kind of uptight around me. I guess because he knew I was a jack-boy. I got that a lot from niggas that knew me from jail and even family. They know I go hard to get it. I would have thought they also knew that I'm loyal to anybody I call my nigga and to my family. Nevertheless, when you have that label as a robber, the only niggas that feels comfortable around you is other jack-boys and killers. To the streets you're pressure. And you know what they say about pressure: It bust a pipe.

Something about the Ave that I always loved was the constant flow of money being exchanged. I remember days coming out without a dime and leaving with a pocket full of money doing shit like housing the dice game to get started, or showing motherfuckers who had the best blow would get you paid. To be broke on the Ave was a sin to me. The Ave would always be special to me. I also liked to be up on the Ave to see who was making moves I liked. I was never a hater. I loved to see niggas shine, and the Ave was where niggas came to show off their cars, jewelry, and to flex their money. I remember seeing Mike Tyson on the Ave with Burt. If you was anybody in Miami streets you made your presence known on the Ave. I remember Trina before she was a rap star.

I'm going to give The Diamond Princess her just due because she was always a ghetto super star among the females. Her mom had a beauty salon on 67th Street. It used to stay jumping up there. They had a weed spot right in front of it called Clear Bag. It was smoking most of the time. I didn't care for it too much because the sacks were small. I think it used to sell out so much because niggas like me wanted a reason to pull up there and flash a knot of money around Trina and her crew. You could even go inside the salon and buy a Fonto leaf to roll your weed in for $1.00. Her daddy had a store on 65th Street. They used to call him Mr. Wonderful. Big boy dice games were held in the back. I never made it to that level in the game to gamble the type of money they were dropping on the table in there.

Back then, the Ave was the place to be after every main event in Miami. Everybody would come through the Ave and then ride over to

JumBo restaurant on 75th Street and 7th Avenue. If you were one of those chosen ones to have a spot on the Ave, chances are your spot could pull at least $20,000 a day or more but, now in 96, 15th Ave was losing its shine. Like I said earlier, 18th Ave was jumping off the hook. Then 61st was jumping. Niggas had weight on the wall in the Pork Beans. The Scott Projects was doing its thing with the Scutter Boys putting the blow down. I used to go through there a lot because my baby-mama stayed over there in the new projects.

After hanging out on the Ave for about an hour, I got bored so I rode back on 60th Street. I knew shit stayed popping in Mackaveli. Just like I thought, the word came around that jump out boys were in the Sub and they were going our way next. We already knew what kind of cars they were using to jump out in. They always try to be slick by taking niggas' cars from previous raids and use them for the next hood but, before they could get to pull that move the street network would put out the description of the cars they were using. Inside the barricade they made for us, we didn't have no respect for regular police officers when they drove through the hood and they knew it, that's why they never stopped.

Now with the jump out boys it was a totally different story. We show them big respect because they didn't play when they came through. First of all, they got their name *Jump-out Boys* because that's how they came through jumping out in ski masks and all black. Some of the older vets didn't even hide their faces. These were some big niggas too. They carried assault rifles, AR-15s, and AK-47s. They would use them at a drop of a dime. They loved to beat a nigga's ass on GP. So whenever we got a heads up that they were out rolling we closed up shop and made it to a night club. The crazy part about it was we wouldn't lose much money. Sometimes we even made more money because when they started jumping out they always started on the outskirts of the city, like Over Town, down south, the Grove, or the Sub. We were in the inner city, so it was always a mad rush for dope because all the dope fiends knew all the dealers were going to be hard to find for most of the night. So we would damn near sell out before we even left the club.

As I pulled up, that's just what was happening. Dope was jumping and everybody was loading up in different cars. One of the real OGs of the hood, Mikeadoo Mac, was talking to Fred. It sounded like he was telling Fred to follow him to follow him to Club Rolex. Mac had pulled with the club management and most of all the hoes that danced there. I already knew what the plan was. Fred was probably telling Mac to get us some strippers for the night. I was going to play it smart and ride with Fred. He was pushing his dark green 96 Maxima. B from JD had one too. Fred had the kit on his with the lights on the back. Yeah it was clean as fuck and low key to move around in. Fred loved the color green on his rides. I guess it was the color of money.

Me, Fred, Boosie, and Red Dawg were riding together four deep in the Max. Bo, Kenny, Kenwa, and Shard were rolling together. Burt, Joe, Herb, and Eddy Bo were in the vert. So all the Veli boys were going to be in the building tonight. Them Loso niggas was coming through as well. Mikeadoo was in his Benz. I didn't see who was riding with him. Old School had them tints as well. It didn't take us long to pull up in the Lex. Shit was already packed. The parking lot was tight. We could have stayed outside and had a good time. It was just as many hoes out in the parking lot as in the club. We didn't have to pay shit, so why not go in and see what it did?

Since I rode with Fred, I reminded myself to be on point. Fred was the big homie, so we had to make sure a motherfucker knew he had them hitters around him all the time. Red Dawg got his chair out the back. Once Fred got on it we moved together. The rest of the Velis were waiting by the other cars until we passed them. They fell in place. Burt stopped us for a second to give us these two-shot Dillinger pistols. I could do nothing but smile to myself. Leave it up to DeBo to think of that. Those guns were so small that mine fit down the side of Bally boots. When Bo seen where I stashed mine, he followed suit he slipped his inside the Clark boots he wore. All the Veli strapped thanks to pushing

Fred through the metal detector whereas we could put the heat on the chair.

When we got to the door, Mac and them Loso niggas was piled in front of the club. We all made it in. One thing I can say about them Lynch Mob niggas was they got big respect whenever they came out and us Veli niggas was getting the same treatment being from the same hood. Them security niggas didn't want no smoke with us. They just let the metal detector go off as the whole crew walked through. Man I thought it was live out in the parking lot, shit was super lit inside. All I'm going to say is the Lex really lived up to its reputation of having the baddest bitches in the game. They had all flavors of strippers you could think of. From Spanish to Asian and all in between.

The spotlight was on female boxing. There was this big ass boxing ring in the middle of the club. When we walked in, the fighting hadn't begun yet, so we hadn't missed shit but, the ring was full of naked hoes dancing and busting it open while niggas and females stood around it throwing money in the ring. They could forget about me throwing anything but looks tonight. Your boy was in grind mode for real. I was on a mission to get that re-up money so I could get back up the road. Fred had Red Dawg to go get some bottles. I got me a beer to sip on while I just looked at all the fine ass hoes in there. I was in real chill mode. I remembered the last time we were in the club together I got us kicked out for touching that red bitch on the ass. I didn't want to be the one always getting us kicked out the club and besides there were too many fine hoes up in there.

I was playing it cool sipping my beer. I was really interested in the boxing match since I was a fighter and loved looking at sexy ass bitches. One was a redbone and the other was caramel brown. They were naked but that didn't stop them from fighting. Breasts were swinging, asses were jumping, and they were just punching away. I couldn't tell who was winning. It really didn't matter as long as they kept looking good. I looked around to see what the rest of the crew was up to. I couldn't miss DeBo, and he was so damn big, He was over in a booth with three bad ass hoes dancing around him. He was smiling ear to ear. Joe and

Shard were in the booth with him. Joe was looking serious, like something major was on his mind. Bro was always like that trying to stay one step ahead of everybody else. Bo was on the dancefloor doing his signature dance move. The best way I can describe it for you is to think about a nigga with rifle shooting up the club while standing on his toes jumping. Watching Bo, all I could do was shake my head. My nigga had a real fetish for gun play. [ Later on I'm going to share with you a part of the story how wild Bo could be with a gun.] For now, back to this wild night at the Rolex.

It seemed like we were going to have a peaceful night followed by some well needed fun with some of these fine ass strippers. I couldn't wait to see what Mac would come up with. Speaking about Mac, I leaned over and asked Fred was Mac still going to make that happen. As Mike was getting closer, I witnessed the body language of the hoes walking with Mac change. It looked like they were saying "No" to him.

I became more certain that they were changing their minds when they all stopped walking. I could see Mike pleading with them on our behalf but, one by one they walked away. Mike came over and laid the bad news on us. To say I was disappointed would be an understatement. I didn't know why, but it seemed like I was the only one mad. I guess the reason everybody was taking the news the way they were was because the night was still young, and because them hoes didn't want to play with the crew. There were still more hoes to choose from.

Mike was telling Fred what the hoes had said when they saw us. Came to find out, these Lynch Mob niggas had a bad reputation with the strippers. It seemed like they love to fuck the girls wild and shit and kept them for long periods of time. Sometimes without paying them fair. It wasn't hard for me to believe that one. I know a few niggas in the hood that got off on beating females' ass. That shit wasn't cool with me at all. The same niggas were straight hoes when they came to jail and be in cells with real his niggas. I'm down with thug passion all day, fucking females rough, you know, pulling hair, slapping ass even down with choking. I love to make females gag when she give me heads but, all those extras have to be consented to or it's a no go with me. While some of the niggas I was rocking with, took it too far sometimes. So that turned the hoes off.

So since Mike dropped the bad news on us it became a change in plan. Every man for himself became the new plan. It didn't take Fred long to rebound. This chick from out the hood named Princess kept a bunch of bad hoes on her team. I don't know if she peeped the play when the stripper hoes broke bad on Mike but, as soon as Mike was pulling off from us, Princess pulled up in her Lac with a four-pack of bad bitches. Two of them were the ones that was boxing that night in the ring. She pulled up on Fred first. She knew who was the real money man of our crew. So that's how Fred got to pick the baddest black bitch out the pack. She was short and thick as fuck. Shorty had a fat ass on her. All I could think was *"Damn, Fred, let's jump that together!"* It was wishful thinking but, Fred wasn't having none of that. Nevertheless, there were still some more bad ones in the car.

Me and Lil Bo ended up following Princess back to the hood. She had this crib on 59th that was known as the "Animal House." Yeah, that's what they called it. I forgot to mention that was the new word in the streets that year for wild ass hoes: *Animals.* Nowadays they call them "Shols" short for "Action." Anyway, we got to the Animal House, and me and Bo went to the back room with two fine ass bitches. I had my eye on the Redbone boxer and now that I was up close on her, I could see she took some hits to the face. Her mouth was a bit swollen. The other one was just as fine. She was caramel with long hair and a fat ass to go with it. You remember earlier I said, I'll tell you a story about how wild Bo could be with his gun fetish," Well this is it!"

We all went into this back room. I was ready to fuck the shit out of Red but, was also ready to see what Caramel was working with. Before the door could get all the way closed, I was halfway undressed. I was horny as hell after being in that strip club all night. I grabbed Red by her arm and pulled her towards me staking my claim before Bo could. When I sat back on the bed, I took my gun out and put it beside me. Being a robber, I knew the rules: Always keep your strap near you whenever you tricking off with hoes.

She wasn't scared of the gun being there. She knew a nigga was on this Thug Life for real. Her only concern was that she wasn't sucking no dick. She made that clear to me. I can't lie, I was a little disappointed but I quickly got over it. When she started taking off that body suit she was wearing my mouth fell open, I was speechless. Damn, little mama was sexy. She didn't have on no underclothes. Her breasts were nice and full, they just sat up on her chest, stomach was flat, waist was small, and that red ass was perfect. I made her turn around and model for me. This bitch had my dick rock hard. She looked down at my dick and I could tell she wasn't expecting it to be that big. I was used to that. I don't know where these hoes get the idea that because a nigga short, he supposed to have a little dick.

As I started to position Red's body on the bed so I could hit that ass from the back. I put on the rubber and grabbed her by the waist and jammed my dick into her pussy. Without foreplay she set me off since she wasn't going to suck my dick. That's all I needed to know. Now I was going to make her wish she could suck my dick. I was pounding that pussy so hard from the back she was trying to run but I had a strong grip on her waist. I looked over at Bo and the caramel bitch. He was making her suck his dick but, here goes the funny part. Bo had his gun in his hand softly tapping Caramel in her saying shit like, "Keep that dick in your mouth."

When I first looked over I had to do a double take because I hadn't ever heard about a nigga gun butting no bitch while she was sucking his dick but now, I was witnessing it, my nigga was wild for real. Hey shit, it looked like little mama was turned on by it because she was moaning and going hard with the head game. Had me thinking if I should gun butt red to suck my dick? Naw, I'm just going to fuck her back out for not doing it, that's how I fixed her! Then I switched with Bo for some head from Caramel. Man, we fucked them two hoes for at least two hours. We did it all to them, tag teamed them both and guess who started sucking dick? Yeah, Red!! Pussy was so sore she couldn't take no more dick and had to suck. I used a pack of rubbers on them when me and Bo finally left the Animal House. Everybody in the front was dead sleep.

Princess and two little kids were out cold on the couch. I was hungry from all that fucking so I told Bo to take us up on the Ave, Duke mama's store on 64$^{th}$ so we could get two of them $2.00 plates that they made up there.

After we got our plates, we pulled up in Mackaveli to see what was popping on the block? The usual morning traffic. Yeah, the spot was picking up. I was done eating, just hanging with the rest of the Veli boys smoking weed, talking shit about last night and them bad ass hoes me and Bo knocked down. It seemed like we talked them back up because at that moment Princess's Lac hit the corner and stopped right in front of Burt's crib. She hit the horn and about a minute later that fine ass short black hoe that Fred rode off with came walking out with her heels in her hand looking like a real foot-dragger. I forgot all about her and Fred but, seeing her then, I still wished I could've gotten a piece of that pussy. Damn, that bitch had a sexy ass walk on her. The way that was sitting in that dress made me want to jump in the car with them and go back to the Animal House. When she got in the car, Princess pulled up to the corner and stopped right in front of us. She yelled out to me, calling me Black Boy. She didn't know I didn't like to be called that, so I walked to the car and hipped her to that. I told her my name was Gigolo, but she could call me Gig with the Dick! All the guys started laughing when they heard me pop that game on her.

We all knew Princess was a female pimp, and real fly with her words, so I was waiting on a slick comeback by her. She didn't let us down either. True to her pimping, her response was, "Yeah, I heard about your dick game but, what I can't understand is why my pocket is light after your dick done got right? What part of the game that is?"

I answered. "Shit, the way I see it, your girl should have broken me off after the way I put her to sleep."

She had a smile on her face. "Oh, yeah, that's how we kick it? I'm going to have to see about that dick game, Gig!" Then she pulled off getting the last word like a pimp! When she left, the homies were still laughing. I looked over at Bo, and said, "Damn, bro, I thought you took care of that tap?"

His response was, "Man, fuck them hoes."

"Yeah, we did that really good." I laughed. I walked across the street to the payphone and called Bone. I needed a ride to mom's house. It was time to check in and wash up. Then I would get some rest. Hopefully she cooked, if not I could always find some leftovers. Mom always saved something to eat. I could tell she was worried about me a lot. I knew I was stressing her out. She was only staying in town, holding the house down for me. She really wanted to be back home in the island taking care of my grandma. I wish that I knew another way to live, than thugging in these streets. I felt like there was no other way. All I knew was to hustle, do whatever it took to get money. Bone came through and I left the homie pushing Mackaveli. I told them I'd be back later on. Bone wanted to know if I had my money right to get back up to P.C.? I told him not yet. He suggested we go on one. That meant he wanted to go on a robbery. He knew I was always down for a lick. I told him my plans on getting some rest and chill with the old girl for a minute. He was cool with that said that he shot over to his baby-mama's house. That way he be on my part of town, when I called him to come back to get me.

Ma was glad to see me. She didn't have to say it. I could tell by the way she looked at me when she opened the door. She asked me was I hungry? I smiled to myself thinking how ma always had my back no matter what. I said "Yes" and went straight to my room. First I checked my stash. I wasn't worried about ma messing with it. She doesn't go in my room because it stayed clean and neat. I wanted to see how much I had saved. I already knew but recounting it made me feel like it was growing. Yeah, I needed to hit this lick. I hoped it was a good one. I was never worried about getting caught. That's how you feel when you're doing wrong. Thinking you could keep getting away until you in jail. Saying, *"Damn I should've chilled!"*

I took out a change of clothes and got in the shower. Ma had my food in the microwave when I got out. We talked as I ate and as always she was asking me about my plans. I could never give her a straight answer. How could I tell her my real plans? I could see her face if I was to say, "Yeah, Ma, I plan on going out with Bone to rob somebody. Then cop me a brick of blow so I can go up the road to sell it." Not happening. So I did my best to talk around the question. The best way was to ask her how Kevia was doing. She told me all the new things that my daughter was doing. All the firsts that I was missing out on because I was too busy in the streets.

Kevia was the joy of my mom's life. Her first grandchild and because she never had a little girl, she raised Kevia as if she was her mother. That was another reason she was staying in town. She loved the time she spent with Kevia. Then she would hit me for some money for Kevia and bills. I loved being able to help ma out with the bills and taking care of my daughter. One of my goals was paying off my ma's mortgage on the house. I wasn't just out here in these streets for the fun of clout chasing, some dumb shit a lot of other young niggas was thugging for. I had people depending on me. Shit was real with my hustle. I called Bone, he told me he would be through in about an hour. That's all I needed to hear because Bone's "hour" meant two. That's why I called him early anyway. Now I could get me a nap. I went straight to sleep. I could feel my ma rubbing oil on my forehead. She did it every time I came home and slept. Then I would hear her praying over me. She would often tell me that was her way of giving me back to God. I didn't mind because I love my ma babying over me and the way I was living in these streets, thugging with killers, seeing the shit I was seeing, I could use all the prayers I could get. I always thanked God for my ma. She was my rock, but now, I needed some rest, so I dozed off with her standing over me. When I woke, I didn't know how long I was out for but, when I looked at the clock, I saw it was three in the morning!

I didn't know if Bone had come by or not? He could have and my mom just ran him off to let me sleep. That would be just like her to do that. Mom worried about me a lot. I was her prodigal son, her baby boy. Her way of thinking was I was home where she could see me. I was safe. So I laid back down, it didn't make sense to call Bone, now it was too late. The next morning, I was up early, fully energized from all the sleep I got. Man, I needed that! Running these streets took a toll on my body.

The first thing I did was call Bone. His baby-mama answered the phone with her messy ass. She acted like she didn't want to give Bone the phone. I came to find out Bone did come by and like I thought, mom told him I needed my rest, see me tomorrow. Well that was cool. I was ready now. His baby-mama was fixing breakfast and I played with him inviting myself over to eat.

"Yeah right," he said. "I'll be through in a minute to get you."

Me and mom ate breakfast together. She was filling me in on my brother Gregg's federal case. She had got him a lawyer and they were working on a deal. Bro had never been in trouble before and the fact that he had served in the Army helped. They were offering him 87 months which was not bad considering he had gotten caught with a brick of hard. Them crackers was giving niggas like me 20 years-to-Life for five grams of crack. Listening to my mom talk about it made me hurt inside because I knew she expected more from him. As for me, everybody in the family knew I was a fuckup! It wasn't a surprise for me to end up in prison. Bro was a straight-A student throughout school. Never been to jail or even had my mom come to the school about him. I was the total opposite. I wanted to help bro so bad. I would've done the time for him if I could have. It was just another reason why I was going so hard in these streets. I felt like I had the weight of the whole family resting on my shoulders.

Right now I needed a joint to relax me, but I never smoked in front of mom. I always gave my mom the utmost respect, even though she knew I smoked. I came home too many days smelling like a pound of loud! I gave my mom a stack out of the money I had put up and told her to send my brother something for his books and do whatever she needed with the rest. I was relieved when I heard the knock on the front door. It was my dawg Bone and I let him in. Then, I went to my room to get my gun so we could go. Mom spoke with Bone about if he had a job yet and all other points of her *do right* speech.

As soon as I got in the car, I lit up a joint. I needed to relax my mind. Mom always laid it on me heavy. Here goes Bone trying to fuck up my high with all his baby-mama drama, telling me about how she wanted them to be together as a family but, Bone liked living with his mom and pop. Bone was the only one of my homies that had both parents living together. Yeah, and my nigga was a full time thug in these streets, he was well respected by real street niggas all over Miami. Yet bro loved staying home with his people. Still, could tell baby-mama was making her case strong because Bone was now talking about how bad he needed this lick so we could get back up the road. Bo had called me before Bone came through and told me to shoot by his old girl's house to grab him on our way to the city.

So that's where we were pulling up now, waiting on him to come outside. Bo jumped in and we went on our way. As we pulled up to the light, something caught my attention. I saw a car driving the wrong way on a One Way street. I pointed them out to Bone. He knew exactly what I was thinking. They were lost. We made a fast U-Turn and went back. By the time we turned around they had figured out they were going in the wrong direction, now we were following them. Bo never been out with us on a lick, but I knew he was down! I told him to chill, sit and watch - I would do everything.

Bone stayed a safe distance from them as we tailed them for what seemed like an hour before they pulled into some warehouses off the side of the expressway. It looked like they were out to do some big boy furniture shopping because that's all these warehouses sold. We pulled in two cars down from them and I jumped out and laid them down in between the cars. I did it real smooth not drawing any unwanted attention to myself. They made it real easy for me. See I knew by now that in a robbery, the victims feed off your energy. If you're calm, they will be calm and everything will go smooth. They had a blue bank bag, so I took it and the lady's purse all in under two minutes and ran back the car.

We were back in traffic heading to the city in seconds. I went through the purse taking out all the money and cards so we could get rid of it. I had already pulled three envelopes of money out of the bank bag. Bo was leaning over the seat looking at the bread asking me how I knew that they were strapped like that? I just smiled and told him, "Gunplay is your game, touching white tourists is my game."

He started laughing. "Yeah, I can dig that!"

Each envelope had two stacks in them and the money in the purse came up to another $450. I gave Bo two bands. Me and Bone bust the rest down even. That's how it goes with me and him. He drive, I go get it. Bone dropped us off on 60th Street. Mackaveli was booming like always. The block was packed already with young niggas. Something about hitting a good lick always gave me a rush, a kind of high! I guess that's how Bo felt shooting his gun? The two stacks I had in my pocket didn't do much to what I needed on my brick fare. I was really back up a stack because I went in my stash that morning and broke the old girl off that stack. Shit, I still needed to hit a good lick to get me where I needed to be on that re-up but, right at that moment I was hyped up feeling live! So I yelled out, "Mackaveli, Mackaveli, weed, bass, and lace: We wide ass open!"

As me and Bo walked across the street to hook up with the homies. Feeding off my vibe, everybody started yelling "Mackaveli!" They were putting whatever they want on it. I heard Bo say, "Yeah, nigga, living out of prison, pistols in the air."

That nigga had his gun out doing that bounce he loved to do in the club. So I upped my shit and started bouncing. All of a sudden I looked around and all the homies had their fire out in the air. I know we looked wild as hell to motherfuckers driving by but, then again the hood knew what it was with us. It was Thug Life for real, and if you wanted it, you could get it ASAP "that way!!"

After we settled down niggas started rolling up and before long a dice game got going. Cars started pulling up. Hoes started popping up, shit was starting to become a block party. Fred had the music booming out the vert. And with the crew, more Mackaveli being sold.

I went against my first mind and got down in the dice game. After all the years I been in these streets robbing motherfuckers, I knew better than to gamble with robbery money. It never failed with me, fast money always go fast and that was exactly what was happening to me.

I was down $500 out the two stacks and was fighting not to lose more, chasing money already lost. The little voice in my head was trying its best to get me to accept the little lose before I lost more but, my eyes were on all that money on the ground. Knowing some of it was mine had me stuck down on my knees sweating rolling dice trying to head crack for my money. I smelled her before I even looked up to see.

Little Sexy Spanish baby was standing over me. That's all it took for my luck to change for the good. 4-5-6 ... Head Crack! My bank. I could've sold the bank for $100 easily, but since Sexy was standing here I didn't want to look petty. So I put $500 in the bank. Nobody stopped it but, everybody got down. It was most likely that they were down more than I was in the bank. So I said as far as this money in my hand go! I rolled and threw a point three, out of all points. We call a 3 "the hoes." So I rolled a hoe in Celo. I guess because my mind was on this sexy ass Spanish bitch by my side. Shit these niggas must be having hoe problems, because they were all throwing dicks to the hoes. A dick was a lose 1-2-3, or any two numbers and a one. Everybody went out to the hoe except two niggas but they were only down $30 and $50. So the bank was growing. I knew I had my money back and some more so I was trying to either throw 4-5-6 again or find a way to cut the bank. My problem was solved when the little homie Red Dawg rolled 4-5-6-, so the bank was his and he wasn't even down that much, only like $20. I was cool with that. I paid all the winners and walked off with Sexy.

I heard one of the homies yell, "Oh you running like that?"

I lied and said, "shit, I lost." Out the corner of my eye I could see Fred smile when I said that. I bet he knew who was winning or losing. Fred stayed on top of the money. I followed Sexy back to the car, she was in a rental. I asked her where her sister and girlfriend was at. She told me she was on her way to Over Town to get them when she thought about me, so she came through to see if I was around here. She said that wasn't the first time she had come by, she had been through a few times since we last seen each other. I explained to her that I had just got back in town a day ago and I had to take care of few things but, I was going to come Over Town to find her. She gave me that *"yeah right look"*.

I told her she brought me luck in the dice game, I liked being around her, she brings me money and we always have a good time. We small talked about nothing really until we got to Over Town and picked up the other two. They were glad to see me, talking about now, their girl could get some good dick now. I was smiling because I didn't know she was feeling me like that... I knew we had a good time last time we were together.

They wanted to grab something to eat and then go by the liquor store to get some Hen. We went to Captain Crab on 79th Street and then we got the drink. We pulled over by the water and ate crab and sipped on Hen. I had a few bags of Mackaveli weed, so I rolled some joints and we smoked. We started talking about getting money, something we all needed. They had run through the bread that we hit for on the last lick. I already figured that part out because I was paying for everything. I didn't mind because I knew they were go-getters and I was going to fuck sexy later anyway. So this was like taking her out on a date. They told me that the Arab nigga did come looking for them and the word was he put money on their heads so, they were watching out for whatever. I knew that was going to be the case. Shit, it's not hard to find out about three Spanish bitches running together in the city hanging around blacks. The streets talk for real and money get them talking fast! That I knew.

So we ended up getting a room on Biscayne Boulevard. Me and Sexy took a shower together. She washed my body and gave me some amazing head! Man, she was laying the sex game down for real this time. I was starting to believe she was looking for me while I was gone out of town. We fucked damn near all night. "I know I used a box of rubbers." She was taking that dick and talking that Spanish shit. She didn't care that her sister and girlfriend were in the room with us. I didn't care either. They could've joined us if they wanted to. I was gone off that Hen, dick rock hard. I gave her all the dick.

The next morning, I treated them to breakfast at Denny's. We talked over pancakes and I gave Sexy $100 for pocket money then told her to take me to Emma's house in Carol City. I had heard from one of my cousins that bro was in town. I told Sexy to swing by Mackaveli later tonight. I should be around there then. When they drove off, I told myself not to be catching feelings for her. I had to keep reminding myself that I had enough on my plate. She needed a nigga with money. I was on the come up!

Everybody but Emma was still asleep when I knocked on the door. She was on her way to work. She told me to go in and keep her door closed, it was too early for traffic in and out of her house. I told her I loved her. "Don't worry, I knew better." I went to Jay's room where Ace was sleeping. I tapped his foot to wake him up. He rolled over looking mad. "What?"

"Where the weed at, bro?" I asked and he pointed to the drawer. There it was. I rolled a joint and the smoke woke him up and we got to puffing. I asked him when he had got in to town? He told me last night and that he was leaving tonight. I didn't respond. I was waiting on him to invite me to come. Still waiting, he never did. So I did the next best thing. I told him what I was trying to do with P.C. and how it's jumping up there. He responded by saying, "Didn't bro get popped up there?"

I told him, "Naw, he got grabbed on the way."

To him that was the same thing. He told me to leave the spot alone, it was hot. Damn, I had never thought of it that way, "but it can't be!" I had just let there. Shit was live. The girl Tee was waiting on me but, smoking with Bro and him running down how the Feds work he'd been doing his thing for a long time. So I had to listen to what he was saying. But shit, he wasn't fucking with me on getting money. He was putting everybody down but me. I just couldn't understand "why?" was fucking with me for real. I wanted to be mad, but kept telling myself that nobody owed me nothing out here. Not even my brother. All it did was make me want it more than before. I was going to show bro that I didn't need him. As we smoked and talked, I didn't let bro know how I was really feeling. I just played it off like nothing.

I walked around the corner to Bo's mama's house to see if Bo was up yet. He was. Bo had this little female I knew from junior high school, fine ass Haitian girl that was black and sexy as fuck. Soon as Bo let me in I could tell he was hyped up about something. He was talking loud and girl was laughing loud too. They were debating about whose name was ringing in the streets harder: Lil Bo or Lil Willie from Over Town.

When I heard what they were talking about I had mixed feelings at first. For one, why does it even matter? And how did they get on this topic? Knowing Bo, and how bro had a big ego issue, I shrugged it off. I used to think it was a little man complex but, after knowing Bo for so long, I knew that wasn't it at all. Bo just grew up spoiled by his family and he had always been used to being the center of attention. He loved the respect he got for being the man. Thinking on that, in some ways don't we all? I didn't give a fuck. Bo's my nigga, so I'm down with him no matter what. So when they pulled me into the discussion for my opinion, I sided with girl just to fuck with Bo for a good laugh. Bro got in his body for real and started saying we got him fucked up.

I thought bro was about to put me out. "Man, that shit ain't that serious," I told him. "Let that shit go and hit this joint."

We stepped out on the porch and smoked. Bo started talking about some nigga he had to deal with over something or another. I was listening but my mind was on what bro was talking about earlier. Was the Feds setting me up in P.C.? Man, shit was closing in on me.

# CHAPTER 8

# County Jail Pressure

Lately I've been waking up in the middle of the night soak and wet from night sweats. I can see myself in this glass room. They were more like windows and I could see niggas walk around in black and white striped jail uniforms. Then I woke up from the dream. It always seems crazy to me because I've never been in any prison or jail where those uniforms were worn. Not in our County Jail or state prison. Or did the Feds wear them? Was I seeing my future? I would just shake it off like a bad dream and think the sweat was because the nights are hot in Miami.

Bo and I had finished smoking and went back inside. Girl was up walking around in some panties and nothing else on. I was looking at her fine black ass and saying to myself, *"Damn I bet Bo had fun with your ass last night."* Bo didn't act like he cared that she wasn't dressed so I guess that meant she was on animal status with him. Nevertheless, I'm going to stay in my lane on this one. Bo got dressed after taking a quick shower. While he was in there, girl was really trying my patience.

She kept coming on to me being flirtatious, at least she got fully dressed. She put on the tight summer dress that just wrapped around her fine ass. Damn, I wouldn't have guessed back in middle school that she would grow up to be this bad! Oh well, maybe another time and place. For now she was my dawg's "Shon!" So I'm going to respect the G-code on this one. Bo was ready and so was I. We all jumped in the dunk. I think that was T's shit, I don't know. Bo had so many differed cars. Who cares, as long as we were riding. We dropped girl off in North Miami, then headed straight to the hood.

Back on 60th they were screaming: "Mackaveli wide ass open!" as we pulled up. Don't nothing change on the block. Dope slinging, young niggas thugged out posted for real ready to put work in for this Veli life. Still me and Bo were leading by example. Burt was telling us how we just missed him knocking one of them niggas on 59th out because they was pulling traffic away from Mackaveli. Them niggas had a weed hole right next to us. They been there, to be honest before we opened up Mackaveli. Yet Burt didn't care. It was time for them to move on or get dealt with! Damn I hate how I missed out on Burt knocking buddy out. They said, he got up off the ground and started running back to his crib, and then Burt took their bomb of weed. I told Burt to give me a few of their sacks of weed. He pulled out a brown paper bag and threw me two sacks of fire ball. That was the name on the sacks. They were fat too.

I walked off to the store on 62nd to grab a backwoods cigar to roll up and see how it smoked. Shit was already jumping on 61st. Traffic came through heavy. A couple motherfuckers drove by yelling out my name.

"Gig! What's up?"

"Gig, what they do?"

I just head nod or threw up the deuces and kept it moving. They weren't talking about shit anyway. For the most part, jokers just be yelling to let a nigga know they out here. Or, to let the people they riding with know they down with a nigga out the hood. So they could feel safe to come through. All I can say is; *Cope and Go.* Nigga these streets ain't no play toy. The city is a jungle full of predators or prey, which one was you? I was a predator. I had to eat. On my way back, I stopped and kicked it with the OG Jeff. We smoked the joint of fire ball. The shit was fire for real. I saw why Burt wanted them niggas to move. Shit, we needed a few pounds of this shit. After chopping it with Jeff, I made my way back on 60$^{th}$. For some reason my mind was on my Sexy Spanish thing.

I was wondering what she and her girls were up to now? I was starting to feel a connection with them. I don't know what the feeling was? Man, fuck that! I didn't have the time to be thinking about no bitch! All the homies were still where I left them holding down the spot. I told Burt how fire the weed was.

He said, "Nigga, I already know. Why you think I made them niggas bounce? and I thought you was going to smoke with me?"

I said, "Nigga, you the one with the bomb. I got some more Backwoods."

He pulled the bag back out and I rolled up two more jays. Burt smoked and went back to the crib. Bo jumped in the car with Joe and they dipped off somewhere. The corner started to clear out a bit. It was still early. The spot would do that all day until nightfall. Then it would stay packed all the way to the morning. As long as jump out boys didn't pop up. I was kind of glad everybody was leaving. It gave me a moment to think to myself.

Red Dawg was still sitting on a milk crate. Me and him were still working the bomb now. I kept my eyes on 59$^{th}$ way. You never know what a sucker might try. The Fire Ball niggas might want some smoke. It was whatever with me! Burt set it off and I'm riding with my dawg. This Veli shit for real with me! As I was saying that to myself, it made me think about what my mom asked me every time we talked.

*"Son, what's your plan?"*

I had plans to get money. I was doing my best out here to stay alive and hustle for the family. Every chance I get I would break her off some of the money I was getting but, it seemed like I wasn't really making no real progress. Nobody was giving me nothing out here. Ironically you need money to make money. I was trying to use the little money I had hustled up so far to make more money. But between putting money into the spot in Robbin Hood, the spot in Carol City, copping work with Bone to take up to P.C., and then breaking mom off to help with bills and Kevia, sending Bro money on his books – there just wasn't enough to go around. I wasn't even buying nothing for myself. I was on a real grind, white tee, Dickie set out the flea market, wearing old shit from when I went to prison, and left in the closet. I still had Cross Color shit I was calling myself bringing back in style. I didn't care about what nobody else thought about me. I always felt confident with myself. Ever since I was a little boy, I always thought big. It was just something in me that always wanted to standout. I could never be a basic nigga. I'm a trendsetter, a leader. That's why I was having conflicting feeling and thoughts right now. Thinking to myself, "what am I doing here? and what was my real plan?" If I could really be honest with myself, I wasn't being a leader, my plan was nothing and deep down I knew it. How could you be a leader when you following your homie?

What kind of plan had I? That depended on somebody else moving with you? I been following from day one when I listened to Burt telling me I didn't have to check in to my PO. Following Bone's lead on going on the road. Creating a plan for myself that depended on another nigga to drive me up the road. All these moves I was making was only digging a hole for me. And when you out there thugging and hustling in them streets you can feel when the hole is getting deeper. You don't know what kind of hole it is: your grave or a jail cell. That's why I smoked so much weed and drink so much trying not to think about that hole. I can only speak for myself though. But if you've ever been locked up before, when your finally in your cell and lying back on your bunk, you think back on all them early sign you ignored; that feeling you get before you sell to an undercover or before you run in on that robbery and yet you went with it anyway because you needed the money or because of the homies with you. I been having them same feelings lately. That's why I started having them dreams but, what can I do about it? Those streets chose me; I didn't ask for this life. All I knew was the hustle. I been doing it all my life. That 8Ball and MJG came to mind: *"What can I do to get out the game?"*

A car pulled up across the street bringing me back out of deep thought. What this nigga want? He came up walking fast with a gold chain in his hand. "You wanna buy this Cuban Link," he asked handing me the chain.

It didn't have no catch on it. "What happened to the catch?" I asked him.

He started fast talking again, running a story down about snatching it off this chico at the mall. That shit didn't sound right to me because a chain this big would have a thick catch on it. That would be hard to break off. I told the nigga that I was good, the shit didn't even look real. Buddy got mad and started talking shit. Why he do that? I upped my fire. His eyes got big as fuck. I don't know why he thought he could talk shit around here. That made me think he wasn't even from the city. Lots of times nigga from down south or Broward County would come to the city to sell slum jewelry. I guess this nigga thought he had a sucker but, now he was slowly moving back across the street talking real slow now pleading for me not to shoot him.

Red Dawg was up telling me to bust a cap in his ass. I had good mind to, but the nigga was doing the right thing getting in his car. Somebody else was driving so I kept the gun pointed at them. As soon as he got the door open, I let off a couple of rounds. He dived into the car as bullets started hitting the side of the car. I aimed up so I didn't hit their tires. The back window shattered for a bullet. Red Dawg was looking at me like he thought I wasn't going to shoot. I wasn't at first but, when he opened that door I didn't know if they were packing or not? I wasn't taking no chances. I don't know if I hit any of them or not. I didn't care either. Those shots brought everybody back out. Them niggas sped away, turning on 61$^{st}$ heading back out the hood. I tucked my gun in my back pocket and started walking to the Pork Beans.

My nigga Oshawn stayed in the Beans on 14$^{th}$ Ave and 65$^{th}$. He was always at the cribs ever since my dawg got paralyzed and been in a chair he had slowed down a lot. Back in the day, Bro was wild in these streets. Now he mostly spent his day chilling on the porch watching his little girl. I always stopped by and smoked a few jays with him and just chopped it up about some of everything. You would be surprised at what Bro knew about the streets just by sitting on his porch. Everybody came through the Beans to fuck with Bro and talk. So when I walked up he was kicking it with another one of my dawgs. A nigga name Noddy from off 103rd Street. We go way back from my Juvenile Hall days.

Noddy was getting real money now. Word on the streets was he was going out of town. He sold me and Oshawn a dream talking about running to his trap to grab some work and he would be right back to look out with some coke. As soon as he pulled off, Oshawn looked at me and said, "You know that fool's lying right?"

All I did was shake my head. "Why niggas be faking for no reason?"

The one thing about chilling with Oshawn was you would always get the latest scoop on what was happening in the hood. Bro could tell you who was beefing with who, who got robbed, and who done it. Who had work, who just got out of jail or prison and who went to jail. If the police knew how much info about the hood came through Oshawn's porch they would have wired it up. They could solve so many cases from listening in on Oshawn's smoke session and here I was telling Bro what I just did to the nigga trying to sell me some slum jewelry. Oshawn asked me what kind of car the nigga was in? I told him it was a Honda Civic. He started laughing and said them cats been running that same chain snatch game on niggas in the Beans. Said he knew somebody was going to bust a cap in them sooner or later and it had to be me. I told Bro I didn't know if I hit any of them. I asked him if he know where they were from? He said what I was already thinking. They were from Broward County. I said it really didn't matter to me, then I pulled out my fire. You know me, I stayed strapped!

"By the way, Bro, you got some 9mm shells?"

"Hold up." Oshawn turned himself around and rolled back inside. A few minutes later, he was back handing me a box of 9mm shells. "Get what you need."

I filled my clip back up and gave him back the box. We smoked some more. His daughter came out on the porch and climbed onto Oshawn's lap. I told Bro I would get back at him later on. I started walking down 14th Ave. I was going to 69th Street to see what was going on. That's where my cousin Frank lived. Cuz was locked up, but I still fucked with the homies around there and that's where Bone was most of the time.

My nigga Curt stayed next door to Frank. He was a funny ass nigga. Curt could make anybody laugh. I don't care what you were going through, or how mad you were, be around Curt for a few minutes and he would have you laughing and forgetting whatever you were mad about. Curt was always complaining about working too hard on his job and not getting paid enough. He would come home and find us on the block smoking, chilling, gambling, talking shit about hoes, hanging out at the club and that shit used to get Curt crunk fast. He would get down in the dice game a few dollars, and then talk everybody into playing cards. Shit would really hit the fan if he lost in the Tonk game too. Some days I would feel sorry for Curt because he lost his money that he had set aside for gas and lunch for the week.

Frank and Bone, Dee, Joe, Curt, Little brother Rod, and Pee Wee, Keith, my other cousin Chico were all the 69th Street homie. Frank and I were the youngest. So now I was on my way around there to see who was on the block. I could lay low around there to make sure everything was good on 60th Street before I headed back around there. For some reason I felt like I was running from something or someone. As soon as I turned the corner, I could tell everybody was out in front of Curt's house and they were standing around Curt's dunk that was parked in his driveway. I knew what they were doing before I even got close. We always use the hood of Curt's car to play tonk. Curt always talked about putting his dunk back in the game. I never saw it running from the time Frank moved next door to now. It needed a motor and some more shit done to it that Curt didn't want to spend the money on.

I walked up on Joe winning the hand. He went down with Bert's hand. He had already been wining because Curt was complaining about how Pee Wee was cutting Joe's deal. I didn't get down because it was already enough of them playing and I wasn't in the gambling mood. I was hoping to see Bone. I knew if I hung out for a while he would be through. Besides, I didn't have nowhere to be, maybe Bone would want to go on out. I could always use a good lick. Still had to get that cope money, right? Curt could tell something was on my mind. "What's up, Gig?" He asked.

I played it off and said that was looking for Bone. He tried to dig a lot deeper and said "What ya'll on, one?"

I knew he was trying to get into my business, but shit, Curt will take a nigga out on one from time to time. It all depended on how bad he needed the money. There have been times in the past when Curt's dumb ass would come home on payday already drunk on beers and lose his check to us. I would feel bad and let him talk me into going on one with him. We came up on a few licks, but I would have to chill with Curt because he wasn't really about that life. He was just trying to get his money back and that's not a good vibe to rob off. It seemed like I may have walked right into one of those moments with Curt needing to get back. That's why he was hitting me with the "What's up?"

It wouldn't be that bad going out to get it with Curt if he wasn't so scary. He always wanted to put you out the car two to three blocks away from the robbery and wanted you to run all the way back to the car. The type of mood I was in back then, if Bone doesn't fuck show up soon I might end up fucking with Curt on a lick. I stood on the side as a sweater not a better, watching the money circulate from man to man. Curt was losing more than he was winning. After every bad hand he got, he would look over at me. I knew what was on his mind. I have seen that look too often in the past.

One of my homies named Ross came through. He was with one of his homie Big Nick. They were in Nick's box Chevy. I know I told you Curt was a funny ass nigga, but Ross was on another level. Bro could easily be a star of Wildin' Out. Ross would make you laugh without evening trying to be funny. He even dressed on some funny man shit. I knew Ross and his brother BJ. They stayed around the way. One of my guys named Yap was from the hood. They all got money around there on 75th and 11th Ave. They would ride through 69th because they knew we stayed gambling.

Ross called me to the car. I went over to see what was on his mind. He hit me with, "Damn nigga, they done fucked you up already, huh?"

He was implying that I done lost my money in the game. I didn't see no need to correct him on what my pockets were looking like. So I just let him talk seeing if he was going to break me off since he thought I was fucked up. Sometimes it's good to play broke out here in these streets. Then you could see who really fucked with you or not but, knowing Ross, he didn't have no money. Ross blew money fast, so if you don't catch him right when he got it you could forget about hitting him up for some. The fat nigga Nick, I didn't know him that well. All I knew was he was from around BJ and Ross's hood. Ross was still trying to see where my head was at.

Then he finally said what was on his mind in the first place. He said, "Damn, Gig, let's go ride and see what it do?" I already knew what he meant by that. I told myself it must be meant for me to go on one. First, Curt was giving me the *look,* now Ross was pulling up ready to fuck with me. FUCK IT! Bone was a no show. It couldn't hurt to ride and look. If we see something slipping it was meant to be.

I jumped in the back seat. Before we pulled away, I looked over and saw Curt look like *Damn*! He would have to catch me another time around. As you could see, when it came to the robbery game, I was in high demand. Niggas knew, I didn't fake one bit when it came to the take game.

While we were riding, I asked Ross, "What's up with Fats?" That's the homie up the road doing a life on a body case. He stayed next door to Ross and they had grown up together. Fats was a real nigga all the way. He been gone about 2 or 3 years now. Ross said Fats was still wilding out, getting into fights. The only thing I didn't like about this lick we were on was being in this box Chevy and Nick had tinted windows. There was no way we could ride on the beach or the airport and that's where the real money was at that time of the day. It was 5:30 PM and getting dark early now.

I told Nick to turn on Biscayne Boulevard. Sometimes you can catch somebody slipping. It's a lot of motels up and down the boulevard as rode down past the motel me and Sexy Spanish had stayed in. I spotted the car she was driving. I made a mental note to have Nick bring me back there to see if it was the same car but, for right now, I was in jack mode. We headed to downtown Miami. It's always packed down there with tourists. We rode around for about an hour before we spotted something worth checking out.

It was at this hotel entrance. There was a group of out of towners checking in to the hotel. They were unloading from a charter bus. Bags were sitting along the sidewalk. Then they had these push carts full of bags. It looked like one of them was a purse out in the open. I told Nick to pull down the block. I got out and made my way back to where the action was. Now the key to the getaway with the lick was blending in with the other guests. And moving at the right time, I had to be fast about it. I did exactly what I described to you. I had the small bag that looked like a purse before anyone noticed me. I made it back to the car. Nick sped away.

I told him to slow down. There was no need to draw attention on us. Ross was turned in his seat facing me. Ross was vet. He knew to keep his eyes on the bag making sure I wasn't cuffing anything out the bag. Needless to say that was never my style. If I didn't want you to have the same cut as me, I would break the bread up in your face and pay you what I wanted to pay you. I was searching the bag looking for cash. For some reason I felt it didn't have any. It didn't take long to prove me right. There was nothing of real value, worth keeping or selling. No money, just a bunch of junk mail and receipts. Ross had disbelief written all over his face. Nick didn't know what was happening. He was glued to the road.

"Well that was a waste of time," I said as I opened the back door to toss the bag out. The only thing I could think was that it was too much pressure on the lick. Yeah, that happens when somebody needs money too bad. I told Nick to swing by the motel where I saw Sexy's rental car.

We weren't far from there. He pulled into the parking lot. The car was still there, but how was I going to find out what room they were in? I took a guess and went back to room we were in the last time. I knocked and the curtain slid back. Then the door swung open. There she was, with her fine ass smiling like she was happy to see me. I walked in to see her sidekicks lying on the same bed together. The one that act like the dude yelled out, "Where the drink at?"

"Go get it. I'm buying!" I told them to hold up and went to Nick's car. I told them I wasn't feeling it tonight. But they could come through in the morning before check out at noon. We could see what it do then. Ross wasn't too happy about that news. But he could take his thirsty ass back out and grab something. I was chilling with Sexy tonight.

They had left the door open and when I got back to the room. The weed smoke was thick. They had a little radio playing an underground station. Butter Love was coming to the jam booming TDD shit. I sat down and Sexy came over, jumping into my lap. She was smoking on a joint and put it to my lips. I took the jay, smoked on it, and she started kissing my neck. Damn, she was coming on strong. I liked this. I pulled out a fifty and told Lil Mama and her other half to go get us something to drink on. I could use a little time alone with Sexy. They got the keys and shot out the door.

I stood up and took my shirt off and flexed on Sexy. She loved my six pack. She wasted no time and dropped to her knees. I helped her out by pulling my dick out. Something about her always made my dick rock hard. She gave me some mind-blowing head. I didn't want to cum too fast, but she was working my solja over so good. I did something I rarely do and pulled her up and walked her over to the bed. She started undressing. I followed her and did the same. For some reason I wanted to feel her skin to skin, yeah raw. I know we wasn't in no relationship, and normally kept a rubber on for safety. Was I catching feelings? Maybe. She turned me on, we had a lot in common. Sex with her was always fire. I was lying some strong thug passion on her right now. She started off trying to take it, but ended up yelling "Ahh papi, yeah papi," while trying to run from the dick. We both came, then laid in our sweat. I needed a shower to help clear my head. She joined me.

Her sister and partner in crime came back with the liquid and some more weed while we were still in the show. They had already opened the bottle of Hen and was drinking. I said, "Damn, ya'll going to party without us?"

They both smiled and said in unison, "Ya'll the ones that started without us." They looked down at my dick back on hard. All I could do was smile. Sexy was cleaning my solja up in the shower and had him back at attention. Lil Mama poured me a red cup full of Hen, no chasers. I took a good gob of the brown. That shit hit my chest quick. We stayed up damn near all night drinking and smoking. They freaked off in front of me. That shit was sexy as fuck! I can't lie, I wanted to join, but Sexy wasn't having none of that shit, she wanted me all to herself. And I made love to her until tears ran down her eyes. I looked over and now we were the freak show for them! They looked like they wanted me to fuck all three of them. Shit, the brown had me so lit I could've gave it a real go. I never fucked 3 hoes at once, but I was young and ready. Neither of them was as fine as sexy, but they weren't busted neither. Shit, sister was small but pretty. Lil Mama didn't really have a shape but that ass was fat under them big clothes she had on all the time trying to hide that body.

We drank, fucked, smoked and talked about coming up on another lick until the wee hours of the next morning. They told me that the room was paid up until next week, so we didn't have to rush out. That was cool by me, after all the rounds with Sexy, I needed some major rest. I didn't tell them about Ross and Nick supposedly coming by to pick me up. Because that wasn't certain, who knows with Ross? Besides they had a car, only thing was the car was over due back to the rental car place. That was the last thing I wanted, to be pulled over with a bunch of Spanish girls in a stolen car. I was already in violation of my probation, and wanted for questioning in a robbery.

I was sleepy and hungry at the same time. I asked sexy was she hungry too? She was. I guess breakfast was on me. The other two were in agreement. They went to the Denny's on 79th Street. Sexy was lying on my chest. It was starting to feel like she was my new lady or something. We were talking about what we were doing as far as being together. But after me eating her pussy and making love to her I swore she said the L-word. I didn't pay it no mind then because I know what good head does to me. So I guess it worked both ways? Now she lay with her head on my chest, her legs wrapped around mine like she was making sure I didn't leave. As I was thinking about all this I had to remind myself that it would never work. Two broke motherfuckers can't do nothing for each other but hold each other down. It had to stay M.O.B. with me. Ain't that what Pac said. Money Over Bitches!! The two Spanish lovers came back with food. We ate pancakes, eggs, and turkey bacon. Full now, I could sleep.

I didn't know at first how long I was out, but Sexy was still sleep, even as somebody knocked on the room door. I got up to see walking past sister and Lil Mama out cold in the other bed. I'm glad prison made me a light sleeper because as they slept somebody could have done whatever to us. I pulled the curtain back to see a wide-eye Ross looking back at me. Damn, bro looked a mess, like he hadn't slept a bit. Shit, I bet I looked the same. It didn't feel like I had a good hour of sleep. I opened the door halfway to tell him to give me a few minutes to get dressed. He kept trying to look past me with his nosy ass. But I wouldn't let him. Sexy didn't have no clothes on and when I got up I pulled the covers back so a part of her ass and legs were visible.

After getting dressed, I woke Sexy to tell her I was going.

"Where?" She immediately asked.

Now I knew she was getting attached to me. I kinda liked it to be honest. When I told her, she wanted to go. Oh well, what the hell? She was down for a lick. Maybe she would be my good luck. It seemed like we get money when we were together. I waited until she put on these tight as jeans and her Nike Airs. Shit, I might put her up to doing the job. She was dressed for it. Naw, I better handle the business. We walked out leaving the other two sleeping. She left them a note, they'd be okay.

"We should be right back." She asked.

"Yeah." I said because I was having second thoughts fucking with this box Chevy.

It was something about this car I didn't like. It wasn't the type of car I was used to going out in. I like rentals or new cars that blend in with the people. Dark tinted windows on a Chevy always drew police attention because they knew niggas be in them. So we couldn't go everywhere in it and we're going to make it fast because we couldn't keep riding past this same place. They call us in fast because people with money move on high alert. I told Nick to take us downtown, to see what's going on down there. He and Ross looked like they'd been up for days. They had the same clothes on, but so did I. But I had been in the hotel room last night. I don't think they had been outside this car. Nick started talking about his gas being low. I guess he was trying to let me know. That confirmed what I was thinking, they most likely had been riding all night long. I started looking over at Sexy and thinking how fine she was. That was another reason to get this over with: Hit a quick lick, bust the money down, and get back to freaking her!

Nick was going by the same hotel where I took the bag from last night. And just like de ja vu it was packed with guests checking in. I told Nick to pull down to the same spot. I jumped out running this time, to hell with being smooth. I was going to snatch and grab one with some money. I did just that. The white lady screamed. I didn't care. I was running back to the car. I jumped back in. It was done within minutes. Nick pulled away heading for the expressway. For some reason, it seemed like the car wasn't going fast as it should. I had a box Chevy. They got some get up in them. But Nick's box was only doing 50-to-55 mph. I know because I was looking at the dash. His fat ass was sweating and wide-eyed. I was hitting the back of his seat telling him to hit it. We had a hero behind us coming fast. I started shaking the pocketbook for money. Ross was turned again watching me like I was trying to cuff. I didn't want to try to open the door to throw the bag out, but I needed to get rid of it fast.

I was backseat driving behind Nick. "Get over now! Hurry up! Let's get off at the next exit." I needed to jump out of the car. I would take my chances on foot. Looking back to see what the hero was doing, my nightmare began: Blue lights. This wasn't no hero, it was an undercover cop car. Shit!

Sexy looked over at me. I could see the worry on her face. That feeling I get when I know I'm going to jail was coming on strong now. Panic started setting in on my chest. I was thinking a mile a minute. *Man, why me? What my mom going to say this time? Who going to take care of my daughter? My brother going to be mad and hurt. Shit! I got to get away! God, let me get away. I'll stop robbing. Please!!*

As if my prayer was being answered, I hopefully looked back. The best way to describe what I saw would be to picture the 1994 O.J. Simpson chase in the white Bronco. It looked like Christmas lights were on with so many police cars chasing us. My chances for getting away was getting smaller as slow as Nick's Chevy was going. He pulled off the expressway on 79th Street, cut through a gas station, right through the car wash part. I told myself it's going to be now or never. I looked over at Sexy as to say I'm sorry I got you into this mess. But baby it's man for himself. That meant ladies too!

I opened the door and kept it cracked really to make my move. Dam, this nigga is not a real getaway driver. That's what I get for fucking with new jack niggas. Come to think of it, this nigga was probably out here trying to rob to get this raggedy ass car fixed.

"Shit, I'm about to jump out this bitch. Come on, man, turn here. Yeah—"Bam. Boom. I took off running through this yard. *What the fuck I'm still holding on to this purse?* I threw it to the side and grabbed hold to the fence. I was jumping it with one leg up on it when I was yanked down by my shoulders.

"What the fuck!? This ain't happening!"

But it was. They were all over me at once. Punching and kicking me like I was fighting back. Telling me to put my hands behind my back. But what's going to protect me from these blows ya'll putting on me if I put my hands behind my back. Naw, Mr. Officer, I want my teeth. But then they were pulling my arm away from my face trying to break them, I'm sure.

"My arm is not supposed to turn that way, sir!" I could taste the blood and dirt all over my face. They had my hands cuffed real tight so I couldn't feel my fingers. They lifted me like I was a prize catch from the hunt! I knew what was coming next. The back seat of a hot car.

They left the windows up so I couldn't get any air. I know of cases where niggas died like this on hot Miami days that could reach 100 degrees. I'm glad it was night time and a little cooler out. They had the whole block roped off. Police cars were everywhere. You would've thought this was a murder scene. Undercover cop cars where in the mix. They had Nick, Ross, and Sexy lined up against the fence. I was the only one in the back of the police car. I can see down the block where Nick's box Chevy was crashed into a yard up against a tree. They didn't make it too far from where I had jumped out. I guess they all got caught still in the car. Now I can see why they treated me the worst. They found the purse near me and figured I was the grabber. They had us wait at the scene until the victims showed up to ID us. But I'm the only one they were looking for. Nobody else got out the car. They pulled me out to let the people see. They got a positive ID and a match on what I was wearing. The Army fatigue pants and black shirt was a dead giveaway.

I felt bad looking at Sexy standing on the fence in a lineup with the boys. I know she wished she had stayed in the room sleep now. Her sister will be worried. They were close and she looked up to Sexy. I hope she was able to talk her way out of this, if they asked me I was ready to take the charge for everybody. There was no sense in all of us going down for this. I'm going to wait until the robbery detectives show up.

They were a little more professional about everything unlike the street cops. Sitting in the back of the police car knowing you was on your way to jail makes you reflect on all the warning signs that God was giving you. Everything started to seem clear. I guess you could call it getting a bucket of cold water thrown in your face. It wakes you up real fast. I was experiencing that feeling right now. Damn, I was a fool. I set myself up to fail. Now I'm heading back to prison for sure! With the new charge, I was looking at more time than just the violation. All I could think about was how I was going to break the news to my mom. She was going to be heartbroken and disappointed. I'm going to admit to something that may not make sense to the average person, but to niggas like me, that live day by day in these streets thugging, going hard, playing with guns, in life and death games, there's a part of you that welcome the time to rest. The time to regroup that jail offer you. Yeah, I know that sound crazy and I agree. But when the other alternative is the graveyard. Jail don't seem like that bad of a deal. The robbery detectives pulled up on a scene because the people I robbed were tourists. Louise and Nelson robbery detectives were the ones that came. They knew who me and Ross were. So he was going down anyway. Nick couldn't beat the ride because he put them on a fake ass chase. The only one who had a chance was Sexy. I told Detective Nelson that she didn't know what I was up to. Since I was trying to help her go free, he said since I was taking the rap he would see what he could do for her. As long as she didn't have a warrant they took us all down in different cars.

I was all so familiar with this ride. So I did what I always did to try and get a good long look at the city before they took me in. The hating ass police was going fast as he could like he knew what I was trying to do. We pulled into the County Jail. If I didn't think things could get anymore worse. He took my personal money as evidence of the robbery. I tried to explain to him that that was my money. He wasn't having no parts of it. To him it was all illegal money, one way or another. He kept booking me in. The rest of the process was routine for me. It all went by in a daze: fingerprints, mugshot, strip search, go in this cell, then that cell. Every last cell was full of niggas checking in to the rent-free motel. Some of us would just spend the night, others like me was facing years behind bars. I already knew what to expect, I've been doing this since a kid now. Sad to say this was starting to be home for me. I just finished doing a 4-year bid up state. Now who knows what they would give me for these new charges. I could see Fat Nick and Ross going through the same process I'd been through. I really didn't want to see them or even talk to them right about now. I was feeling set up in a way. I did my part, they supposed to have got us away. Fuck I could've been so dumb. I didn't need to go out with them. Why I put so much pressure on myself? I could have just made the trip back to P.C. with a half and let Bone put up the other half. Tee didn't have to know the whole think wasn't mine. This is what I got for doing too much.

Would've. Should've. Could've. What good was it to be thinking about all that now? I was back in the belly of the beast! No matter how hard I try to tell myself that this ain't my life, I'm better than this, smarter than this, I always find myself in here. *God why? What is it you trying to tell me, or better yet, what is it you trying to teach me?* Those were the kind of thoughts that were going through my mind as they moved me up on the housing floors.

The Fourth Floor was where they put me for now. They stuck me down the wing first, I had a chance to look in the cells. There were 4 on A-Wing and 4 on B-Wing and 2 down on C-Wing was locked down and safety cells. I was on B-Wing looking into 4-B-1 cell when somebody yelled, "Who that?"

"This Gig," somebody out another cell yelled.

"Who, Gig out the city?"

"Yeah, this me."

"Boy what they do?

"Who that?" I asked.

"Nigga, this Mazon."

He didn't have to say no more. That was my nigga. We went all the way back from Juvenile to high school, and we got money together on a few licks.

He said, "Tell them to put you down here in B-4."

"I'll see what's up." I wanted to finish checking out the other cells first. Going down there with Mason, may or may not be a good idea. Bro was wild ass fuck, and love to fight so I don't know what the politics on the floor was yet. I wanted to be hip before I jump right into some shit.

4-B-2 is where they put me. I was cool in there. It was laid back. There was a nigga named Rabbit from around the 40s where my cuz was the O.G. Charlie Parker aka Bobba. And a nigga name Orange Man, he was out the 40s too. They had the cell and it was laid back. It was just what I needed because I was still trying to rap my head around the fact that I was back in jail, on my way to prison. The cell was made to house 20 men. But it was never full up in the County Jail. Naw, niggas didn't stay in the county unless they were flight risks. Miami had four major jails that housed men: Dade County, TGK, Metro Dade, and the Stockade. Dade County was the hardest as far as violence. The Stockade was next. The other two was day care for men. Juvenile Hall was harder than them.

In the County we ran the jail. We had everything we wanted except our freedom and cars. IF you had game, or your money was right you could get pussy from a C.O. or your girl at visit. There were plenty of drugs and alcohol. We wore our own street clothes and shoes, everything was good in the County. I rather do all my time in our jail. But freedom is always better. With that gone I had to get into survivor mode. Bring that beast out. But first, I'm in a peaceful, friendly environment. I need to get myself in fight shape. That calls for working out, training, shadow boxing. I knew I had enemies, also I had a rep that niggas would want to make a name off. Then I was a Veli, so that brought on my dogs' beef to my plate. So I knew I was pressure in here and that niggas act out in different ways.

Me and Rabbit worked out each morning. Then Orange Man joined us after dinner time in the evening. Me and Rabbit sparred a lot, both of us keeping our set right. We had yard with the rest of the cells on the wing. There would be fights on the yard every time we went. Shit be over anything; somebody from one cell didn't send somebody in the next cell some smokes when they asked. Or there was a hit out for one or the other. Yeah, that's right, niggas had hits on their heads for snitching from old beef. Somebody's enemy can't get to them because they're on a different floor, so they send a hit up to people on your floor and a fight would break out on the yard because of the basketball. Oh yeah, gambling was always a reason. No matter what it was for, you could count on a fight happening every day.

I been blessed with time to get back in shape before I had to defend my rep. I hated it for my first victim because I had a lot of pinned up rage from being in jail. I haven't even worked up the nerve to call my mom to let her know where I was, that I was bothering me the most because I

know she was worried. It's been two weeks now. And I still haven't called her. I told myself I was waiting to hear how bad everything was in my case.

The next morning, at the first bond hearing the next morning in jail my bond was denied due to the probation violation. Ross and Fat Boy

Nick were in court also. The first time I had time to speak to them. They had us on different floors. Ross looked like he aged overnight with bags under his eyes. Fat Boy kept asking if Pretrial came and seen us yet? Pretrial was like probation before you go to court. They make your bond if it's under $15,000. It was a service put in place to help prevent the jail from being overcrowded. They helped Ross and Fat Boy get released. I wasn't so lucky. I was stuck like Chuck, like the old saying goes.

Now here I was, two weeks later, about to put hands on a nigga because we had unfinished beef from one of my last bids in the county or from some other time. All I know is they came up on the floor lying about he whooped me before. I got the word asap. Niggas were asking me if I wanted them to handle It for me because he was in another cell and I had to wait to get him myself. The nigga name was D.C. He was out these projects called Seminoelea in Hialeah in a Spanish hood in Miami. The nigga was taller than me and a little bigger than me. The fight was set to go down on the rec yard. It was well advertised about the fight all over the floor. My named carried some weight in jail and on the street. There were a lot of niggas hoping I lose the fight. I made me a mouth piece out of toilet paper. Got my mind right on how to beat this nigga's ass. I knew that I would have to put a real example out to let niggas know I still had it. Since the nigga D.C. was the one with all the mouth talking,I had an edge already. He was trying to prove himself. I was going to be patient and let the knock out come to me. When they popped the cell doors for the yard, the wing was packed. Everybody was going to yard today. That gave the C.O. a tip that something was up, so they would be on high alert.

The rec officer, Steve, was used to us fighting. He looked forward to a good fade. As long as it was one on one. He let us get it. We came down the stairs to the yard, the nigga D.C. was playing the back of the line. I caught him trying to size me up when we were in the hallway waiting on the gate to be popped. He knew not to make a move on me before time because in here I was a made nigga, for real! When we got on the yard since I was in the front I was the first one on the yard. When C.O. Steve saw me he spoke using my street name, "Gig."

"I see you back home." He joked.

"Yeah, for a minute. But dig this, I got a lil rec going on first. You cool with it?"

"Shit, let me see what you're working with."

As everybody entered the yard they automatically formed a ring around me and D.C. He was already smiling like he had won already. I wasn't doing any talking. My mouthpiece was already in, my chin was tucked and I was in my fight stance. The move was on him. He came at me swinging hands fast trying to take me out. I ducked under him and came up with an upper cut that made his eyes roll back. That was my power hand. The right. Then I followed with an overhand left that knocked him back. As he stumbled back, I heard niggas on the side scream, "Damn, Gig!"

I caught the side of his head with a right hook. That dropped him. The left cross didn't connect. To be my size it always amazed me that I could hit so hard. I was never really one to kick a nigga when he was down unless you really had it coming. I did stand over him to let him know that was easy work. And that I had more in me if he hadn't had enough. As I looked down I could see blood leaking out of his left ear and that side was swollen. If I had to guess, he had a concussion. Steve knew buddy was done and needed medical attention. He told us that was enough and gave him a nod that I was good.

I took out my mouth piece and threw it down walking to the back of the yard. I started doing pull ups and pushups with dips at the end. We had an hour, but sometimes they let us go for two. But I needed to get my work out on before we had to go. I watched how new niggas were giving me the eye. Some were wondering if they could take me down? I was happy with my knock down, but I knew I had to put on some weight because there were a lot of touch hawks aka Knock Out Artists from all over Miami to down south in Carol City running around the County Jail. Most of them were cool with me out of mutual respect. But I still had to hold my own. That meant accepting all call outs to fight. When we got back to the cell from the yard, Rabbit pulled me to the side and said he wanted to help me with my footwork. He said he I looked good and had power behind my punches. He liked the way I knew how to get low and bob and weave with my head. But I was too flat footed.

We fooled around for an hour. He was showing me how to move on my toes. It made me quicker. Next he showed me how to step into my punches. We trained every day and worked out like we were prize fighters. Because of my family, and me being a real street nigga from all parts of Miami, come to find out I had two cousins in the County with me. Word had come down for me to come to the chapel for church services on Sunday. That was one of the meeting spots for all the floors to pass information and whatever else you were trying to move.

I got the kite from the trustee on my floor. It was my cuz Pookie Black. He was a Parker on my brother Ace's side of the family. So I came out on Sunday to holla at cuz. In the chapel, niggas be paying close attention to who was vibing with who so they knew their surroundings better. Pookie Black was on the 6th Floor. He told me Corn Flake, our other cousin, was on the same floor. I heard cuz got jammed up on a robbery he didn't even do. I told cuz I was good for now, that I was chilling on the fourth floor with Rabbit from the 40s and my niggas Dawy Hound, Heavy, and Orange Man. I gave him some weed to smoke and told him to chill. I'd be up there soon.

The 6th Floor was known as the House of Pain because it stayed going down 24/7 in all the cells up there. It was where I belonged and I didn't mind doing all my time up there. But I had to get ready so I was going to give myself some time to get my jail weight up. I know this may sound crazy, how you could be a free man, doing free world things that matter, to moving and thinking like a locked up animal worrying about jailhouse madness! But that's what Thug Life and street nigga shit called for. You already know one minute you free, the next you in a cage with animals. Now three weeks in and I was preparing myself for jail life. I knew I wasn't going nowhere no time soon. There were niggas in our county that been riding for 10 years fighting their case. Staying in for 2 or three years was nothing in our county. You could go a whole year without stepping foot in the courtroom. Sometimes it worked in your favor; the case became weak and the time was always counting. What I wasn't expecting happened the next morning. The CO came to our cell and called my name to pack up. They were transferring me to another jail.

Rabbit and Orange Man told me they were doing it like that now trying to fill the other jail. To say I wasn't upset would be a lie. I didn't have much to pack. Rabbit had given me a sweatshirt, and a pair of shorts when I first got to the cell. Orange Man had some new boxer shorts he gave me with a pair of new socks. That's all I had: No food or mail yet. I was living off the land for real now.

I told Rabbit and Orange Man that I would be back soon. I yelled over to the next cell and told Mazin and Heavy that they were transferring me but I would get up with them soon. I told Dawy Hound and Heavy the same thing. I didn't know then but my words would be true. I will make it back and faster than I thought. They took me down to the holding tank. There were a few faces that looked familiar but I was looking over the group for any enemies. When you moving through these walls and cells it's best to do less talking and more watching and listening.

I could tell you a story where a nigga would be talking shit about another nigga and that nigga was sitting right next to him and then shit jumped off. Or where somebody talking shit about somebody family or dogs and his people right there. So I just moved in silence. But it's hard to do when you know a nigga in the streets and in jail. I always hated being in transit, for one the smell of unbathed, stank mouth niggas piled up in a small cell with a stinking ass toilet overflowing with piss and shit. I was glad when they got us chained up and on the bus. They had me going to Metro West Jail. I ain't never been out there,, but what I heard was all bad. They treated niggas like kids in a big dorm with bunkbeds. They had two CO's in the dorm with you at all times. Shit sounded like Juvenile Hall to me. Then I heard the CO like to jump niggas out there too. I was going to have to find a way from out there.

When we pulled up to the jail, I could tell this wasn't for me right away. The CO waiting on us to get off the bus got slick with me as soon as he read my card and called my name. "Oh, you a thug, huh?"

I was looking at him like *what the fuck you talking about?* When I didn't take the bait, he said, "I'm talking to you, convict!'

I just smiled because I didn't know what else to do. There wasn't no good answer to what he was asking. He took my card and stuck it in his pocket. Well, shit, if he wanted to fuck with me, I'm going to make it work to get me back to the county. If I had a problem with staff, they may transfer me back. When the line was ready to go, the same CO put me in front of the line. The first dorm they tried to put me in, the officer looked at my card and refused me. So here I was standing at a desk in front of this quiet dorm. It was clean, but cold as hell. I was wondering how they got everybody to lay in bed in the middle of the day and to be so quiet. The CO was looking me over, up and down, like he was still thinking about if he should keep me or send me on my way. Out of curiosity I wanted to know what my card said about me that had me on the spot with the CO. He wouldn't tell me, but said that he wasn't having any trouble maker in his dorm. He called some nigga named Head who slept right there by his desk, near the TV. So this was the so called house man. The CO told Head to get me a mat. I followed buddy to a closet in the back of the dorm. I could tell he was sizing me up by the way he looked at me when we got to the closet. Buddy called himself getting gangster with me about a mat. He was trying to hand me this pissy, beat up mat. When I could clearly see a stack of new ones up against the wall. So I asked him what's up with them?

He just smiled and said there's a ticket on them, meaning he was selling them.

I politely told him, "Nigga, you got me fucked up. Let me get my issue!"

After that, I was through talking. When he didn't get out my way so I could get a new mat, I hit him with what me and Rabbit had been working on. It's called the Chicken Wing: a right upper cut, followed by a short right hook to the chin. See, most niggas when they fight, they used to taking off with a straight jab or a two-piece. Most times all that do is stun a man, dazing him. Then you have to keep working him to put him down. But if he can take a punch, then you got a fight. I learned to go for the knock out the gate. If he leave it open, why not take it? It saves you time and energy. And if he's still standing after hitting that chin or catching him in the temple. One or two more hits will put him down. At least with the type of knock out power I had, my punches always did the job.

That's how I got a rep for being a knock out artist. And the chicken wing was one of my favorite combinations. And this nigga laid up against his closet door was proof that my power was there. The dorm came to life with the commotion in the closet. That brought the CO running. Once he saw his house man leaking from the mouth and me standing over him, he already knew what had happened. He yelled for me not stand still and not move. He was trying to get buddy to tell him what happened to him. But his mouth was too full of blood to speak. So I told him.

"Your man was trying to give me a fucked up mat to sleep on when there's new ones right there!"

"So you hit him for that?"

I said, "Naw, I hit him because he wouldn't get out my way."

"Oh, you a tough guy?" He snarled. "I got something for you." Then he hit the deuces and a few minutes later in came a whole bunch of CO's and white shirt Lieutenants, all for me! They handcuffed me and roughly threw me to the ground, patting me down with knees in my back. I knew to just take it or it would get worse. They pulled me up and damn near ran with me in the air. Most of this was for show, to keep the other inmates in line.

Once we were out in the hallway, the LTs took over. They wanted to know what the problem was. I told them the same thing I told the CO. All I wanted was a good mat and not the old, pissy one. The LT had my card in his hand and he looked at me and said, "You're not an inmate, you're a convict. This is not a good place for you. I'm going to help you out. Just chill out and do what my officers tell you and I'll have you back on the next bus going back to the County." True to his word, the LT had me put on the morning court bus run.

I was tired of the whole ordeal. The past 24 hours was taking a toll on my body and mind. News of my latest knock down was the main topic on the bus ride to the County. It seemed the nigga Head was a known nigga in that jail. He was having his way for a while and the CO was letting him rough dudes off. He had whooped a few drop shots and considered himself to t be a touch hawk until the day he met a real touch hawk. I knew a few niggas on the bus from prison and the hood. But I didn't feel like talking, especially not yelling back and forth on a bus. They have us chained together by two. So, I gave the *what's up* head nod, then closed my eyes. It didn't take long to pull up at the County. I had made up my mind to call my mom and give her the bad news. It had been three weeks, and I know she was worried sick. That was part of the reason I was so quick to fight because I was hurting inside and the pressure of knowing I let my family down again was weighing heavy on my mind. I had so much pent up rage inside me and the only way to get some release was fighting. At least that was the only way I knew of then. But I had to let mom know, and tell her where I had my money hid.

I was so disappointed in myself that I didn't want a dime of it. I will let her use it to help the family. I can live off the land in here. Besides this was my second home, it was some real niggas in here that was like family to me. They put me on the 5th Floor this time around on B-Wing. For some reason I preferred B over A-Wing. I felt lucky on this side of the jail.

When they popped the wing and let me down, I went to the first window and looked in. There was a pair of eyes looking back with a smile. My nigga Cooda Hound from off 61st was in 5-B-1. That was good enough for me to see. I told the CO, B-1 had beds open. He knew that's where I wanted to go. He came down and popped the cell. Hound blessed me with a care package with hygiene, shower slides, and some food. I was good. We sat up and chopped it up about the hood well into the night.

The house man was a young nigga named Fonzo. He been riding the County for 5 years now on a robbery and a body case. Then there was this Columbian hitman who had been in the County since the 80s (like ten years now). Everybody else was dopeheads and petty theft niggas. It was no more than 13 of us in a 20-man cell. Hound was on some chill shit. He put me up on game. He said the morning shift CO was cool, but the 4-12 PM shift was the assholes. They were jumping and setting niggas up to get fucked up in the wrong cells. He said the best thing to do was sleep their shift out.

I took his advice, then asked him to make a 3-way call for me. It wasn't easy, but I broke the news to mom and told her where the money was. She was mad and relieved at the same time. She said she had been praying that God saved me from the streets. With that out the way, I could settle down into jail life. The cell was laid back, Hound wasn't into the workout tip. He played the phone and watched TV all night. I got into a routine. I took Hound's advice and worked around the suckers' shift: 6 AM-to-12 PM. I worked out doing everything from pull ups, pushups, to shadow boxing in the yard. I went without a fight for about a month. But I knew that wouldn't last long. I came to realize that my presence in a cell or in the streets made weak niggas intimidated and that made them defensive. That's what end up causing me to fight. That wouldn't be the case with my next fight.

This was Veli work, mixed with old beef. The sound of the wing door opening and closing woke me up. I always pay close attention to the goings and comings on the wing. In the County you could hear through the walls because everything carried in the air; smoke and sounds. You could smell a woman's perfume or smoke on man's clothes entering the floor from your cell. So when the nigga Zay off 58th came on the floor, I knew he was there before he knew where I was. I waited to see where they were going to put him. I made sure to stay quiet and out of view of the window. Hound knew I had Veli beef with Zay. Everybody out the hood knew he was on top of Veli's hit list. It was on site with him. He was the same nigga that shot Shar and Joe. Now he was walking into the cell with me.

When the CO rolled the cage door open, I stayed in the back of the cell. Out of site. As soon as the cage closed and the door was locked, I came from the back of the cell. Zay looked like he seen a ghost. He said, "What's up, my nigga. You still on that old juvenile shit from back in the Hall?"

I smiled and shook my head no. "But I'm on Veli business, for sho!"

He had a confused look on his face, like he couldn't make the connection. It was possible that he didn't know I was down with Veli, but he was about to find out the hard way. He dropped his mat to the floor. Hound was standing on the side. Fonzo was sitting at the table. I could tell he didn't want me to fight the nigga. I put my mouth piece in and threw up my set. He was still standing there looking like he didn't understand, so I faked a move with my left shoulder that made him step to the right; right into my right hook. I doubled up my hooks with two rights. The first hook sent him into the bars by the door. The second right hook didn't connect all the way because he was falling away from me. This nigga didn't even fight back. He balled up. So I let off a fury of punches. Right. Left. Trying to open him back up, but he just lay there so I had no choice but to kick him a few times. I let him know this pain was for Joeaveli and Sharaveli. Even though this was my enemy, I felt sad for the nigga. He supposed to be this real ass killer, thug nigga, but take the nigga's gun away and he straight bitch, balling up like a sucker instead of fighting back. Wait until I tell the homies about this, and Hound was a witness to it all. I told the nigga to get up and get on the door.

"You can't stay here!"

That was a County rule that the loser had to get on the door. Yeah, I put him on the door. That would be the word throughout the County. A week after putting Zay on the door, my homie from the Sub came to the cell. Vee was back from prison. He got there on the morning shift and came down the wing as loud as he could be dressed in prison blues. When the cage door rolled back and Vee dropped his mat I knew things in the cell would get wild from then on. Vee didn't want a bunk. He laid his mat next to the table near the phones on the floor.

Me, him, and Hound started talking about everything from who was dead to who was up the road in prison. We tried to put Vee up on the lay of the floor, which CO was tripping on petty shit, to how laid back the cell was. But talking to Vee was like talking to a wall. Vee was going to do shit Vee's way, no matter what the consequences were. Hound gave Vee a Fila sweatshirt because it stayed cold in County. Vee act like that sweatshirt was made of gold. Bro been down for 11 years now. And he was making a big deal about everything. He wanted to know about cellphones, CDs, and what niggas were driving now? Vee was happy to be back in the County. To him it was like coming home. He told us that he purposely set his prison cell on fire so they could charge him with arson. That way he could come back to the county to hang out. And that's exactly what he was doing, everything was all fun and games to him. Me and Vee would become real tight over my next 2 years in the County. We would take cells and give officers hell. Starting with this cell, I was cool with Fonzo so I kept the peace as far as it was with him. Hound was good with us all, so he did whatever.

Since Vee was playing the day room, I brought my mat out there as well. We would lay out there and watch TV all night long. Vee wanted to watch anything that had women in it. Volleyball games, track and field, as long as he could fend it off. I didn't have no problem with it, I was fending them off myself. But Vee had it bad, to the point he didn't want to let nobody watch nothing else. Hound liked music videos. I didn't really care about the TV like that. Everybody knew the TV was one of the number one reasons fights start in jail or prison. That's why the nickname for the TV was the "Trick Box." I knew it was bound to happen.

It was already understood in the cell that the Columbian hitman could watch the Spanish news at 5:30 PM everyday. It's been like that before I came in the cell. It was cool because this time me and Hound only slept because this was the sucker CO's shift. Well like I told you before, Vee don't listen to nobody, so when Fonzo woke me up he said I had to try to talk to Vee about the TV. I couldn't do nothing but shake my head. It was too late for talking even if I could've. Vee and the Hitman was already standing toe-to-toe facing off. Vee turned the TV from the news and the Spanish nigga pulled the cord out the wall. So now it was no TV on for nobody. The plug socket was outside the bars.

Before I knew it they were fighting. I mean getting it. This was a heavyweight match up. The Hitman outweighed Vee by more than 50 or more pounds. Vee was 6'2", anywhere between 200-215, cut up muscle. The Hitman was 6-feet about 260-280 fat boy. They fought from the front to the back of the cell. We all watched as the fight went on. There weren't many blows thrown other than the first 2 piece Vee got off in the beginning. They were tied up wrestling flipping each other over as they tried to get the upper hand on each other until the Hitman flipped Vee over and had his whole weight pinning Vee down. But he wasn't trying to swing a punch. I was just about to jump in and help Vee when he surprised the hell out of me. "No, Gig, I got this ... It's was getting good now."

Like he caught his second wind kicked in, he started growling like some kind of animal and twist his body flipping the Hitman so he was now on top. Then Vee pinned his arms down with his knees on the Hitman's arms. The Hitman's face was now exposed and Vee started dropping big blows on the Hitman knocking teeth out, just fucking him up big time. It took Fonzo and Hound to help me pull Vee off dude before he killed the man.

The Hitman was a bloody mess, he needed medical. That meant he would have to bang on the door for the sucker CO's. This wasn't good. They were already looking for a reason to bust me and Vee. People were dropping kites on us. They didn't like how Vee, not me, was controlling the TV. And I had my bed on the table when the CO did their rounds, they always had something to say about that, but I didn't care. I still stayed up there because the fight happened on the sucker's shift, now they had a valid reason to move us off the floor. They weren't going to move the Hitman since he had been on the floor forever. Moving us was easier. I wasn't fucked up with it. After this, how could I sleep in the same cell with the Hitman? We would have had to sleep in shifts.

They moved us just like I thought, to the 6th Floor (The House of Pain). They sent Vee down A-Wing and I got on my lucky side: B-Wing.

As soon as I walked on the wing, niggas were yelling for me to come to their cell. Don't get it twisted, they weren't all friendly yells. Some niggas wanted to see me put in work. They knew what time it was. On the 6<sup>th</sup> Floor, niggas fought all day long just for fun. There wasn't a chill cell on the floor. I was ready. I'd been under this kind of pressure my whole life. I'm always representing, putting on for my hood, my name, my dogs. They put me in B-2. My nigga Cheesie Will from Over Town was in there with a few other niggas I didn't know. I came in and made my bottom bunk, I heard an announcement: "Tell the softest nigga to get off the bottom bunk!"

In most cases somebody would step up to fight. It would be the nigga with the most pressure on him; the one with the most to prove. When you a real touch hawk you don't respond to indirect call outs. A real nigga already know they ain't talking about them without putting a name on it. But Cheese being the smooth nigga he was already had me on the workout.

"Come on, Gig," he said. "I got you a bunk in the back by me." Bro was happy to see me, now he could sleep better knowing a nigga had his back. The cell had some Spanish nigga in it. They was hitting licks on the floor. So niggas were letting them rock on the floor. They were going to visit and jamming the door on our side. And their people were slinging packs under the door to the wing.

Cheese put me on the whole lick. He told me chill had the chicos on his team. One thing about Cheese was that anybody that knew him would tell you that Cheese had the gift of gab. He could talk a "Cat off a fish trunk" for real! I had known Cheese for a long time, a real street nigga, always kept it G-code. So I fell back and chill. The Chico's name was Gordo. He was the one running the show and the other two were his do-boys. I peeped that Gordo kept the pack on him at all times up under his stomach. Every time they fire up, he would bring Cheese a joint for us. Cheese always included me. I didn't feel right about the way things were being handled by the chico. They would smoke two or 3 joints at a time while they expected us to share one. Cheese was trying to make it work.

He called one of the other niggas in the cell and let him smoke with us. I know it was their pack and they were the ones busting a move to get it. But we were all in this cell together. See when the COs smell smoke they don't care who was smoking. They start by unplugging the TV or coming in and shaking us down. They did all kinds of shit to make our time hard. So if we're going to be punished together for smoking, let's all get high together the right way. I started turning the weed down and started working out more to relieve my stress. The chico started moving different around me. Then this Haitian nigga jumped out there with me. He slept on top of me. In fact, he was the one Cheese made get up to give me the bottom bunk. I guess he was feeling a way about that now? Whatever the case is, I asked him to not step up on my bed by the head part. But he kept doing it so slap the shit out of him. Then I walked out to the day room. He followed me talking about he "Live for me!"

I asked him what the fuck that mean? *"You live for me?"* I jumped with a leaping right hook. It knocked him back. Then I hit him with a two piece that split his forehead open. Cheese was like, "Damn, Gig, buddy shot leaking for real."

He was bent over with blood pouring from his head but he was still talking. Now, he was saying, "Look at what you done to me."

I said, "Naw, you the one talking about 'live for me."

We knocked on the door so they could take him to medical. The only thing I liked about the 6th Floor was the COs didn't trip about this type of shit. They brought this so-called "Solution" and threw it on the blood spot. It was a bleach mix with other chemicals. In the course of my stay in the County Jail I made them bring out the Solution to clean up most of my fight scenes. After the Haitian nigga was gone, Gordo pulled out some weed. This time he gave Cheese 3 jays for us to smoke. That let me know he had a little fear in him. A little violence and he moved different. Just when I had enough of Gordo bird feeding us with the weed, look who was looking through the window, my nigga Vee.

Yeah, Vee got into it with this big nigga over in 6-A-1 from what I heard. It was a thriller, they say Vee was putting hands on buddy. When they locked up, some kind of way Vee was on top. When buddy pulled out a banger and started hitting Vee in the head and shoulder area. But Vee was able to work the banger out the nigga's hand by bending it up. But he still was bleeding from the head. So he had to be taken to Ward D at the hospital. They put a bandage on it and now they were moving him in with me. My nigga, I knew once Vee see what was going down in here we would take the cell and Gordo's sack. Vee came in the cell. This time he had a small bag of clothes with him. And gone was the prison blues. He had a matching Fila sweater to go with some shorts. But he still had the prison black boots on. He would fill me in later on how he had been collecting all this Fila stuff. It seemed that Vee thought everybody should donate their Fila clothes to him because he had a sweater to match it! Nevertheless, it gave him something to do while he was in the County, I guess.

They brought lunch and after Gordo pulled out the sack, he gave Cheese the usual 2 jays. Cheese smoked with me, Vee and two of the other young niggas in the cell. Cheese knew Vee from the streets. See we all were dogs. The whole time we were smoking, Vee kept his eyes on the Spanish niggas. I knew he was seeing how bigger their jays were compared to ours and the fact they had their own jays. I didn't need to convince Vee that we should take Gordo's sack. Like minds think alike. He was trying us anyway by bird feeding some real niggas. He would've been better breaking us off from the top and let us smoke how we wanted to. So we stopped Gordo and told him what he should do. He tried to play hard at first, but I could tell he was scared. He already seen what I could do, and Vee's name was spreading through the county for being a touch hawk and knock out artist. I was stamped that same way.

But pride is a terrible thing. And because of that Gordo and his two guys got their ass whooped and the pack took. Cheese wasn't down with it at first, but once I took off it was on. Me and Vee had Gordo cornered in between the first bunk and the wall. I mention that because when I threw my famous right hook, I connected on the side of Gordo's temple knocking his head up against the wall. You had to see this to believe it, but Gordo was knocked out standing stuck between the wall and the bunk. Anybody that ever done time in Dade County know that cut between the first bunks is real tight. And Gordo's big ass was stuck knocked out on his feet. Vee pulled his pants down and the sack fell out. Cheese and one of the young niggas had did quick work with the other two Spanish cats.

We rolled up their shit with the mat and set them and it by the cage door. Gordo recovered and was still a little dazed. But I think his pride hurt the most. He kept trying to ask Cheese, "Why, papa?"

Cheese just gave it to him real raw. "Man, I kept trying to tell you everybody wasn't going for the pinch game."

When the CO came and moved them out, they waited until they were in the hallway to start making threats and talking loud. We did not care. We were already rolling a jay, we all were. Vee and me would last about a month or two in this cell before the CO came through with a shakedown and found some buck (jailhouse liquid) that Vee was making. I did not really care for the stuff. But Vee swore by the fact that his batch of buck would get anybody drunk. I let him have that and kept smoking weed.

They moved me back on the 4th Floor. But this time they put me in 4-B-3. My cousin Pookie Black was down there and guess who pop up in jail, Bo-aveli. Yeah, I knew Bo was on the 4th Floor. The whole jail knew. I sent word for him to come up on the 6th Floor. But he refused. Shit was too sweet on the 4th Floor. Dawy Hound and Heavy was shaking packs on the regular. Breaking all the boys off. The nigga "best" from Alinda project was busting a move also. And Bo himself had a line coming through. So it made all the sense in the world for me to stay down here. The only thing about the 4th Floor was the CO on the day shift didn't want no fighting with niggas getting hurt and shit like that. They didn't care about us smoking as long as we kept some smell good in the air to cover the smoke. When I came in the cell, Pookie Black had already arranged for this nigga from down south name Snow to give up his bottom bunk. But I guess when the nigga looked at me. He sized me up and thought maybe he could take me, So he changed his mind and made it be known he wanted to fight for his bunk.

See, niggas looked at my height and think I'm not working with nothing. And I admit it looks that way with my shirt on. And I always wore big clothes so that made it hard to tell. Pookie Black started to argue with the nigga Snow over him changing his mind. But I stopped him and told him Snow was entitled to fight over his bunk. Snow was a big nigga and he was already worked up for the fight. I knew I needed an edge. I always kept a readymade mouthpiece in my pocket. Never knew when you have to get one in. Snow was standing right next to me, but he knew better than to start the fight until I was ready. He was from down south in a city cell. However, I was never on that. I fuck with real niggas all over Miami. So I told him to give me a minute so I could tie my shoes. I bent down and started untying my shoes to retie them. When I looked up, I saw that I had a clear shot at his chin. I took it. I came straight up into an uppercut. It was the edge I needed. It caught Snow off guard. It was so hard that I saw his eyes roll back in his head. One of his teeth came flying out. I split the bottom part of his chin wide open.

Bo yelled, "Damn, Gig. You fucked buddy up!"

The nigga Snow was so dazed and blood was gushing from the cut under his lip and from his mouth. He needed to go to medical, but I couldn't let him leave right then. Not on this shift, they just gave me a warning not to fight or they would move me off the floor. So I told Snow to go get in the shower and wash the blood off and try to stop the bleeding. I kinda hate that I did that to him, but he really didn't give me a choice. I been riding the County too long to be on a top bunk, plus he made it seem like a call out! Bo was fighting an attempted body case. He was waiting on his lawyer to get him a bond. We smoked a few jays and Bo put me up on Mackaveli business. It seemed that the hood was on fire ever since the police got shot. Yeah it happened on New Year's 1997.

They had police cars sitting in everybody spots on 61st because that's where it happened. But we were still good on 60th Street. So Mackaveli was booming and the Veli click was growing. There were young niggas coming in and out the County claiming Veli. Bo told me we were all up and down 14th Avenue, even up on 62nd Street. Bo called Joe and told him that I was in the cell with him. I got on the phone and Joe ask me what I needed. He broke Bo's girl Angel off. Something for me and Bo, and had me some shoes and clothes sent to the County. He had some bad news for us. Burt got jammed up on a gun case at the Club Rolex. He was on the 5th Floor on A-Wing. I found later on that he was in a Carol City cell. He was good. Them niggas fucked with us and Burt could handle his own wherever they put him. We just had to get him I got the nigga Zay for him. But I know my nigga wish we would've got him on the streets. Burt wasn't the only Veli with a new case. His cousin Shar-aveli got picked up by homicide. The word was that his codefendant was snitching on him. He was a young nigga down on the Thug Life line. He was up on the 6th Floor wild as ever. They picked up my dog Charlie Boy for shooting the police. It was a fucked up beef they were trying to pin on my dog. Word in the hood was niggas snitched on C.B. out because they wanted him off the street. My nigga was for sure pressure out there.

Yeah, C.B. had a lot of niggas shook. So they fed him the cracker to get him out the way. They went so far as to have this smoker, base head hoe, that got hit the same night the police got hit on new year's to say she seen C.B. shooting a big gun; like an AK-47. C.B. was up on the 6th Floor too in 6-B-1 cell. But for now, I was good chilling on this sweet as floor with my little cuz and my Veli brother Bo.

We finally got Snow the help he needed when the second shift came on. He told them he slipped coming out the shower. They didn't care one way or another. They just moved him and counted us, then put dinner in the cell. Weeks went by and Bo's bond hearing was coming up. His lawyer was confident she would get him out on bond. When you got a paid lawyer things move faster for you in the County. I hada P.D. that I hadn't met in the months I'd been in the County.

My mind was already set on going back to prison. I knew there was no other way out. With a violation alone, I was going to prison. They already let Fat Nick and Ross go on the new charge. The County Jail had a way of exposing niggas that was one way. I'm going to give you an example. This nigga Best, out of Alinda Projects was on the 4th Floor with me and Bo. We both knew the nigga from the hood. He used to always pulled up on 60<sup>th</sup>, stayed strapped with fire and would put in work on the streets. He was known for flipping niggas, putting stripper hoes on out-of-town niggas. I always had the up most respect for my nigga's gangsta. But that changed after the County exposed his softness. Dig this! Best's little brother got killed up on 15<sup>th</sup> Ave. The word going around the County was it was over a female. They say he was fucking with my homie's girl, Little M. Well, him and this nigga named Frog got into it. I won't go into much more of that, nevertheless, Frog caught the body charge. They put Frog on the 4<sup>th</sup> Floor with us and Best.

When the news that Frog was on the floor came to me, Bo and Pookie Black, we were betting Best was going to fuck buddy up asap. Best wasn't in the cell with us, but he was on the same wing as Frog. Matter of fact, they were in the same cells next to each other. Best was on the bars chopping it up with dude like they were old buddies or something. We could hear them talking way on the other side. We all thought Best was tricking him into thinking everything was all good. And he could go to the yard. That had to be it? But it wasn't.

The next morning came and everybody went to the yard looking to see Best put that work in. When we were in line in the hall, I told Pookie Black, "Cuz, that nigga ain't about to do shit to dude." I could tell by his body language. When we got to the yard, Best fell to the back of the yard by the water fountain. That's where we all went to smoke, not fight. Instead of whooping the nigga Frog, Best was smoking weed with buddy and showing each other pictures. I couldn't believe my eyes. None of us could. It really didn't matter to us either way it went. But we all knew how it was supposed to go. We smoked Best's weed up. Shit, far as I was concerned, Best was fair game now. He showed me that he was a one way nigga. That's what we called niggas that was "like that" with a gun or when they had numbers. Basically a nigga that's one way is hard when he on the street with a gun. But when he in jail or prison, he soft as fuck!

Me and all my dogs were 2-way niggas. I'm pressure in and out of jail or prison. With a gun or without one, I'm going to be a real one.

Standing out on the rec yard, smoking this soft ass nigga's weed. I just started laughing, Pookie Black shook his head and bust out laughing himself. Before long we all were laughing. The nigga Best didn't know we were laughing at him. All I could think was *these niggas are so funny.*

My stay on the 4th Floor wouldn't last long. Bo made bond and a few weeks after he left, they bust our cell for too many fights. Also because a few niggas got accused of gunning a female CO down (jacking their dicks on her). I think that was main reason they bust the cell up. Even though I wasn't accused, they still sent me back to the House of Pain on the 6th Floor. I went right in the cell with Charlie Boy, my cousin Corn Flake. The cell was B-1 (6 Bout It 1) or just C.B. The 6th Floor was turned up as usual. This was the first time I really got to bond with Corn Flake.

They had cousin on a bum ass fake robbery charge. He was actually innocent, but since the police couldn't never get him on shit they knew he did they jumped at the opportunity to pin this beauty salon robbery on him. The owner picked Flake out of a picture line up with the help of the police. Flake was real laid back in jail. All he wanted to talk about was his babymama and his two boys. He was totally opposite from the nigga he was on the street. Cuz was from Over Town and he was real pressure out the swamps. That the most gutter part of town if you ask me. And most people would tell you the same.

Flake was known for jacking niggas. Word was he had a few bodies under his belt. He was cool, but when he got on that blow and start drinking, he becomes a beast and anybody could get it. Don't get me wrong, Flake was a "two-way" nigga. In jail he still carried his weight. Cuz would fight whoever. But he always kept a banger on him. He knew a lot of niggas had it out for him about street beef. Somebody's family member wanted to get even with him for something he had done to them. He was good up here with me. I had his back and with that came Veli love out the city. Charlie Boy was shaking the pack in the cell. The nigga B over John Doe was shooting C.B. whatever he asked for. C.B. only smoked weed, but he would still get blow in the cell. I didn't have to worry about nothing. Everywhere I went in the County niggas showed me love.

Me and my crew ran the County Jail from 97-98. There was so many of us calling each other *Cuz* that some of the officers referred to us as "The Family." Others thought that L.A. Crips had put down in Miami. It was just that every floor had a Parker or a Veli. So that gave me influence all over the County. That came in handy when the shit in the streets turned wild and war broke out. If any Parker or Veli enemy got locked up and came to the County Jail, I made sure they got dealt with. But then some bad blood came between Veli and Loso J.D.

It was '97 and shit was going crazy in the city. Niggas were getting knocked off left and right. All the hoods were into it with the body count rising. I'm not going to go in full detail of what I know about the fact that led up to Veli and Loso J.D. falling out. That's not my story to tell. But I'm going to say this, I hate it ever happened. Real G's died on both sides. I most definitely miss my Veli brothers and sisters that are gone. Even though shit was crazy with Veli and Loso J.D. on the streets. All of us who were locked up with each other didn't flip. Me and Charlie Boy had a long talk about where we stood on that. We knew too much had happened out there to squash the beef and there was nothing we could do from the inside. A lot of new wannabes claiming Veli or J.D. was bumping heads and getting into it. But the real Velis and J.D.s, who knew how deep down we were before this beef shit - like me, C.B., Cooda Hound, Dawy Hound, and Heavy – we still had love for each other. I can't lie in a way I felt like God saved me from something worse than what I was facing with this robbery case. And after it was all said and done, I would know he did.

*\*\*\**

My mother's prayers came through for me. I ended up riding the County Jail for 2 years and catching a mandatory 7-year sentence. To me that was a lot of time. I never had been locked up for that long. But when I look at all the things that happened while I was gone like Veli homies getting killed and others getting life sentences, it made me feel blessed and I knew when I got out I was going to have to come up so I could look out for my homies still locked up. I would have to show love to my dead homies' kids and mothers. So here I go again added pressure to already pressure. And all I know is the hustle and thugging in these streets. I thought about how hard this was on my mom and daughter. She had two sons in prison now, one in the Feds and the other on his way to state prison. What bothered me the most was here I was riding this bus, on my way back to prison was I had only stayed out a total of six months. After this bid my number of years in prison would be 11 altogether. I was 24 years old. If all goes well and I make it back out of here, I would be 29. Still young with whole life ahead of me. But first I got to get through this bid.

Prison is all about survival, to remain alive and not catch more time while you're in. I did it before and I do it again. This time it wasn't going to be as easy as the last time. I had no money coming in, so I was going to have to live off the land. I wasn't worried. I've been getting it how I lived from day one! I went back to South Reception Center. This time I was an adult. They sent me to the Annex side. Like usual there was a lot of homies from the hood and Miami. Once we were up the road, no matter what part of Miami you from we all were homies. I didn't stay at the Reception Center long this time. Once you been through the system before it more easy to process you.

They added a letter "A" to my prison number: It was now A-193503. That's how it worked in the prison system for A-z. I saw a guy with a "G" and I think that's the highest letter I could remember. But I'm sure there were much higher ones. I can't lie, I was kinda embarrassed for being back in prison. And so quick with no money. I played it off. I wasn't going to let nobody know how I felt. So, whenever me and the homies were around, I talked about how wild me and my dogs was thugging out there. It was a good reflection too on how I really flopped out there. Inside I felt like shit.

This wasn't how I was supposed to be living. I knew I was smarter than this and I wasn't last at all. I didn't mind working for a living. I just had to be a job I could feel respected on. I always wanted my own business, I didn't know how to start one or even run a business. And what kind of business? I knew before I got out I would need to have answered those questions! I had enough time to think on it with the five years I had left on this sentence.

I was designated to Madison C.I. prison in North Florida. I really didn't care that it was so far from Miami because I wasn't planning on getting any visits. The only person that would come see me was my brother Gregg, and he was still locked up in the Feds. When I arrive at Madison C.I. it was lunch time. I was glad to get off that funky ass Blue Bird prison bus.

A group of inmates had bunched up by the gate to see the new inmates. I glanced over the sea of mostly black and brown faces, one familiar face was my cousin Pookie Black. He did leave the County Jail before me. But I didn't know where they sent him until now. Having family there was cool because I know Black would have already worked his hand on the pound. And just like I thought, Black had a little crew of wild niggas running under him. Before I even made it to the yard good word of me being there had already spread. All the young niggas from Miami and Hollywood were ready to get down. They gave me the yard, so that made me the Shot-caller for Miami. The older O.G. from Miami, that wasn't on count, didn't oppose the move. They knew somebody had to keep the young homies in order and had respect for me. Like the big homie Big Rick from down south, I knew him from the County. He was the head cook in the chow hall, but he knew I was a fighter, but also a thinker. So he would pull up on me if something was in the wind with the homies that I needed to get in front of.

For the most, it was easy running the Miami car at Madison. Everything was chill. There were cases where one of the young homies got in over their head with gambling debt and didn't want to pay. I would make them honor the bet or fight a fade. If the dude who was owed the money didn't want to fight for it then it was over. Can't make a nigga pay what he don't have and I wasn't going to pay it. All I can say is don't gamble him no more. But I would also tell the young nigga to stop bringing petty shit to the car. I was working in the kitchen. Black and Big Rick also worked there. That's where I got down with the money man.

I had seen him around but I didn't know he was from Miami until we started working on the same shift in the kitchen. His name was David (I won't even try to pronounce his last name). He was from Wynwood, off 36th and 7th Ave. Everybody from Miami know that's where that work come from, talking about "Bricks of Blow!" We started talking about who we knew from around there. He was surprised to find out I knew a lot of the homies like B-Boy, Spencer, Leo, Alex, and the Twins. All of the times I was in Juvenile Hall, I got down with real niggas all over Miami, out of every hood. David was mixed with Spanish and Russian. He had that money, and his family was caked up too. The only reason he was working in Food Service was because they made everybody get jobs or go to the box. David paid other inmates to do his job. Once I found out that's what he was doing, I got his work detail changed to work with mine; shit I could use the money. Like I always said, I'm not lazy. Besides the work wasn't really shit; just wipe down the service line and we were done. He started sending money to my account. Not just for doing his job, also for having more money on hand. Because they only let us spend so much a week and I never used my limit. So if he needed it, I'd have it for him, if not it was mine.

David loved to smoke weed and so did I. But I wasn't about to let us be customers. He had the money and I had the connect. We had this old homie that was busting licks on visit. His name was Boatwright. He had a Life sentence and was cold with the law. That was his job. He was a law library clerk. It's crazy because he helped so many brothers get back in court and win some time off but couldn't find a loophole in his own case. But he kept fighting and sold weed on the side to help with all his legal fees because it costs to file motions and get paperwork you need to help with your case. Not to mention the books you have to buy on your own. Because most of all the books in the law library are outdated. Boatwright had this young gay guy coming to visit him. From what Boatwright told me, he used to date the boy's mom when he was free, and he was the only daddy dude knew. So Boatwright kept it that way and looked at him like a son. I didn't know if that was true or not. He told me about it one day when we were smoking. I didn't care anyway as long as he kept us with weed to smoke.

I worked it out with Boatwright, that's how we would buy whatever he wanted to sell. That was cool for him because he could stay low key and still get paid. All he wanted was a little percentage for himself and the rest was ours. He would sell us a couple of ounces each week. Me and David would break them down and I would give a pack to Pookie Black to push. We keep a percent for ours, and made David his money back and more we broke that down. And it went like that for a while with no problems. But you know nothing lasts forever when there are jealous hearted niggas watching your moves. The heat didn't come down on us, they put the man on the O.G. Boatwright.

Niggas in his dorm was mad he wasn't serving them so they dropped a kite on him and got his visit knocked off. I hated that for the O.G., but I guess his time had ran out at Madison. Where one door closes, another opens. That's just how the game go! Come to find out, the homie Big Rick had a C.O. on his line and he had the trees for sale. So I made a deal with him and the crew kept eating and smoking good.

Everything was flowing smooth and prison life at Madison was sweet for me and my car. I had some young hitters down on my line. One of main ones was from Broward County, Florida. His name is "Big Jit." He was a real nigga and well known in Hollywood. He had been down for a minute, ever since he was like 16. He loved to fight, but I had him under my wing. He loved me because he knew I was the type of shotcaller that didn't love to send young niggas out on dummy moves, and I was a frony line nigga myself. And my hands speak for themselves. From the time I arrived at Madison, I didn't have to put an example out there for my respect because my name carried weight. But there is always somebody that just had to see it for themselves. And when they do, I make sure they don't ever forget me – them and whoever witnessed.

There was this OB ("off brand" dudes not from Miami who we didn't fuck with) ass nigga who worked as a cook in the kitchen. He was a big light skinned dude that loved to horseplay with whoever let him. I never played around with nobody because that was a way for niggas to size you up or try to disrespect you and act like they were only playing. This dude used the playing to do both and I had him figured out. So the day we got into it started like this.

The cooks made hamburgers and French fries for all the kitchen workers. So we made a line to serve ourselves. I had my hamburger and all I needed was my fries. As I reached for the pan with the fries, the big light skin nigga cut in front of me and grabbed the pan. Then he looked at me and said nobody else was getting none until he got his. He was smiling like this was a game. I was mad because I didn't play with niggas and I wasn't about to let him chump me off. So I put my tray down and told him to get out of my way so I could get my fries.

He started puffing his chest out like he was supposed to put fear in me. Then he gave me the shot I was looking for, he turned to his right to put the pan of fries down. When he turned back around, he stepped right into my famous chicken wing combo: upper cut with that right hook. I put my hip into it when I turned that right hook. I'll say this, he could take a punch or I didn't put as much as I thought I did. The power behind the blow still dazed him, but it didn't drop him like it should have. While he was trying to regroup, I quickly grabbed me some fries and put them on my tray and walked off into the dining room of the chow hall. If he wanted some more I'd give it to him out there. It was more room for me to work him on. And also I was trying to get away from the C.O.'s office station. He wanted to because his pride was hurt. But now Pookie Black was right by my side ready to jump in if I needed him. But Pookie knew that wasn't my style. If shit got out of hand it was good to have him nearby.

Big Rick came into the dining room behind dude. I am standing ready to fight when dude started explaining that he was just playing. And why I hit him? I let him talk and stayed in my fighting stance not trusting what he was up to. Big Rick took over and told dude to back off.

He shouldn't have been playing in the first place. "That playing shit always led to fights." I told them both I don't play at all. Pookie Black wanted to know what happened and I told him. He was glad I sparked dude. He said dude had been trying him too, but he kept his distance from buddy. Word spread all over the compound. It seemed dude had a lot of people fooled. They thought he was some kind of kickboxer. He used to be on the rec yard training doing kicks and splits. Niggas was looking at me like I had just whooped Debo like Craig in *Friday*.

After that fight, everything was going smooth. Me and David was still hanging tight. We were always together. We stayed in the same dorm and Black lived there too. It was the Food Service dorm. We were getting money. I would call home once a week to check on mom. She was holding everything together the best she could. I wasn't making enough money to send some home but I wished I was. We were smoking and living off it. David didn't want to do nothing but get high all day. We stayed on the water out of fear of a piss test. The year passed and things was still good for my team.

I was running the South Florida car with dudes mostly from Dade and Broward County. You had to be a real nigga to even rock with us. There were no rats ("snitches"). I expected everybody in the car to be a fighter. I worked out a lot so most of the time you could find me and the guy in the weight pile or hitting the punching bag. It was 1999, and the homie Little Fame from Over Town just hit the yard. We went back to Juvenile Hall and Jackson High school. We were real cool. Fame was a hitter on the streets. He was known for slinging that iron. He was fresh off the street with a light 2-3 year sentence. They were sending him to the work camp across the street so we didn't have long to kick it. He kept me laughing, telling me about the Over Town and Carol City beef. He was rolling with these two known hitters from Town – Rah Rah and Lil Bam. They were into it with Black Boy aka Boobie, E-4, the twin Boobie little cousins. I had been hearing a little bits and pieces of the story. But when you wind way up the road, tucked away in the woods all you get is second hand parts of the story. But now I was getting one side of it from one of the real players involved. It was not Veli or Parker business so I was neutral. I was cool with niggas on both sides indirectly.

See, Boobie and Chico were my older brother Ace's homies, and I was cool with Fame. So I just listened while Fame told his version of how the war was going. The way he was painting it, they were getting out on Black Boy. He told me how he saved E-4 and his daughter from being shot up at the red light. He said they had him spotted up, but when he saw the little girl head he pulled back the stick. That was some real shit, how it was supposed to go. No kids, no women, no innocent bystanders. Those were G-code rules.

Nowadays these young niggas want to be "Gs" and live this Thug Life that they don't know nothing about. He told me how he made the news by escaping out the backseat of a police car. I remember seeing that on the news. He said the cop put the handcuffs on loose. Fame is a little dude for real. Him, Lil Bo, and Lil Willie were all the same size. Fame said when he got away it got back to him that Black Boy was talking shit about how he was lucky them crackers got him first. But when he heard Fame got away he went back into hiding. I can't say I believe him, but since we were smoking weed and high as hell, I let him give it to me however he wanted to. Besides, it was his story, if he wanted to put 12 on it, then go ahead. It's all war stories to pass time. So he had some more beef to talk about.

This time it was about the homie Bob out of Alenda Projects. The same Bob who was tight with the nigga Best (I told ya'll about him early on in this book). Let Fame tell it, Bob was having a sucker attack over a stripper bitch Fame said he pulled from Bob. Beefing over a bitch wasn't hard to believe. Niggas do that shit all the time in the hood. Believe it or not, most of the beef that take place in the hood be about a bitch. I'm talking about real wars that go on for years. I know about cases where a nigga call his girl from the County and another nigga answer the phone, and there you have it: War! Then the nigga that's having the sucker attack, don't tell his homies what it's really about, letting them think it's over money or some real shit. So now Fame is telling me that he and Bob had words over a female. To the point they talking gunplay on site.

I knew of Bob, and everything I heard was real nigga shit. True money getter out there in the streets. But other than that, we weren't connected in no way.

Like I said, Fame was a short-timer headed for the work camp. So he chilled out for a week with me and Black before being sent to the camp. We made plans to meet up at the law library. They bring a van of campers over on the weekends to use the law library. Now here is the twist to this part of the story. I couldn't make this up if I tried. When the next Blue Bird prison bus pulled up to the prison, you would not believe who was on it. Yeah, none other than Mr. Bob himself! Like the young people say: "No cap."

I couldn't believe it, nor could Black. But it was him. Like any real nigga from Miami, when they get off the bus at Madison the homies always bring them to me. I was on the rec yard hitting the heavy bag, getting my cardio on when Bob walked up with a few of the young homies. I took off my gloves and we walked the track. Pookie Black fired up a jay. David did the same so we had two jays in rotation. Bob opened up to us. He had a light sentence. I was starting to feel a little funny inside because here I was smoking and kicking it with Bob, but two weeks ago, I was walking this same track with his enemy. Even though I don't owe him no allegiance, I still felt the need to at least let him know that Fame was here and was still at the work camp. But on the flip side, I am a loyal nigga at heart, and Fame is my dog! I really just met Bob on some person to person tip. As I was thinking about what to do, Bob must have picked up on my vibe because he addressed the subject at hand.

"I heard that nigga Fame here?" He said it as a question waiting to see what I said.

But I just shook my head and let him finish talking. He confirmed the beef between him and Fame was over a hoe. But everyone thought it was the total opposite to how Fame saw it. I didn't know who to believe at this point. It was all humorous to me. Just something to listen to while I was doing time. Pookie Black told Bob how his main man Best was punt faking in the County. I stamped it and added how I couldn't understand how a real nigga let a nigga that knock your blood off make it around him and didn't handle his business. Bob agreed with us and felt like that was a real sucker move on Best's part. After catching up with Bob, I went back to the dorm and time went on like usual. I kept the Miami car on point. Then shit hit the fan!

I was getting off work from Food Service when Black, Big Jit, and a few of the other young homies came up to me. It was this nigga name Junkie out of Scott Projects who was from Miami. But I didn't fuck with. But Black was super cool with him. I always had a funny feeling about Junkie. He was something cause he only came around when shit was good with us. But stayed to himself most of the time. He was there before I got there. But he was from the crib as far as I knew, he wasn't hot ("a rat"), so when it was brought to my attention that some Spanish dudes pushed up on him and was about to jump him, I made the decision to have his back. I asked Junkie what happened? He told me it started over him sitting on a Spanish nigga's bed.

It seemed that Junkie was playing skin, a gambling card game and sat on the dude's bed. When dude said something to him, they had a few words then his homeboys stepped in to jump Junkie. So Junkie dipped out the unit and got with Black. Now they were coming to me for the green light! When you're running a car, it's a lot of responsibility. You have to think moves through with everybody in mind. Green lighting a move like this could blow up the yard because everybody will be transferred. The guys in the car that ride may have legal work on their cases being done by somebody else. There are niggas in relationships with women C.O.s. Dudes had shit to lose. But on the other hand, I know how these Spanish boys think. You give them an inch, they take a yard. And there were other cars watching to see how we handle the diss to our car. So I had to at least see what was on the Spanish nigga's mind. If they want a head up fade with Junkie, I got to see if that could work before I pushed the green light button. I was big on seeing if a nigga was going to ride for himself before I ride with him. Because if you don't then I know you won't ride for me if I need you! So we all fell out to take the rec yard where the Spanish niggas were grouped up.

IF you ever been in a prison riot you know how quiet it get before it pop off. Everybody can feel it, even the guards. I walked and asked to speak to their shot caller. He was this big fat Spanish nigga. We stepped off to the side near the horseshoe pit. My guys already knew what to do if shit went left with me and dude. They all knew I wasn't good at prison politics, so if they see me take off then that was the green light to push on them. I offered to let Junkie fade the Spanish dude one on one. But like I knew already, these Spanish boys don't like to fight one on one. So it was a no go on that end. So, I told him that they wasn't going to fuck with Junkie and we were down for whatever.

He responded. "Fuc—"

Before the words left his lips, I took off. He was standing too far back for my upper cut to connect, so I led off with a straight two-piece. It caught him off guard in mid-sentence knocking him into the horseshoe pit. I didn't stop there. Before he could get back on his feet, I kicked him in his head with my boots. As I went to kick him again one of his homies came from the right. He had a banger in his hand and I jumped out the way as he tried to stab me. The only thing I saw to defend myself against the weapon in his hand was some horse shoes lying on the ground, so I picked up two of them. I threw them at him. One missed and the other hit him in the face. I used that moment as the chance to rush him and grab the banger.

There was fighting going on all around me. I was on the ground wrestling with the guy when Big Jit came over and helped me beat the shit out of him. I wasn't trying to kill him, that's why we didn't bother with the banger. I took it and threw it across the yard. But me and Big Jit stomped him to sleep. I was so caught up in the fight that I didn't notice when it was time to run off the yard. A lot of homies got off the yard before they locked the gate. But there was still a few of us left on the yard with all the Spanish dudes. Now we were outnumbered, but we still held our ground until the Doom Squad came and surrounded us. I gave up since it made no sense catching a new charge for fighting against the C.O. We all did. Even the Spanish boys.

They cuffed us and dragged us off to the hole. They closed the prison down because it was so many of us going to the box. This was the reason I got transferred from Madison C.I. and put in Close Management ("C.M"). They keep you locked down 24 hours a day. We showered and was allowed rec 3 days a week. They put all of us on C.M. and sent me and a few of the homies to the same spot: Tyler C.I. They sent Pookie Black and the other homies to another prison that had C.M. They gave me 12-24 months on C.M. The messed up part about all of this was after we were all locked in the box, I found out that Junkie hadn't even fought when shit jumped off, and the entire situation was over him. He was the first one to take off running off the yard. I put the word out that he was a mark, fake ass nigga. And that label will follow him always in the Florida Prison system.

C.M. wasn't as bad as you may think once you get in to the groove of things. I made the best out of it. Reading played a big part of keeping my mind free. Being on C.M. you had to learn how to deal with the guards on another lever if you wanted to make it off there. What I mean by "another level" is, the guards had the control over everything you need. They brought your meals, change of clothes, mail, and let you out to shower. All of this depended on how you interact with them. It was all a psychological game with them. When you first get on C.M. they try you with head games. Talk to you crazy over nothing, get all up in your face. Test you to see if you take the bait. I witnessed C.O.s jump on dudes because they didn't answer them with "Yes, sir."

One of their favorite moves was to drop your tray when they opened the chow hole flap. Then say you threw your tray and you refused to eat. Now they put you on what they call the "loaf!" It was a baked loaf with tomatoes, carrots, and whatever else they put into it. Most time it was burned black and hard. I saw guys grow to love eating the "loaf." Somebody was getting pepper sprayed everyday on C.M. So, we all grow grew immune to the pepper spray. That stuff was so strong it used to peal the paint off the walls in the cell. I used to feel sad for the brothers that got the full dose of that stuff. When they pulled them out the cell to take a shower, their whole face and body would be orange and snot would be running down from their nose, tears coming from their eyes. You would think the water would help, but it only flared up the pepper spray again. They be inside the shower screaming for the C.O. to turn the water off. I made it a point not to get on the C.O., bad side.

To me it didn't make sense, how could you win, when they had complete control over when you get out of C.M. or stay back there your whole bid? They had niggas that been on C.M. for 5 years or more. I still had 4 more years left on my sentence. I wasn't trying to do it all on C.M because I stayed out the way and never gave them no problems. They made me an orderly on the 2<sup>nd</sup> shift. I had to hand out the dinner meal, and also the laundry for shower so that gave me the opportunity to hustle cigarettes. The money on C.M. was stamps. Our homies on the compound would send us cigarettes in the food trays, or the laundry cart. I would get them out. If the packs weren't for me, whoever they were for would have to break me off for getting them. And I would still make more stamps for selling the cigarettes for them. But I wasn't the only one doing it, there were other orderlies working too. Some on different shifts. You had to be very careful not to get caught. There was always somebody behind the door that didn't like the fact you was out making money, or for whatever reason they wanted to hate. They drop kites to the C.O. on you and get your cell shook down. So I never kept nothing in my cell, I was always one step ahead of them suckers hating on me. I had a homeboy named Gator from Over Town, that was on C.M. before me. He was the orderly on the 3<sup>rd</sup> shift and passed out morning meals.

Gator was a real nigga and we go back from stockade Jail, and we were at Baker C.I. together. Gator used to always be in his cell writing rap songs and working out. He would look out for me on his shift with extra trays and I do the same on my shift. He got off C.M. six months before me. But when I got out on the compound, Gator was still there. My time on C.M. went by pretty fast hustling and making money. I did 18 months all together with my D.C. box time added to the C.M. time. I lost a lot of weight on C.M. I got out 162 pounds. It wouldn't take me long to get my size back. I got me a job in Food Services. Taylor C.I. wasn't that bad outside of C.M. Gator plugged me up with Big Black from down south Miami. I knew who he was from hearing about him in the County Jail. We never did no time together until now, but his codefendant, Shrimp, was my dog.

Me and Shrimp had been locked up together in Belle Glade C.I. on my first bid. Big Black was the go-to nigga from down south back in the day on the 10th floor. Niggas from all over Miami had respect for him. He would end up doing 28 years before he got out. For now, me, him and Gator was chilling during this bid. There was some more of the homies there, another one of my guys was Teddy Sission from South Miami. Me and his older brother were cool in the County. So that's how me and Teddy got tight.

Things at Taylor C.I. was more laid back. I guess it was because the thought of going back on C.M. was always right there to remind you. Almost everybody that was on the compound came off C.M., so we all knew how easy it was to go back. I spent my days working in Food Services and working out with Gator and Black. Sometimes Teddy would join us. Other than that, we walked around and tried to holla at the female C.O.s. They were giving up all kinds of play. I didn't stay at Taylor after C.M. but another 6 months. Then they transferred me to Cross City C.I.

It was 2000, a new year. We all thought that we were going to die in prison because of Y2K, the end of the world. One of the prison scare theory was that the government was going to execute all prisoners. That year was a turning point in my life. I was becoming a thinker. I have to give credit to the time I spent on C.M. It helped with my reading more, also it made me use my mind more. I had to think before I acted and I was able to reflect more on my past actions. So when I got to Cross City, I was in search of a spiritual connection with God.

My homie Bushwick had a brother named Santa (R.I.P.). Fred and Santa were road dogs. They was getting money back in the day. I remember when they had them Boyz in da Hood 64 Chevys dropped on Daytons with 16-inches on them. Nobody else in the city was coming through like that. Well, back to Bushwick, he was the Iman over the Muslim community at Cross City. Bushwick had a 30 ball sentence on a body and robbery case. He had been down about 10 years by this time and converted Islam Sunni Muslim. I could see the change in him and the peace he had even with such a long sentence. I would have long talks with him about the streets and the homies. He would listen but then he would always ask me tough questions like was I tired of being locked up? He would say shit like keeping it real with the homies is loyalty to the hood, but keeping it real with yourself is loyalty to God! He would ask when was the last time the homies went around to check up on your mom and kids? Or when was the last time the homies sent you some money on your books? But you would put in work for the homies right now if they asked you to. Or if somebody diss the hood or disrespect Veli you would ride on them right? Talking to Bushwick on a daily basis started making me think about my life in a different way. Here was one of the homies whose brother had helped so many niggas on in the game. But nobody was really showing him love. There were a few. He would tell me about them. He always talked highly of Bayla and Choppa off 15th Ave and Fred. But overall, he was like after his brother got killed niggas fell back off him and the family. I knew how he was feeling. I was going through the same thing with my brother being locked up. He helped put niggas on. I even put a nigga down with him that wasn't getting no money until bro took him in. But this same nigga wouldn't send me a dime.

I was doing good at Cross City. Instead of getting a job in the kitchen, I decided to get a job in the Maintenance Department. I was given the job as a boiler room attendant. My job was real easy, all I had to do was monitor the pressure on the gauges of the boiler. It left me with a lot of time to study. Bushwick gave me a Quran and other Islamic books to read. This kept me busy and out the way. Ever since I got off C.M. I had lost interest in running the Miami car, or even being involved with the prison politics. I just wanted to use my time focusing on myself and building a relationship with God. The more I studied Islam, the more humble and at peace with myself I became.

I wasn't getting into any trouble or fights. I liked the fact that Islam required discipline to be a Muslim. The first thing I wanted to learn was how to pray. When I did learn, I took my Shahada ("Testimony of faith") stating that there is "No God but Allah and Muhammad is his messenger!" Bushwick gave me my Shahada, and just like that I became a Muslim. One of the older brothers – Aleem – gave me my Muslim name, Abu Shaheed. The name is an attribute for "Witness." I love the name and what it meant because I always been big on representing for myself, my hood, my homies, and my city. So now I was given a name that said I'm a witness of Allah Lord of the worlds. I was proud to be a Muslim. I went hard on my studies and stayed around the older Muslim brothers.

A year went by and it was now 2001, and I've devoted my life to Islam. My brother Gregg was out of the Feds. That gave my mom the help she's been praying for. My good behavior and the fact that my time was winding down, I only had 2 years left on my sentence. They transferred me to the work camp. It was a bittersweet feeling, because on one hand I wanted to feel some freedom by going to work outside the gates, and on the other hand, I was going to miss the brothers. I'd grown used to being around the brothers learning about Islam. Brotherhood is a very important part of Islam. At the work camp there was only three of us Muslims, and even though I was a new Muslim I had the most knowledge of the religion so that put more responsibility on me.

I had stopped smoking and drinking. I didn't even use profanity. I took my new role as a Iman over the other two brothers very serious. I can't say that I was all the way changed, but I was putting forth the effort. Looking back on it now, even though I accepted Islam as my religion I didn't fully submit. I was still gambling and hustling on the side. Doing time at the work camp was real easy and time went by fast. Going out in the world each day made time fly. Everybody at the work camp was a short timer, so there wasn't many fights. Guys were trying to make it home early as possible. We mostly gambled to pass time when we wasn't out the gate working. We also played dominoes and handball.

Then September 11th happened.

I remember seeing it on the news. That was big news. I thought because I was a Muslim, the government was going to add my name to the watch list. They did have the prison chaplain remove a lot of our religious books and videos. And they started monitoring our service. A lot of officers started harassing me and the brothers. They even went so far as to try not to let us have Fridays off to attend Jumah service. It's fair to say, us Muslims weren't popular among the staff. I really didn't care as long as you didn't put your hands on me or become real disrespectful.

When 2002 came in, I was really ready to be free. I was back in contact with my brother Ace. He was still living up in Tennessee and he gave me his word that when I jumped this time I could come up there and get my grind on. That was good news to me because I really didn't want to go back to Miami. The streets were on fire out there. They killed my cousin Corn Flake. Man, I took that one hard. Because when I was in the County with cuz, he told me how he just wanted to make things right with his babymoma and help raise his two boys. I really believed him too. I could tell he was serious this time around and from what I heard he was doing just that. He wasn't robbing no more or getting high or drunk. Cuz had got put on with some work and was going up the road to flip it!

The whole thing was a set up by some niggas cuz had shot but didn't kill back in the day. It seems that while cuz was down doing them 5 years these niggas got their weight up with their hate and when cuz jumped they stuck a young Jit on cuz to make it seem that he looked up to cuz and wanted to see cuz get some money. So he gave cuz some work, and when cuz came back to grab the second time them niggas were laying on him. The word that came to me in the pen was "they fucked cuz up bad." He laid dead in the streets for a minute without no help! That made me think about all my enemies that wanted me dead. Some of them were out there getting their bag up while I was still broke doing a bid.

After two years in the County putting hands on niggas from all over the city, I knew my list of enemies had increased. And the last thing I wanted to do was get out and walk into a death trap. Then add to the fact that my Veli crew had ongoing beef with other crews and they had people out there laying. So as my time began to come to an end, I was already making plans to get back into the game. I knew my plans were not in accordance with Islamic teaching, but I was feeling the pressure of my past trying to destroy my future. My brother Gregg came to visit me. He brought my daughter to see me, my

mom came too. It was the first visit I had my hold bid.

Bro was doing good now, he had two jobs and was talking about going to college. I told him I was a Muslim now, he just gave me that look like "I believe it when I see you living it!" I know it was no sense in trying to convince him with my words. Bro knew me to well. He could tell I wasn't done with the street life. Mom was just happy to see me. She didn't care that I was locked up, as long as I was alive and well. I know that's sad to say but when you grow up in the hood and your mom seen so many of your homies die young , she is content with you being locked up in prison. My daughter was acting real shy with me and I can't blame her. She barely knew me, but she could tell I loved her. And I could tell she loved me. When she was sitting on my lap she went straight to sleep like a baby. She was 12 years old now, very beautiful and so smart. I was proud to be her dad. But at the same time, ashamed of who I was and where I was: Just a broke inmate.

Bro was living in South Miami and mom was making plans on moving back to the island. She needed to go look after my aging grandma. So the house in the city, where I grew up, was about to be sitting open waiting on me. So, I had a few options open to me as to where I would live. No matter where I go there was still the issue of money. If I went home to live, I would have to pay all the bills and still have to worry about my enemies laying on me. My best move would be moving up the road with bro in Tennessee.

The good part of when I get released is no more probation. I'm a free man. I can go where I want to. I had a fresh start in life and I planned on doing things differently. No more robbing. No more smoking. I wanted a real girlfriend. A ride or die on my team. During this bid I started playing a lot more chess and sat down with some real O.G.s who broke the game of chess down for me in terms of living life. One of them told me like this, "Young blood, chess and life is one of the same game." He said, "put yourself as the King, the most important piece on the board." Then he asked me what would be my next important piece? And why?

I said, "My Queen because she is real powerful."

He said, "those are reasonable answers, and by making that main choice, making choices and planning your move is a smart way to play chess, the same way with life." But then he said something that really made me think. He said his most important piece is all them from the pawn to the Queen because they were all on his team. "And like to be a real king, and a master of the game, you got to use all your pieces and care about the sacrifices every piece makes for you to win. And that's how I always beat you, knowing what choices to make and when to sacrifice while caring about all my pieces. That's chess and that's a life lesson."

It was talks like that with the O.G.s that helped me. I wanted to make better choices and getting me a queen on my team was one of them. But always looming in the back of my mind was pressure of having money. I knew a job wasn't going to offer me the type of lifestyle I felt like I was entitled to. Not only that, I didn't see nobody giving me a good job, but I also never forgot when I got out of boy's school with all my certificates and trades that nobody gave me a chance. All I could find was a dishwasher job. To me, looking for a job was just a waste of time. My mind was made up. I was going to Tennessee to get my grind on, get me a bag. Then I was going to fix my mom's house up so I could move back home. Maybe make enough money to start me a big time commercial landscaping business.

I always loved cutting grass. I guess that's because my Uncle Joe's teaching me landscaping like a father would do for his son. To me, selling dope was going legit and they wasn't giving a lot of time out for drugs on the state level. I was feeling confident on my new outlook on life. I had Islam, that was giving me peace and making me humble. I could tell because I've been chilling and no fights. Ever since C.M. I think a lot more, it made me more in tune with myself. I love being by myself, just sitting and thinking of new ways to hustle and get money. What I wanted out of life, I guess you could say I had a vision now.

My time at Cross City came to an end. It was 2003, and my release day was here. There would be no bus ride this time. My bro Gregg was out front in the parking lot waiting on me. I had the biggest smile ever. Seven years. Wow. That felt like forever. It was 1996 when I went in, now here it was 2003. I'm 28 years old and had already spent 11 years in the state prison system. Bro was doing his best to show me that I had support on our way back to Miami. He stopped off at Nike, Fila and a few other outlets. He bought me a couple pairs of shoes and 2 sweat suits. He also bought me some underclothes and hygiene. We had a good time riding home together. I told him my plan to go to the island to visit our grandma and spend some time with my mom. Then when I got back, I was headed to Tennessee.

He was cool with all that. His only concern was my action and words around his boys. He didn't want me to use the N word in their presence. Bro was doing the real family thing. He married the longtime girlfriend. She was there for him during his bid in the Feds, and when he came home she held him down until he found a job. So I was happy for bro. It's rare you find a real Ride or Die that really has your back in bad times. I wasn't planning on being at bro's spot for too long. I just left one warden in prison, I wasn't about to be under new rules and regulations. But, I could respect bro's house rules for a week. I had bro stop off around my other brother's house in Carol City.

Jay Jay had the hood on lock. Bro was the man in the hood. Everybody was happy to see me. My brother and sister were all there. My nieces and nephews had all grown up and were teens now. Jay Jay pulled me to the side and told me that my older brother Ace gave me a stack. He had to tell me that a stack was $1,000. When I left the streets, we just called it a grand. Ace told him to tell me to jump on the

Greyhound bus whenever I was ready to make that trip. Jay Jay gave me an ounce of that loud green. He promised to break me off when I was ready to make that move up the road. I had to cut my visit short with the family because bro was ready to get back home to his fam.

I hollered at that lady, Miss Emma, that's my brothers and sisters' mom. She was my second mom and her house was always open to me. I love that lady. She always told you how it was, no cut card! You could always depend on Emma to keep it all the way 100% with all of us. If we had a problem with each other, and wanted to know who was wrong we'd just go to Emma. She gave it to us raw. Things were looking good for my first day home.

This time around I had some new clothes, money in my pocket, and some weed to smoke while I thought about my next move. I didn't let Gregg see the weed because I didn't feel like being judged. I knew the first thing he would have said: "I didn't know Muslims smoke weed?"

I know I shouldn't have took the weed, but what else would I have to relax me over while I was stuck over Bro's house? There were so many rules, I felt like I was still in prison or at least a halfway house. No drinking. No smoking. No females. No profanity. No N-word. Curfew. I was scared to even ask him what time I had to be in. He didn't give me a key so I took that as when they were in that meant I was expected to be in as well. I was cool though because I didn't have a car and they didn't have an extra one I could use, so I just stayed in and watched movies. Bro had a major collection of movies. My new sister-in-law, Londa had a few girlfriends that were single, so she invited them over, two at the same time one day. She introduced me to them.

Ann was red and very pretty, but she was on the heavy side. I didn't mind at all. I never had nothing against big women as long as they smelled good and took care of their hygiene, they could get the dick. Remember, I'm Pig's son!! The other one was the full package. She was brown skin and fine as hell. But she was boogie and stuck up. She gave me a look like I was beneath her. I'm pretty sure Londa gave them the run down on me. So I guess she was used to niggas taking care of her. She looked like she was high maintenance. Well she didn't have to worry

I was going to gladly stay in my lane. I wasn't looking for a new bill and I wasn't a trick. But big girl couldn't keep her eyes off me. She was giving me me that, *you can go home with me* look.

It had been a week since I been out and I hadn't had sex. Yeah, I know that hard to believe, a real street nigga jump out of prison and have not got his dick wet right away. I could have if I was in Carol City with my other brothers. They would've had me in the strip club the first night. The offer was made but I declined. I wanted to spend time with Gregg and his family. Me and Bro was real close. We grew up together. In so many ways Bro was like a father to me. So here I was flirting with Big Pretty. Me and Ann end up going to her place. So my sister-in-law's plan had paid off. She got me out the house and hooked me up in the process.

Ann stayed in a duplex that she owned. She lived on one side and rented the other side out, She was a real businesswoman. She had a pick-up and drop-off service for kids. With two vans operating. She drove one and had hired a driver for the other one. She also had an ice cream truck she hustled in from time to time. Ann was a real go-getter and I liked that about her. She was clean. Her place was nice and she cooked. She would make any man with any sense a good woman, I know that. But, still, I wasn't planning on locking down with her. We could kick it and have fun, but my mind was made up. I was going to get this money out in Tennessee.

The same night we went to her place, I fucked 7 years of pent up sexual rage out of her. After that she was hooked. She went on a shopping spree, bought me throwback jerseys, Sean John jeans, Nikes, a cellphone, you name it, if I wanted it, she got it. She had two cars, so she let me use one and took me to get my driver's license. I was living like a king at Ann's place. She cooked and catered to me. All I had to do was lay up during the day, and lay pipe during the night. We did that for a week until I made the trip to the island to see mom and my grandma. I told Ann that when I get back, I'll come through and chill for another week before I made that move to Tennessee. She didn't really want me to leave, but knew there was nothing she could do or say to stop me. I fucked her real good that night and she was ok with whatever I said.

It felt real good being back in the island. The weather was great. Mom was so happy to see me. She wasted no time hitting me with the big question: "What's your plan?"

Here we go again. I didn't want to lie, but how could I possibly tell my mom that I was planning on selling dope to get on my feet after just being released from doing 7 years in prison! So I told her as close to the truth as I could. That I was going to live with my brother Ace in Tennessee and find some work up there. She said it wasn't a good idea and that I should come live over there with her and find work on the island. She would help me find a job and I could stay in my granddaddy's old house. But I wasn't trying to stay over there. I love the island, don't get me wrong, but I needed fast money. I was under pressure of catching up to everybody else my age. I had cousins over there in the island that were younger than me with their own homes and businesses. So how would it look for me, who was born in the States to be doing bad?

I was not ready to see the change life had on my Big Ma. Old age had made the big strong lady of my childhood vanish into this sweet little, gentle old lady. My grandma was now fragile. All I wanted to do was take care of her. Seeing her like that really upset me. I was so mad and disappointed in myself for just now coming to see about her. And I was mad with everybody I knew. She always took care of everyone and they weren't helping her now that she was old. I stayed at my grandma's house the whole time I was there. I washed her feet. I sat and talked with her. We laughed about old times. I wanted to stay and take care of her, but I told myself if I go get this money I could do more for her. I built my grandma a bathroom and added onto her home. I used every dollar I had to get supplies. My mom pitched in too. She was already saving just for that. Seeing my grandma after all these years made me happy, but at the same time ashamed. This wasn't supposed to be. I was 29 years old. I should have been able to renovate my grandma's whole house. That added to the pressure I was already dealing with, trying to fix up my mom's house so I could live there.

I wanted to be near my daughter, so I could help raise her. I needed money. That's all I could think of to help make my plan come through. While I was on the island, I started networking with some of my cousins and childhood friends. Dope was real cheap on the island, that was a fact. So I was trying to get a plug with some of the big ballers over there. If I could get a connect to sling me the work it would be on. I spent my days sitting and talking with grandma and ran around at night. Meanwhile mom was still trying to convince me to stay and find a job. I can't lie, I was tempted. I loved eating my mom's home cooked meals and being around my grandma. And there were some sexy ass island women all around me. But the only thing about them was they didn't play when it came to dating. They were very possessive of their men. Dudes were the same way. They have real sucker attacks over a woman. I stayed away from the island drama. The last thing I wanted to do was have to fuck some nigga up because his girl was on my line.

While working on my grandma's house my funds ran low. So it was time to get back state side. My trip was only planned for 2 weeks but I extended for an extra week. When that was up, and it was time for me to leave, it wasn't easy saying goodbye to mom and grandma. I promised my mom I would be back soon and stay out of trouble. She wanted me to stay. My grandma just smiled at me. I was choking back tears as I kissed her cheek and pulled away from her, not knowing if this was the last time I would see her alive. I told myself it wasn't and I would be back with more money to help her do more work on her house. I had to go!

My mom's husband, Silas, drove me to the airport. My flight to Miami left an hour later. I was on my way to get my grind on in a state I had never been in. They say it snowed up there a lot, so I needed to bring a real jacket. My sister, DayShawn, came to pick me up from the airport. I didn't go back over Ann's house right away. I went to Carol City to Emma's house. It was time to get down to business. Jay Jay was there to meet me. I told him I was ready to make that trip to see Hound. So the plan was set for me to leave the next day on the Greyhound bus. Jay gave me $500 pocket money, and some weed to smoke on the trip. I call Ace, he Ok'd the trip, but with a long speech on what he expected out of me. I agreed to his rules. I had no other choice. They weren't the same as my brother Gregg's. Hound only cared about me not coming up there with all the wild street shit, like robbing and gunplay. I let him know what time my bus was going to arrive in Knoxville.

CHAPTER 9

# **Dope Game Pressure**

It was a 22-hour trip with plenty of stops in between. I didn't care. I had the money Jay gave me and some smoke. It gave me more time to think. I knew that I was a hustler and given the chance I could make a dollar out of nothing. I would just have to learn the town first. So I couldn't afford to be drunk or high all the time. I got to stay focused on getting money. I was counting on Ace to put me on so I could get started. Jay dropped me off at the Greyhound station. He told me to hit him when I got up there. I called Ann. She was mad that I didn't come back like I said I would. I smooth talked her and let her know that I had a change of plans because I needed the money fast. She wanted to help, but I told her to let me see how it was up there first, and that I would call her every day and not to worry because I wasn't thinking about no other women.

The bus ride to Knoxville wasn't too bad. We had a three-hour layover in Jacksonville. I called up one of my dawgs that I was in prison with. He came through and we smoked a little, sitting in his car. He was trying to convince me to chill in J-Town, talking about the money being good. All he needed was that Miami plug. I told him I had to see what it would do up the road. I lied to him and told him I was headed to

ATL[Atlanta]. There was no need in putting him all the way up in my game room. This nigga knew my real name from hearing it called in prison at mail call. I couldn't chance him getting caught with work then maybe flipping on me. Far as I knew he was a real nigga in the pen, but you never know what a nigga would do when the Feds grabbed them. Nevertheless, I just wanted to kill some time, not go into business with him. My bus was ready to go, so I dapped bro up and told him I would be in touch.

When I got to Knoxville, I did what Hound told me to do. I gave him a ring. Bro was there ten minutes later. *Damn, was Knoxville that small, or did bro stay close by?* Whatever, he arrived in a Suburban vehicle [SUV] with his girl's cousin. Rob aka M-30 was about my height and build. I could tell right off that he was cool. Bro was all smiles already joking around which he did right off the back going in on my old Michigan Starter jacket and backpack. I didn't bring any clothes because I figured I would buy a couple pairs of Dickie suits and some underwear here and I would be good. The less I had the more I wanted, and that meant I had to hustle hard. But bro was enjoying my starting-from-the-bottom look.

Rob spoke up in my defense. "Didn't you say he was just getting out the pen? So what you expect?" He then told me not to worry because he had a few extra jackets and whatever clothes I may need. Rob would play a big part in me coming up in K-Town!

We got back to my brother's house in no time. So he did stay close by. I was already observing my surroundings. If I had to, I could drive us back to the bus station. My bro's wife, Punkin, was real pretty and down for whatever. She was cool as hell and we got along right away. She made me feel at home and like one of the family from the very beginning. There was her baby girl Dajah and my little niece Saria. It was a Friday night when I got there, so Rob said we should all hit the club. He said a club called Platinum in the old city was always jumping on Friday nights. Bro was down, Punkin had to stay and watch the kids. Bro took me in his room and told me pick something out of his closet to wear. Bro had like 500 pairs of shoes: Nikes, Reeboks, Adidas, Filas, Timberlands. There were sweatsuits, jerseys, Polos among other name brands that made me feel like I was in a store at the mall. I grabbed a pair of Timbs and a brown baseball jersey that I would wear with the jeans I had on.

Bro changed clothes and grabbed some money out of his safe. Rob stayed right around the corner from Bro so he went home to get ready. I still had some weed left from the trip. Bro want to smoke some, he said, "Let's see what Jay working with."

About an hour later, Rob pulled back up. He got fresh and put on his jewelry with a big boy watch. It seemed like everybody was eating up here. I hoped they let me get a seat at the table. Me, Bro, and Rob loaded up in Rob's truck and headed to the club.

I was chilling, playing my position and let them show me the town. Rob was really outgoing and loved to club. He thought of himself as a lady's man; a player. Bro really didn't hang out or do the club scene but made exemptions because I was fresh in town and he wanted to show me a good time. Rob was right, Platinum was packed and the parking lot was thick as hell. Rob flashed a .44 Bulldog before placing the strap in the stash spot. I was starting to like Rob more and more. He was my kind of dude.

Bro paid our way in and bought bottles of Moet for us. The club was just as thick as the parking lot. Bad bitches everywhere. I could tell by the love Bro was getting that his name carried weight in this town. They were giving me the eye as well. I guess they were trying to figure out who I was? I will have to admit I was in good shape. If I had to describe myself at this time in life: Let me use 50 Cent. We were about the same size. Far as looks, I never had problems with ladies. Added that to the fact I was rolling with two niggas that was getting money I could see why all the attention was on us. I still play it cool, and fell back in the cut so I could watch everybody. I sip on that Moet all night slowly. I wasn't trying to get drunk. I got with this fine ass brown skin female who was sitting alone. So I agreed to hook up with her sometime that week. Bro was making his rounds in the club. I kept my eye on him because I could tell he was tipsy already. Punkin had asked me to keep an eye on him because he couldn't handle his liquor. But I thought she was just playing, but it looked like she wasn't. Rob was by the bar in between two females talking. Looked like he was trying to make a play for us! I hoped so. I would love to see what kind of freak these Tennessee hoes were. I was already digging how they talked, then Rob came over real fast.

He was trying to tell me something, but it was too loud. I was near one of the wall speakers. They were blasting that Bird Man joint "What Happened to that Boy?" So I motioned to Rob to walk outside with me, but first I wanted to get Bro. I grab Bro and we went out to meet Rob. I could tell something was up because Rob was pacing back and forth. He told us that the nigga that killed one of his homies was in the club. And this nigga came by him saying the Bird Man hook, "What happened to that boy?"

I was ready to prove my worth right then and there. But Rob talked some sense into me. We were in the open and there was off duty cops working the club. We waited by the trunk, Rob had the strap out the stash spot. I could tell Bro was a little tipsy. The two girls Rob was talking to in the club came over to where we were parked. They were sisters. The one Rob was talking to was named Stephanie. And her sister was Tonya.

Tonya was coming on to me strong. I was feeling her, but I still had my mind on buddy that knocked off Rob's homie. Bro had posted up in the truck. It was time to go for real. Rob gave me the eye, and nodded his head at Tonya suggesting that I go with her. I really wasn't feeling going home with a female in a new town that I didn't know nothing about. So I pulled Rob to the side and explained that to him. He assured me that she was cool and I had nothing to worry about. She had her own place and she didn't stay in the projects. I asked him to let me keep the strap, that would make me feel a whole lot better.

Tonya was a pretty redbone. She had a little stomach, but she wasn't fat. You could tell she had kids. The ass was fat enough for me. I was down for a little fun. We walked to her car. It was an old beat up Buick. Tonya was tipsy. I wasn't sure if she could drive us to her place. The last thing I needed was to get pulled over with this gun on me. I hoped she didn't stay too far, so I asked her just that. She told me not to worry, she got us: She do this all the time! That worried me, hearing her say that. Did she mean take different guys home after the club? I was glad Rob had some condoms in his truck. Safe to say we made it to her place with only one stop. Her car cut off at a red light, but started right back up.

She stayed in the hood, but not in the projects. When we stepped into her house, it was dark except for the TV glow in the living room. Her teenage daughter and baby boy were knocked out in a makeshift pile of blankets and pillows. She stopped and picked her son up and took him to a room in the back of the house then came back and woke her daughter. She gave me a mean mug face then stomped off to the back. Shit, why she mad at me? I'm not the one who woke her up! I sat down on the couch and watched the movie they fell asleep watching. Tonya went to the back to her bedroom. She came back in a white tee and a smile. She had a blunt rolled up when she sat next to me.

I grabbed her and pulled her on top of me. I could feel that the tee was the only thing she was wearing. That made my dick stand up. I started kissing her around her neck while she smoked on the blunt. I could tell that was one of her spots by the way she wiggled when I sucked on her neck. I put my hand under her tee shirt and felt her pussy. One of my fingers slipped right in. She was so wet. She started riding my finger then she put the blunt in my mouth and I took a big puff. She got down on the floor and unfastened my belt. She unzipped my pants, pulled out my dick and gave up some fire head.

I finished the rest of the blunt while she smoked my dick. I was ready to beat that pussy, so I pulled her off my dick and stood up letting my pants fall to the ground. I let her put her knees on the couch and get in doggy style. I was fucking her so hard I had to reach around and cover her mouth. I was scared so would wake the kids. We switched positions and I sat back down on the couch so she could ride cowgirl style. She rode me like she was on a pill or something. We fucked in the living room and again in the show. We finally ended up in her bedroom, then we slowed it down. When I came for the third time that night, I was exhausted.

I fell asleep with the condom still on my dick laying across Tonya. She was out of it herself. We slept well into the next day. When I woke, I was staring eye to eye with her 4-year-old son. Tonya was already up and cleaning her house up. I asked her did she have an extra toothbrush? She told me to look in the bathroom drawer. While I was in there, I took another shower and freshened all the way up. Now let me call bro so he could come through and scoop me up.

Bro told me he had me once he got up to make his rounds. This would be my first understanding of how Hound moved. He took all day to show up. It was 5:30 PM when he pulled up. Tonya had been making runs all day and I noticed her phone stayed ringing. I wasn't no fool. Girl was a hustler and I wanted in. She kept smiling at me. She fried some chicken wings and French fries. Bro chilled with us and we smoked a few while I got to know Tonya better.

On the ride back to Bro's crib, he once again reminded me of what he expected. Then he laid out how I could make some money. I was all ears. He said it was good that girl was feeling me. He told me she was a real go-getter and that I needed to hook up with her. He was fronting me the work and I could give him his on the back end. I couldn't beat that. I wasn't looking for no hand out. Because nobody never gave me one, family or not. We made it back to Bro's house. I played with niece until I went to sleep.

My ringing phone woke me up at about 11:00. It was Tonya asking if I wanted to come over. She said her kids were gone over to her mother's. And it would just be us watching a movie or whatever. I was down. What else I had to do? She came over and got me. Before we left, Bro pulled me to the side and gave me the work. He dropped me an ounce and told me to break him back $800. He also put me up on the break down game. Everything up here was $20 or better. He told me to watch how Tonya cut her rocks. She showed me how shit went down. That's how I got started in K-Town.

Me and Tonya jumped in her car. Her phone was ringing nonstop, so we were on the move right away. She ran through her work after two stops. She was real cool about letting me get off my work. When shit slowed down we went to her crib to chill and get to know each other better. It was more sex talk than words. Tonya was gone off the dick. She could fuck all day if I let her. But I was feeling the money over the pussy. After showering and letting Tonya suck my dick clean, we made plans to buy some more work. She liked the way Bro's work looked but didn't like the high price. I convinced her that we still could flip off his work. I got the scale out and she took out the last 3 grams of hard I had left of the ounce. I cut 20 rocks out weighing .02 a piece, that way we could make $300 off every 3 grams. Instead of doubling our money we would be tripling it. Now that I had her seeing it my way she was ready to be my Trap Queen.

A few more calls came in and it was time to go see Bro. I had $2,400 and all I had to do was give him $800. I was going to keep my money separate from Tonya. That way she could do whatever she wanted with hers. I was in grind mode; it was all about stacking. I went down in Bro's basement and found a hiding spot for my money in the meantime. I put up a stack and kept $600 on me. Bro dropped another ounce on me, and Tonya grabbed one for herself. We had enough work for the rest of the night. I told Bro that I would be over Tonya's place, so I was good for the night. He just smiled and said, "Be easy."

I still had Rob's .44 with me, so I was good. I still hadn't heard Tonya talk about no other nigga in her life. But I wasn't no fool either. She didn't make them kids on her own. I reminded myself to find out about her baby daddy. It was time to "Cop-lock-and-block" as the pimps put it in Donald Goines' books. I couldn't believe my good fortune in meeting Tonya on the first night in K-Town. Things were finally looking up for me. But I still had Ann's phone and she had been calling me left and right, leaving messages. I talked to her a few times from Bro's house. I just couldn't bring myself to tell her the truth. That I was kicking it with Tonya and that I didn't plan on coming back to Miami no time soon. So I just told her I was busy getting money, and didn't have time to be on no phone all day. Even though that was hard and mean she still wouldn't lay off the calls. So I went and got me a new phone and stopped answering her phone.

Things were going good for me in K-Town. Me and Tonya were sticking to the plan that I had drawn up and was tripling our money. I got Tonya a better car, a used Maxima from one of her homegirls. As much time as I was spending at Tonya's house you may as well say I lived there. Her kids loved me already. I won them over by the way I treated their mom, not to mention the toys and clothes that I brought them. Her daughter was about the same age as my daughter. So every time I went shopping for Kevia, I bought Tonya's girl something. She would take me to Londale Projects where her mom lived on the west side. The hood belonged to the Crips. They were cool with me because Rob M-30 was 52 Hoover. I even got away with wearing red around there. Niggas would look over that saying, "Yo, that's Miami, he ain't on nothing." They knew I wasn't claiming any set. I was a hustler bringing work to the hood. Then once the word spread that I was Ace's brother, shit got even sweeter for me.

Bro had pull all over the city. Niggas would pull up on me and tell me how Bro put them on back in the day. So that gave me a pass all over K-Town. On the east side was mostly Bloods, The GDs were big in Augusta Homes Projects on the east side too. The Bloods had Walter P Projects on lock. All this was new to me. I'm a Miami nigga. We didn't have the colors in our hood. Only thing I knew about that type of gangbanging was from the movie. In Miami, we had money making clicks. I guess when you look at it broadly, they were almost the same.

I didn't care what a nigga claimed, if I could get money with him, let's get it! That would be my approach to moving in K—Town. I guess you could say I was in all the gangs, whichever one was fucking with me on the money tip. But before it was all said and done, I had a falling out with different members in each gang. And you can best believe I made a name in K-Town for not being the one to cross. But that's a little later in the story.

For now, things were beautiful. When I wasn't with Tonya, I was rolling with Rob. Me and him became real tight. We even made a few trips to OKC. That's where the other half of Rob's family was from. And they were all Crips. He had a cuz named Short Dog. He was Rob's O.G. and had real pull in OKC. Real ass nigga. We became cool too and went out on a few licks together. All of them didn't pay off, but he knew I was bout it. I just didn't want Bro to find out. He told me, "No licks."

I started learning K-Town. It was a money-getting spot. But what stood out to me was how so many females were in the game. It seemed that a lot of niggas in K-Town was on some pimp shit for real. To me, a lot of dudes were acting like niggas out of Memphis. They were riding around sitting low on the passenger side of the car while their girl or babymama drove them. They didn't have no problem serving their babymama's work. I saw niggas sell their babymama's pack of whip up work that sweat away in the bag because it was water whip too much. Now their babymama took the loss! And the nigga didn't care. That happened to Tonya's sister.

She was in tears when we came over. She was on the phone with him going back and forth. I told her to flush that shit and broke her off. She started copping her work from me. It was so many females getting money. I couldn't believe it. Way different from Miami. We spoil our ladies and take care of our babymamas. I was brought up to believe you made sure your girl was straight. She was a reflection of you. I guess it was why so many out of town niggas was getting on in K-Town. You had niggas from the Chi, Detroit, New York, Memphis, Florida and we all had pulled K-Town females. That helped us get money. Another thing I noticed was that these Tennessee dudes were into white girls heavy.

But then I got up on what was really king in K-Town: Pills. All of them. Z to X pills. That was where the real money was at. Everybody was on some kind of pill. Tonya knew all about that game. She schooled me good. I was about to start seeing real money now. I never knew much about pills; cocaine rule in Miami. But we also was becoming the city for X pills. Tonya was already dealing pills on the side. I knew about it but never really felt a need to see what was up with it until I put a trip together to go to Miami. Me and Rob would take Tonya and her sister with us. Rob wanted to grab a whole one, and my money was up there. I was ready to do the same. The plan was for us to drive down together, grab the work, then let the girls ride back alone. Me and Rob would fly back. Rob had a girlfriend that worked for the airline, so we got some cheap one-way tickets from Miami back to K-Town. Hound found out about the trip. Rob opened his big mouth not knowing I was trying to keep it a secret from Bro. I didn't want him to know I was copping my own work from somewhere else. When he heard about the trip, he called me and asked me about it. I let him talk me into bringing some work back for him. I wasn't mad because now I would let him pay the girls for moving it for us. Even though Tonya would've done it for me anyway. I still want them to be paid. It was only fair considering the big chance they were taking.

When we got to Miami, Tonya started asking about X pills and what was the ticket on them. So I asked around and found a plug that would give them to me for $5 a pill. When I told Tonya she started smiling telling me they went for $20-$25 a pill up in K-Town. When I heard that, I changed my plans and decided to get half work half X pills. This move would be a game changer for me. Before we left Miami, I had to show Tonya and her sister the real Miami. I took them to USA Flea Market in the heart of the city to let them see where niggas out the hood shop for just about everything. I also had to pick up a few things for the hustle. They had these stores in the flea market that sold fake work, stash spots, that look like everyday household stuff; like water bottles that came apart so you could stash an ounce in the middle. They had candles with false bottoms, soda cans with removable top ... all kinds of stuff that I knew they wasn't up on yet in K-Town. And my pill plug was doing her thing in the flea market.

The girls enjoyed all the places that I took them, but they got a real kick out of the beach. We took a lot of pics. It was their first time visiting Miami but wouldn't be their last. When it was time to go, we followed them to the highway, told them to do the speed limit and be careful. I reminded Tonya to always remain calm and no smoking. And when they stopped for anything, stay cool, don't look like you doing nothing wrong. Because them troopers be looking for body language. She felt me and promised to be on point. Me and Rob had my brother Jay take us to the airport. We would beat the girls back. They had a 16-hour drive ahead of them. This trip would be the first of many. But not for all of us. After this trip, Rob would do his own thing. Me, Tonya, and her sister would remain a team. When Tonya put the word out that we had X pills, the phone never stopped ringing. They went so fast. I was mad I didn't get more. I was back on the road heading to the Flea Market. This time I was going to buy a "tank" (1,000 pills).

It was 2004. I was back in Miami grabbing me a tank of X pills and meeting up with my dog O.J. from Robbin Hood. O.J. had that work and he was fucking with me way back. I didn't grab much this time because I was really down here for the pills. But no need to pass up the blow when the homie was giving it to me for the low. I could tell something was upsetting O.J. For one, he was in all black. So, I asked him what it is? He explained that some niggas he was fronting some work to was going back and forth to North Carolina. But was sneaking down behind his back to re-up somebody else. And he wanted his money. He told me that he wished he knew I was out a long time ago. He would have fronted me the work instead. I was cool trying to stay off the radar and out the way. I didn't even let O.J. know where I was going. I lied to him and told him I was up in GA. It was always best to let less people know where you were hustling. When you playing in this drug trafficking game you never know when somebody might flip and start working for the Feds. I didn't know that then but this would be my last time seeing my dog O.J. alive. Later, I would hear about him being shot in the back of his head in his own house. I hated to hear that because I knew he was a father with a young son. It was just a reminder to me what kind of game I was playing in. I got my tank of pills and some blow then I was back up the road. K-Town was jumping. I was making a name in the streets, everybody knew me as "G" the Miami Boy.

The money was pouring in. I had more than enough to go back to the island and build my grandma a new house and start me a legal business. But just like so many other dope boys, I got caught up in the lifestyle and started buying things I didn't even need. Yeah, first was the clothes and jewelry, then the cars and guns. I was wasting money gambling. Fast as I could make it, I found new ways to spend it. And with all the new toys, cars with rims, jewelry came the hoes. They were sweating me hard, not only for the money but because I had the pills. That was the real reason so many hoes were hitting on me. I knew what they wanted and I played with it, but I always got my money. I may give a discount here and there, but I wasn't no trick. Money over bitches was for real my motto.

With the attention I was getting from the females, came envy and jealousy from the niggas. Bro was trying to warn me about being flashy, riding around with rims on all my cars, wearing so much jewelry. He wasn't worried about the attention I was getting from the streets, he was more concerned with the Feds getting on my line. See, Bro had been doing this way longer than me. He seen niggas go fast and play themselves right into the Feds or die. I was being hard headed thinking nobody wanted to see me shine. This was the first time in my life when I was getting easy money. It felt good, I felt like I was legit. You couldn't tell me I wasn't living the right way. I was still living with Tonya, but I was in and out. Some nights I stayed over with one of the many women I was sleeping with.

I didn't feel like I was cheating on Tonya, I never told her we were a couple. And I made sure all her bills were paid. I even paid her moma's bills a few times and took care of her kids, to me it was a hustling team. It was hard not to mess around with other women because about all my clientele were females. Like I said before in K-Town there were more females hustling than niggas. That's how my first conflict started with this GD nigga from Rockford, Illinois.

He was claiming the Chi, but I found out later on the sucker was from outside of Chicago. I was doing business with his old lady. She was grabbing an ounce from me. She always made little passes at me being flirtatious saying shit like, "Damn, what up, Trick Daddy, when you going to take me to Miami?" She wasn't bad looking, but I didn't like the fact she was coming on so strong. I just felt like shit wasn't right with her. I had already heard about what her boyfriend and his guys were doing around K-Town. They were known as the Chicago Boys and their game was to come down with a brick of blow, sell it, then turn around and rob the customer back for the work. They called themselves pulling rank on the GDs out of K-Town because they were from the Land ("Chicago"), but the whole time they weren't. So when they ran out of work or couldn't rob their work back they would send their girls out to grab work from niggas like me, or get them to set up niggas. Well, it was my time.

His girl came to grab a two-and-a-baby. I served her the work and she gave me the money. She pulled off and before I could walk back into the house, she was calling me back saying it was short. She claimed it was just 2 ounces and asked me where was the other half? First of all, everybody that I ever done business with me know that I'm always on point. And I take forever to count my money. So I already knew she was lying. So I told her straight up, "Baby, you got me fucked up. Everything was good when you left here."

I hung up.

We had already said too much on the phone already. She called me right back yelling and cursing me out so I told her to pull up! I waited in the same spot for her. I had my .40 Glock on me just in case. Something just didn't feel right about all this. I watched her car pull back around the block. She stopped right in front of me. I walked up to the passenger side window and said, "Where the work at?"

She pulled out a ziplock bag with what looked like just an ounce and said, "Right here." That's when I knew something wasn't right for real. So I stepped back from the car just in time to see the white van coming the same way she did, but was slow rolling. She pulled away from the sidewalk real fast. Something in my head told me to pull out my gun ... this was a drive-by.

I had my gun behind my back as the van pulled near, but instead of these coward ass niggas jumping out right there in front of me, they pulled down past my house and jumped out at the corner. I reacted at the same time. No cap. I was shooting at the van and the one nigga jumped out. All I could think of was a verse from B.G.'s *Heart of the Streets*: "You can never say you bust at me and I didn't bust back!" I let about 17 go at that van standing in the middle of the street in broad daylight.

All I could say was mom's prayers were being answered and God had his hand of protection on me that day. Because the nigga shooting at me was busting some kind of stick. There were bullets holes all around me that hit the house. I would find out later that bullets went into my neighbor's little boy's bedroom. I hurried back in the house and grabbed my extra clip then jumped into one of my cars. I wanted to get out of there before the police showed up. I knew they were on the way. There were too many shots fired. In my mind, it was on! Nothing else mattered to me now but getting at Little Mama and her nigga and whoever else was involved.

I called Bro and put him up on what happened. He wasn't happy to hear the news, but he did agree with me that I needed to bring all my cars around his house. My plan was to put up the cars and grab me a rental car. I knew how some suckers play. They loved to vandalize a nigga's property by shooting up his house and cars. I call them fake killer, bystander and property shooters. Just like the one that jumped out on me, if he was for real about it, he would've jumped out right in front of me instead of pulling down the street before he started shooting. But they picked the wrong one this time. I don't go out of my way to look for trouble, but I do the one who get there. In other words, I don't run from nobody. They had my full attention. The hustle came second now. Next, I called my dog M-30 Rob. He came through and we hooked up at Bro's house. We went and got a rental car like planned. And later on that night after the police had left we went back.

Me and Rob sat on the porch all night. I had the AR-15 out and my .40 Glock on me. Rob was strapped too. Them suckers didn't come through none that night. I put the word out on Little Mama asking anybody to let me know where she and dude lay their heads at? It didn't take long before I got the info I wanted. So many people wanted them to get fucked up because the word was the Chicago Boys was doing all kinds of fucked up shit. I did a few drive bys to see if I could catch them slipping, going or coming from the crib. But I never got lucky on that tip. But I did catch that van on the back road. So I took that opportunity to send a message of my own.

My girl was driving, so I leaned out the passenger window and came up on the top of the rental we were in. I had a .40 and my baby .9mm on me. I let them go. The niggas in the van were caught by surprise. They turned off the street and my girl went right behind them. We gave chase for about a half a block with me still shooting at the van. When both of my clips were empty, I told my girl to turn off. About an hour later, my phone rang.

It was some nigga named Tee-Bone. He was a GD. I asked him who gave him my number. He didn't answer my question. He just went on to say that he was the one driving the van today and he didn't have nothing to do with what happened at my house, and that a lot of the homies used the van. I stopped him and said that I didn't care. They needed to park that shit because far as I know they could use it again, and hung up. This little beef I had going on with this nigga was starting to cost me money. I bust one of the rental car side window when I was shooting at the van a shell from one of the bullets kicked back and cracked the window. I was spending unnecessarily money on renting cars, now I was paying to fix a window. This is what I was doing when the nigga Tee-Bone called me. After I hung up with him, my phone rang again. This time it was my Bro Hound. He told me that GD niggas had reached out to him to see if he could talk to me. It was the same nigga Tee-Bone. Bro said the nigga Tee-Bone claim that he and his guys weren't fucking with the nigga Cain. That was the name of the Lil Mama's boyfriend. I already knew who he was and what he looked like; light skin, bald head. Put you in the mind of a broke Suge Knight. I told Bro I would ease up on the van, but I got to have the nigga Cain on site.

Later on that night, the matter would solve itself. It seemed that the Knoxville GDs was into it with Cain and his crew. The word was that Cain had finessed some GDs from K-Town to go in on a brick of blow then took $25,000 and fled to Rockford with the bread. He had left a few of his homies to deal with the fall out. They ended up having a shootout at this spot called the Hall of Game, a spot on the eastside where niggas go to gamble. So the nigga I was after wasn't in town no more. I would hear about him some years later. He got fucked over by his homies in Rockford.

He was doing the same shady shit up there running off with dope and money until it caught up with him. They say niggas tied him up behind a car and dragged him. I went back to getting money. A lot of street niggas was coming up to me telling me that they were glad I ran that sucker out of town. They were giving me the credit for Cain and his homies leaving. This only made me cockier. I now kept my gun on me everywhere I went. But that didn't feel like that was enough. I felt alone in them streets. Bro didn't come out the house but once a day, to pick his kids up from day care after he made his rounds. Even though I could call Rob to have my back, he was making money moves on his own. So, on my next trip back to the crib it was time to see if any of my Veli homies was ready to come up the road with me.

Back in Miami, I needed some more pills. I always went to 60th, to Mackaveli to see if my dog was out yet and checked on his mom, Auntie Blanch. I always broke her off a few dollars when I came into town. But this time Bert was out. He had been home for a month. Damn, I was happy to see my dog. Bert was damn near 300 pounds now. Once I put him up on where I was hustling at, he was game. I didn't have to convince him. He wanted to get from down bottom. We got some work, I got some pills, and we were back on our way to K-Town.

Bert was trying to get back on his feet. Fred was in the pen on a gun charge, but he was waiting on the judge to overturn his case on appeal. In the meantime, I was going to help Bert out. He had two spots moving a little work for him in the city. They wasn't doing no real numbers. Up here with me going to get things moving for him, I was happy to have my dog with me. These niggas up here better stay out of my way now. They thought I was hell by myself, now they would understand what real Liberty City pressure is!

I put Bert up in my trap house. It was called the Blue House named after the paint color. It was a duplex I had my care keeper Cee Cee and old man Pop staying in on one side of it. They both got high. But they did anything I asked them to do, and on top of that they both brought me money. Cee Cee turns tricks on the side, and Pop workedcthe hood for whatever hustle he could find. Pop was real good at fixing things around the house. I often used him to do work at my place. Bert was cool with staying at the Blue House because it was always live there. Yeah, the spot was jumping 7 days a week, but on the weekend shit really got wild. Good part about the Blue House was it being on the end of the block. So, all the traffic from cars going and coming didn't really mess with the neighbors. I just made sure we kept the noise down, no loud music, or gun shots. So nobody ever put the cops on me there.

Things were back to normal. I was getting money around this time and I started seeing this woman. She became a big part of my life. But out of respect of her privacy, I'm not going to mention her name or go into details in her role in my life. But it's safe to say she changed my whole plan of what my priority was. My intention was to get my money up and go back to the island to build my grandma a house and fix my mama house in Miami. I'm not going to put all the blame on meeting this woman because I could've been left and took care of that. But after meeting her, catching feelings, I was stuck. Call it love, or whatever. I can admit it happened to me. When I told Bro about girl, he was the first to tell me I was a sucker for love. I stopped messing around with other women. Even cut Tonya off. I was a one-woman man. She had kids, so now I was playing step daddy too. It didn't matter to me because I only had my daughter and I loved kids anyway. For once in my life I was thinking about having a family. This was the best time of my life so far. Me and Bert was getting money together and we would go back and forth to Miami. Bert would stay some time to take care of his spot in Miami.

I would go Over Town and hook up with my homie Cheese and Hen. Cheese would lookout when he could. Me and Hen would go to the clubs or South Beach and kick it until it was time for me to get back on the road. Sometime I would bring ole girl and the kids, so they could see the city and do some shopping. Back in K-Town the pills had my name ringing, I had the best X pills around and niggas from other cities couldn't touch my pills. They were from all over: New York, Detroit, Chicago, Memphis, Atlanta – you name the city and if they were in K-Town with X pills they wasn't fucking with the pills coming from Miami. And I had them. My shit was so good them same niggas from other cities would get their personal pack of pills from me. So you already know where there is love, hate is not far away. It showed its face in this Crip nigga who just got out the joint that didn't know me. I was making my night rounds to all the after-hours spots in town. I stopped at this spot on the west side of town in Londale Projects, right next to the yellow house on the hill.

It was always love for me around here. This where my nigga M-30 and my ex Tonya was from. I was looking fly as hell. I was driving my El Camino black on black sitting on 22-inch rims. I had my little yorky Booker T with me. He was fresh with his Burberry dog jacket attached to its matching leash. When I walk into the club, it was packed. Some niggas and a few females was shooting pool. Other people were sitting around in the booths talking and the bar was full. So I made my way over to the bar, so I could ask the female bartender to sell me some of the flavor ready to roll blunts. A few of the females that knew me was coming up to play with Booker T and to buy pills from me. That's when this nigga I ain't never seen before tried me with an insult to my swag.

He said, "Who this nigga think he is coming in here looking like a fake ass Trick Daddy?"

I heard the nigga when he first said it, but I didn't pay it no mind. I kept on doing my business with the ladies. I wasn't strapped because I was in one of my cars with rims on it and the police loved to stop cars with rims. So I was trying to stay out of shit. But this nigga wasn't having it. He came close to me and said, "Nigga, what you got?"

I told him what I had and if he was copping, wait until I'm done with the ladies. He got mad and pushed past the girls, that's when I took off hitting him with a two-piece. He stumbled back so I kept swinging. Then he grabbed me in a bear hug pinning me up against the bar, I wasn't about to let him slam me. So I grabbed him around the neck and wrapped my legs around his legs. He couldn't do nothing, when I saw that he was giving out of breath I let go of his neck and hooked him with right and left hooks to the side of his head. The nigga start biting me on the chest. I screamed out in pain. He was tearing my skin off my chest. A couple of niggas came over and broke us up. I looked around to see where Booker T was. This girl was holding him in her arms. I hurried over and got him. I turned around and made my first mistake of the night. I told everybody they better not be up there when I get back. It's crazy how things could go left so fast. Here I was just chilling, doing my thing, minding my own business, when out the blue, here comes a hater. The reason why I was so mad was because the nigga bit me. I don't know what he had. He could be infected with some kind of disease. What kind of nigga go around biting niggas in a fight? Then I was mad with everybody in the club because they didn't stop it fast enough before the nigga bit me. That's why anybody still there when I got back could get it.

I drove home and grabbed my AR-15 and my .40 Glock. I parked the El Camino and got in my Durango. My mind was made up. I was going to shoot the whole club up. I didn't care who was in it. I wasn't thinking straight. I was out for blood. I drove by the club one time first to see if they heeded my threat. It looked like they did. There was less cars in the lot and the lights were off. I should have kept going, but I couldn't leave well enough alone. I had to make my point and leave a message that I was true to my word and I was nothing to play with. This mistake almost cost me my life.

I came back around and pulled right up in front of the club. I jumped out with the AR-15 blasting into the front door and windows of the club. All of a sudden, I could not feel my right arm and the AR was falling out of my grip. My arm was dangling loosely by my side. At first, I didn't know what had hit me. I thought the AR-15 had backfired. But then I kept hearing shots and I wasn't shooting anymore. When the second bullet hit me in the back, I knew exactly what was happening. I walked right into an ambush. They had been lying in wait for me. And I let them know I was coming back. I had to act fast because these country ass niggas weren't playing. They were trying to kill me.

So with my left hand, I grabbed my .40 out my waistband and shot back in the direction they were hiding in behind some parked cars. Then I jumped back into my Durango, leaving my AR-15 on the ground. I had no choice with only one arm. I had my .40 in that hand. I pulled off bleeding all over from my wounds. The white shirt I had on was turning dark red. I had to get help before I passed out from losing so much blood. First I had to get this gun off me. So I pulled over and threw it into some bushes. Then I pulled in to a gas station, fell out on the ground and yelled for help. People at the pump came over asking what happened.

I didn't answer. All I kept saying was, "Help me!"

Somebody out the crowd said, "Help is on the way."

That's when I heard sirens coming near. The police were there. EMT transported me to the hospital. They patched me up then the police came in with their questioning. You already know I had a lie to give them. I told them I got robbed and shot, but I got away. They took the report, but I could tell they knew I was lying. I didn't care. I live by the G-code. What happens in the streets, stays there: No Snitching! When the police left, I lay there thinking I got shot tonight. I could have been dead. Damn, shit is real and I'm playing these country niggas too close. What was I thinking telling them, *I will be back*. That was dumb on my part. And I should have been strapped from the jump. That's Veli rule in my hood. Well for now on, I stayed strapped. Fuck the police. I rather be caught with it then caught slipping by one of these country niggas! Then I started thinking about how it felt like hot rocks passing through my flesh. I didn't feel no pain. The pain came after I was in the hospital. This the shit I was thinking about when my brother Hound walked in. His girl Punkin was with him. They were the only real family I had up there. I checked myself out the hospital against doctor's advice. He wanted me to stay a few more days for checkups.

I was on my 2Pac shit. Five shots didn't stop him from checking out. I wasn't about to let 2 shots stop me. You couldn't tell me I wasn't a real thug. Mackaveli solja for real. But the next night I would be back at the hospital, because I became weak and faint. It was my protoplasm level had dropped real low in my loss of blood. They gave me a bottle of protoplasm pills and told me get some fast. But I was still being hardheaded, so I had my brother take me to the Blue House and I stayed there. I had my guns and CeCe and Pop would do whatever I asked. Me and my girl was at odds, so I didn't feel like being around her. This way I could heal up and still trap money. I worked my phone getting all the info on the nigga I got into it with. The Town was talking, and waiting to see how I would respond. This happened on one of the times Bert was not up here with me. But I called and let him know what went down. He was back in Miami, Fred was out now, and they were taking care of family issues.

I already knew how I was going to handle this beef, it was SOS. I wasn't going to put up no cars this time. I would keep hustling and making my rounds and if I see him, it is what it is. I didn't know who else was shooting at me that night. But what I did find out was the nigga name who I had the fight with. He was a Crip from the west side. His name was T.K. He had just come home from the pen. The nigga didn't have no money because he stayed getting locked up. From what I heard this was his M.O.: Fighting and doing dumb shit to look hard. All he cared about was gangbanging, not money. But it also got back to me that he wanted to make peace because he looked up to my brother and all his guys were Crips and so was my brother's people.

He gave my Ar-15 back to Bro as a peace offering. But I wasn't feeling the peace shit! I wanted to let him feel that lead like I did. It was too late for me since I got shot. I was on some 2Pac in *Juice* shit. You could call me Bishop because I had the juice. This was the most dangerous I had ever been in my life. Because I felt vulnerable without my gun. My nerves in my right arm were messed up, so it made my hand not work all the way; the little finger and the one next to it. So, when someone try me, there was no more thought of fighting, it was shoot first. This was my mind set going forward.

After the shooting, I got better and I took a quick trip to the island. Because word got back to my mom that I'd been shot, and she was hitting my phone up daily checking on me. I knew I had to go and let her see that I was okay. And besides, I needed a break to get my mind right. I grabbed a few stacks for pocket money and headed home.

I always loved going home to the island, spending time with my grandma. It was precious. I didn't know then, but this would be the last time I'd see my grandmother alive. I enjoyed the time with her. We sat and talked for hours. I stayed for a month and then I made my way back to K-Town.

Things were the same. Everybody was hustling, getting money. It took me about a week to let my clientele know I was back in business. I didn't have nothing to worry about. They were all loyal to me because the way I treated them. CeeCee and Pop held the Blue House down like I knew they would. I had other traps that I hustled out of too. Like my K-Town mom's spot. I call her that because she always treated me like a son. Her name was Miss Lisa. She had two daughters that were in the game. The young one had a thing for me. But I kept it as friends because I was in a relationship at the time. But that never stopped her from coming on to me. Miss Lisa's older brother was a kingpin in K-Town back in the day before the Feds got him. The word was he had a million dollars stashed away on one of his properties. His name is Goodie. They gave him life in the pen.

Well, his sister was my K-Town mom, and her place be booming on the weekend. That's the only time she let her white people come down and get high at her place. And they be spending a couple grand. She would split the sales up between me and her daughter. I always took care of her, even during the weekdays when nothing was moving at her place. Sometimes I came through to cook up over there when I didn't feel like being bothered with the Blue House. So, when Miss Lisa called me to help out one of her nieces that was getting evicted from her apartment, I came through to help. Besides, her niece copped work from me.

Her name is Chat. She was cool people with six kids and I think like four baby daddies. She was a young girl in her 20s. Yeah, she started early. Matter of fact, like a month before she hit me trying to pawn a flat screen TV to me for $500 to bond her boyfriend out of jail on a robbery case. I didn't take the TV, but I lent her the money on her face. She was good for it. I knew that because she spent about $500 a day with me on 8-balls and breaking them down. But this was different now, because her dude was out. I had just seen them in the club the night before. *And they were getting evicted.* I just couldn't understand this. She was doing better by herself with her kids when he was in jail. His name was Nook. He was a Blood and ran with a crew of local stick up boys. They were hitting licks almost every week. Robbing dope boys, home invasions, carjacking, you name it. Lil Nook and his boys was in on it.

When I first met Lil Nook, he came to the Blue House. His girl Chat came through with him, she wanted to buy some work and he supposedly wanted to thank me personally for helping bail him out of jail. But I got the feeling he was trying to get a feel for me and look my spot over. So after I served Chat, I told her to step out and let us men talk for a minute.

I could see the budge in Lil Nook's pocket to know he was strapped as I was. He was sitting on my couch with this smile on his face like he was looking at his next lick. So I jumped right in front of him and stood right over him. I had my gun out but not pointed at him. I told him straight up, "Lil Bro, I'm not the one to fuck with. I'm a good nigga to the people I'm down with. But my enemies fear me for a reason. I don't care that you a robber because I'm one too. I just choose to hustle now because the money good here. But don't get it twisted, I stay strapped and I'm bout that life for real."

He was looking crazy now. I guess no nigga ever rushed him like that, or he could really see in my eyes I wasn't playing. Whatever it was we had an understanding for now. Fast forward, I would see Lil Nook out and we would speak and keep it moving. He and his girl would be in the club, chilling. They bought pills from me. So I was surprised to hear they were being evicted. The reason Miss Lisa called me to help was because everybody knew I had a truck. It was an 87 model, clean and in good condition. I used it for my lawn service business. I was trying to do things smart by cleaning up my dope money through the lawn service. And I could move around town better in the work truck without the police on me. So the truck was why I was asked to help Chat.

When I got around to Chat's apartment, they weren't just being evicted: All of their stuff was outside in big heaps and it was drizzling. I felt sorry for her and her kids standing out there. Shit was embarrassing and there he was, Mr. Jack Boy himself – Lil Nook – standing inside the doorway out the rain. I couldn't do nothing but shake my head at him thinking *what kind of hustler let his family get evicted?* He had this wife beater on with some Dickies shorts and I could see his gun hanging out his pocket. I was in my Durango truck and I had Pop driving the F-150 truck. I had my jewelry on, chain and big boy bracelet with my rings on. I had a few stacks in my pocket. They caught me the next morning after hustling pills in the club. I always got fresh when I did my rounds in the club. It was part of the deal. The people expect their pill man to be fly. At least that was the excuse I gave myself for doing it. So I knew I was a walking lick to a jack boy in need. But that came with the game and I stayed ready. I had my baby .9mm. It was a Cobra model. I had on a black tee with Army fatigue vest, black Dickies pants, and Timberlands. My gun was inside my vest pocket, you couldn't tell if I was strapped or not and it made it easier for me to grab it when I wanted to. Since Lil Nook wasn't taking charge like a man should do when his family was in a crisis, I did.

I started by instructing Pop to help me load up the TVs and all the electrical products on the truck. Then we put the kids' mattresses on next. I wasn't too concerned with Chat and her man's mattress getting wet. Once we had the truck loaded up for what would be the first run to the storage. Without Lil Nook's help, I can't lie, it did bother me that he stood by as we worked to help them move. But I didn't say nothing because I felt bad for the kids. I let him and Chat ride with me in the Durango. I made him sit up front with me so I could keep my eyes on him. He wasn't talking a lot like usual when I was around. Me being a robber myself, I could sense when you trying to work up your nerve to pull a lick. And he had that look. So I was just playing it how he wanted it to go waiting for him to make a move.

We dropped the first load off at the storage, but it didn't go smooth. Me and Lil Nook started having words because I had enough of his I'm-too-cool-to-help act. The kids weren't with us so there wasn't nothing holding me back from checking him. I asked him what made him think it was cool for me and Pop to help and he didn't, when we were doing his family a favor?

This fool had the balls to say we "weren't doing shit for him."

I couldn't believe what I was hearing so I made him say it again, but he added that I was doing it for his girl. It's like he thought I was fucking his girl on the side. I laughed but I was getting mad. For one, she didn't even try and step in when he said that, and then who the fuck this young nigga thinks he talking to? I had to take a deep breath and remind myself it wasn't worth the problem. So I just looked at Chat and shook my head thinking why would I want to fuck you? I told them that I was dropping them off and they could find somebody else to help them with the rest of their stuff. I had other business to take care of and needed my truck. When I got back in the truck I moved my vest over so the pocket was open near my hand. Chat was still in the back and Lil Nook was in the passenger seat. He was still running his mouth about how fucked up it was that I wasn't going to finish moving their stuff. I wasn't feeding in to him with answering, so he started fucking with my CD player. I told him to leave it alone, but he wouldn't. So when I pulled up at a stop light I told him to get out. We were in front of his hood Walter P. Projects. He told me, "No." That I had him fucked up. So I pulled off when the light turned green. I didn't even respond, something in me had already clicked. I had had enough of this nigga's disrespect. So I sped up like I was trying to hurry up and get us back, and he said something else.

I slammed on the brakes sending him into the dashboard and Chat into the backseat. When he straightened his body I had my gun pointed right at his face. His eyes became big as hell. Then he fucked up by going for his gun. I shot him twice in the pelvis near his reaching hand. Then I snatched his gun from his waist. Chat jumped out the backseat and swung open my passenger door. She jumped between me and Lil Nook begging for me not to shoot him again. She didn't know I was about to shoot her and him, but by the door being open in broad daylight reality brought me back from kill mode. People were all around on MLK and Chestnut in the parking lot at Holiday Market. They had all witnessed the shooting. I wasn't trying to drop two bodies right in front of everybody. I told Chat to get him out my shit.

She grabbed his little ass up like one of her kids and I reached over and closed my door. I hurried and drove off. The last thing I wanted was to be pulled over with two guns in my possession. I knew somebody had called the police and I was driving a red truck that was easy to spot. I jumped on the expressway and put some distance between me and them.

My phone was ringing nonstop. Word traveled fast in the hood. I answered one call from this girl that I was cool with just to see what she had heard. The first thing out her mouth was, "G, you shot Lil Nook?"

I denied it.

She said, "Stop lying! Everybody talking about it." She told me that the whole hood was saying that it was good that somebody got him because he was robbing people left and right. I didn't care about all that, I was worried about what they had told the cops.

I parked the Durango and went to take a shower. I could hear my phone going off. I kept replaying the shooting in my mind trying to remember was Nook's eyes still open after I shot him? But I could only see Chat holding him like a baby. I had to find out how he was doing so I could know my next move. If he was dead, then I was getting out of town for real. I got dressed then checked my phone. A long list of numbers was in my log. I knew some was money calls, but most of them were people being nosey trying to find out why I shot Lil Nook. I called my brother back. He would know if dude died or not? Word traveled fast in this little ass town.

The first thing he did was ask me what happened? I explained it to him. He still found a way to make me be in the wrong, telling me I shouldn't have been so friendly: What the fuck I'm doing helping that nigga move for? He couldn't see I wasn't doing it for the nigga, it was for Miss Lisa and them kids. Nevertheless, all I wanted to know was if the nigga was dead or not? Bro told me to come over to his house because the police was definitely looking for me. He heard that everybody up there at the corner where it happened stayed and made statements on me. So, now, a warrant was out for me for the shooting.

This was a real turning point in my time in Knoxville. They were still trying to investigate what happened the night I had been shot. Some detective came to visit me at my house and when I didn't give them what they wanted they let me know I didn't get robbed and that they knew I was in a shootout at that nightclub. They also knew about the fight I had with KT. If I think about it all honestly, I had brought all this heat onto myself. My days as a free man were numbered. All this gunplay had my name ringing in the streets and it wasn't for business. But I couldn't see it then. I was caught up.

I started popping X pills and drinking. I don't know what made me take a pill. I guess it was the mounting pressure. But the pills only made me more reckless on how I was moving. The night they took me in on the shooting case, I was rolling off a 3 stack X pill. I should've known something was wrong by the way the bouncer was acting at the door when I came in. He usually kicked it with me on some joke time. But not tonight. He had a surprised look on his face. I was too high to catch it, so I went on in. Not even ten minutes went by before the police rushed in the club to get me. I was slipping big time. I had a pack of X pills on me and a gun outside in my car.

It's something about being arrested that sobers you right up. I was sweating and nervous as hell. Some reason when the cop patted me down, he didn't feel the pills on me. But I still had to get them off me. I knew better than to stick them in the backseat. When they found them there they still give you the charge. They took me back to the police station, and put me in a room for questioning. A white detective came in to ask me what happened in the shooting of Lil Nook. I knew this would be my only chance to get the pill off me.

So, before I let him know I didn't have nothing to say. While he was playing nice cop, I asked him to let me go to the bathroom. He took me down the hall to the restroom and as soon as I was out of his sight and in the stall, I flushed the pills down the toilet. Back in the interrogation room, I asked for my lawyer to be present. He didn't like that move so he let me know that he didn't need me to talk because he had statements from Chat and Lil Nook. So I was charged with Aggravated Assault with a firearm. They took me to the County Jail. I made a $5,000 bond and was out the next day. Even then I couldn't see the rope tightening around my neck. Now I had known enemies, one on the east side and the other on the west side of town. One was a Blood and the other was Crip. It didn't matter to me; they both could get it.

I kept my .40 Glock on me at all times. You would think that I would have slowed down and stayed out the streets. But not me. It's like I was looking for someone to kill. Being shot and now taking pills to deal with it all, I was always paranoid with my gun close by. I wasn't just worried about my enemies; I knew the police was out to arrest me again. I couldn't leave town because I was on bail. I kept hustling, fighting the case was adding up. I hired a lawyer to represent me, that was $8,000. Not to count the $5,000 I spent to bond out. It was all a waste for trying to help somebody out! Me and my girl at the time was always arguing over everything from me going out to my drinking and taking pills. I hate to admit it but in most cases she was right.

It was during one of these arguments after about a month of me being out on bond for shooting Lil Nook. I had been out all night in the club hustling pills and I got in around 6 in the morning. I laid down on the couch in the den, when I woke my girl was vacuuming the floor and opening blinds sending the sunlight right into my face. I could tell something had her mad. And I knew it had something to do with me staying out all night. But I wasn't in the mood for it. So I got up. I needed to smoke a joint to chill me out and relax my mind. Lately I've been dealing with a lot. With this case over my head and still at war with these two niggas out here in the streets, to come home and fight with my girl was the last thing I wanted to be doing. Today was shaping up to be not so good.

When I went to my weed box, it was empty. So I made a call to my weed man. I put in an order for 1 ounce. I had to go meet him on the east side. He wanted me to come to Chestnut Park. I was in my F-150 pickup truck. I got the weed, and since I was in no rush to get back home I stopped by the Blue House. It was a Sunday afternoon and things were jumping already. I looked down at my phone and I could see the missed calls now from CeeCee and Pops. Damn I had my phone on silent. Lucky I always kept some work on me, so I jumped out and took care of a few cars of smokers that Pop had parked out front of the Blue House.

Pop was glad to see me and so was CeeCee. They both needed a wake up hit from me. Pop let me know that he was out of dog food for my two red nose pit bulls Remi and Red. I loved those dogs. I had raised them from puppies. Remi was my girl and Red was the boy. I went back outside to smoke a blunt. Being in the yard with my dogs always relaxed me and gave me a peace of mind. I guess it was because I could feel real love and loyalty coming from them. I filled their water buckets then jumped back in my truck. They needed some ice for the water and some dry dog food. I was thinking about adding some red meat but I would ask CeeCee to cook it for them later.

I sat in my truck and rolled another blunt. For some reason, I wasn't feeling right. I couldn't put my finger on it, but it kind of felt like I was in a dream and none of this was real. I shook it off thinking to myself, *Damn this some fire ass weed, it got me tripping for real*. I was considering hitting buddy back to cop another ounce … only if I knew it was my gut feeling trying to warn me of what lied in front of me. Like so many street niggas, I had ignored that warning feeling before the big fall.

I didn't have to drive far for what I needed. My Muslim brother, Kalem, was an Arab from overseas. He had a spot called the spot, a Quick Mart located in a strip mall down the street from the Blue House. The brother owned the whole strip mall. He had a store and a sub shop in it. The good part about his location was it being right off the interstate on Cherry Street. A lot of the young niggas that hustled up there got their work from me. But on a Sunday morning and afternoon, all the dope boys were still sleeping off the clubbing from Saturday night. So when I pulled up there, I got bum rushed by smokers wanting to buy work.

Normally I didn't get down out in the open like this because it be hot as hell up here. I leave all the rock sales for the young niggas, but for some reason I decided to go against my better judgment and made some sells. That's when I went into the store and grabbed the dog food. I had just paid for my order when the police car pulled up into the parking lot. I knew that I had fucked up. I was thinking one of them smokers had to be an undercover. The officers that pulled up knew me from the club, the night I got arrested for shooting Lil Nook. He called me by my real name so I turned and answered him. He started asking me about my red Durango. He wanted to know when was the last time I drove it? These questions had me confused because I thought he was up there about me dealing drugs. I told him I haven't drove the Durango in months and that it was my wife's car.

As I was answering him, I kept walking towards my truck. He yelled for me to stop walking. That's when I got nervous and took off running. He came after me yelling for me to stop.

He could forget about that! I wasn't going back to jail. I had a gun and some more drugs in my truck. Later when I learned the law, I had no reason to run. My Fourth Amendment right protects me from illegal search and seizure. But being a street nigga, what I knew about the law was the police could do whatever the hell they wanted. So I got out of there quick, fast, and in a hurry. He wasn't about to catch me. I had always been fast. Even in high school, my PE coach wanted me to run track. Once I shook the police, I circled back around and made it to the Blue House. All I could I hear were sirens from police cars riding around the hood trying to find me. I wasn't about to come back outside until I knew they were long gone.

I called my girl letting her know what happened. She was pissed as usual at me. It seemed lately I couldn't do nothing right. I don't know why, but my world was becoming a nightmare. I didn't know that, but it was about to get even worse. This was the beginning of the end. As I was on the phone with my girl, she was driving by the Quick Mart where they were towing my truck. That meant they found the gun and drugs. Damn, now I had a new case hanging over my head. I was wondering how much this was going to cost me? It's true what they say: When it rains, it pours. My girl was telling me that there were a lot of police action going on when she passed by. I already knew I had to call my bond man to see what he could do. I knew he didn't want me to run. So I hung up with my girl and made the call. As soon as he answered I got right into it.

"How much is a bond on a gun and dope case?"

He let me know that he would have to wait and see what type of charges they hit me with. But made sure he told me to sit tight. He was going to get right on top of it, and don't worry he would cut me some slack on the bond. That made me feel a little better for the time being. But deep down inside I could feel the walls closing in on me. I knew the feeling. I had had it so many times in my past. When you grow up going in and out of jail as I have you know the pressure of being on the run from the police. It's like somebody throws a bucket of cold water in your face. And all you could think of was how you got yourself in this mess? And why you let this happen? You're questioning God, and yourself: Why? Why? Why? Then, you stop and try to look back over everything you see. All the missed warning signs from God, family, and loved ones. That's when you feel stupid and lost at the same time.

I was going through all these emotions when she walked in. I guess she could tell I needed some love and comfort because instead of coming in and arguing like normal, she hugged me and we laid down. I had to fight back tears. I truly loved this woman and now I may lose her because the dumb decisions I made out in these streets. After lying in silence after a while, we got up and started talking about what happened. I told her why I was up there at the Quick Mart in the first place, and how all the smokers bum rushed me for work. Then, the police showing up as I was about to leave. She told me what I already knew. That I should have never left the house and what the hell I was thinking about dealing rocks to smokers in the first place, I let her say her piece, then I changed the subject to what I needed to do to get out this mess.

I told her I was waiting for the bondsman to call me back. He was going to tell me what I was being charged with and how much my bond will be. After that I was going to call my lawyer and try to work out a payment plan because I knew he was going to try to tax me for this new case. I wasn't even done paying him for the shooting case. Damn, this shit was putting me in the hole for real. I had to stay free just to pay my bills. I got the call I'd been waiting on and it was all bad news.

They had charged me with the gun and dope. I knew that much already, but when he said he had to move fast, and I had to turn myself in because his people down at the police department told him the .10mm was stolen from Georgia. Since the gun had been carried across state lines the case was being referred to the Feds. So, if I wanted to make bond and have time out to get my money right, I better walk myself in and get booked so he could place my bail. Shit just got real with that one phone call. I looked over at my girl and didn't know if I wanted to tell her everything.

As soon as I hung up she was all up on me, asking what did the bondsman say? I was never good at lying or keeping anything from her. So I told her what he had said. That I needed to hurry up and turn myself in because they was walking my case over to the Feds. The look she gave me was hurt and disappointment all in one. She knew more about niggas catching fed time than me. After all this was her town. And she seen so many of her homeboys go Fed. We used to talk about that from time to time. But foolish me never thought it could happen to me.

I don't know why I felt like that. Everybody but me knew it was a fed charge riding around every day with a gun and crack. I even heard people in town calling the east side the Feds Gun Zone. But I never thought nothing of it. I thought about running. Going back to the island and live there until the statute of limitations ran out on these charges. But I didn't really know how that worked. I only heard about that before.

And besides, what would I do on the island? It's hard over there without money. It was ok to visit, but to live was a whole other thing. I knew niggas that was over there doing just that. And they were stuck forever, couldn't leave and their paperwork was fucked up by now. I didn't want to live like that. But I didn't want to go to federal prison either. I needed time to think, just as that came to mind my phone rang.

It was the bondsman again. He must've felt me thinking about running? He was asking me when I wanted to turn myself in because he would go with me and that would speed up the process. I made up my mind and decided that I would do it the next morning. I just needed another night with my girl. We went home an hour later. I took a bath instead of my usual shower. As I sat in the tub, I reflected on the past few months. With my mind being clear, I was able to see how things was steadily spiraling downward: Street hustling – police- jail – prison ... So much had happened within a small period of time. I was having real bad night sweats where the whole side of the bed would be soaked and wet with sweat.

I remember some of my dreams. They seemed like nightmares. I would be in some kind of jail with glass windows everywhere and I had on this old prison jumper with black and white stripes. I always seen that part of the dream as clear as day. Like I was really there. I got out the tub, and went into the room. My girl was still dressed lying across the bed looking at TV or was the TV watching her? She looked as if her mind was somewhere else. I wanted to have sex to help take my mind off everything I had to face starting the next day, but it didn't seem like she was in the mood. You would think she was the one going to jail not me! I rolled a blunt and jumped on the bed next to her. We talked about moving out of town once this was all over. We talked about everything that happened leading up to this. And both of us agreed that it was time to find new ways to hustle. The dope game was playing out.

Somewhere in between talking and smoking we ended up making love. After that we both fell asleep. It was morning before I knew it. Shit, it was almost noon. I checked my phone and there was 25 missed calls and half of them was from the bondsman. I woke my girl up and we showered together and made love in the free flowing water. I threw on a Dickie set and some Timbs. After my girl got dressed I called the bondsman. We set the time for 1:00 PM and met at the Penal Farm Jail on the east side not far from where I lived. I can't lie, I was nervous as hell. Never in my life had I ever turned myself in to jail. It felt strange. I kept telling myself I would be back out in a few hours. They would just book me in and I would make bail. He charged me $6000 for the bail. I wasn't even trying to think about the money right now.

I already had plans on selling one of the cars and grabbing a half a block. Then it was all about the grind. No more fucking off. I just needed to get this part over with. The part that was really messing with me was that the police officer that I ran on insisted on being there when I turn myself in. The bondsman had told me that part. And I just didn't understand why. He wanted to be the one to handcuff me. Damn, that seemed kind of personal to me. But I would have to let him get that off so I could get on with making bond. But I should have known something was up with that. Once I was in custody and locked in jail, that's when they played their trick card.

After spending the whole night in jail waiting to make bail, they moved me to the main County Jail a guy that came after me made bond. I didn't. I started having doubts as to me being able to get out like I had planned. I couldn't understand. I kept running everything over. The money was there. My bondsman was with us. What could be holding me up? I needed to make my phone call. I wanted to talk with my girl. They wouldn't let me make a call until the next morning when my wing was scheduled to come out for an hour since I was on 23/1 (23 hours locked in, 1 hour out) with no TV, no nothing.

There were 8 of us on the wing in two main cells. Every time I heard the guards' key rattled down the hall I thought they were coming to get me. That night was one of the worst nights of my life. I didn't sleep a bit, not knowing was like torture to me. When the morning finally got there I couldn't wait until they popped my cell. I rushed to only the phone we had to use. My girl answered on the first ring, she was waiting on my call. She had been up all night herself. I knew something was terribly wrong by her voice, she was crying as she was telling me the bad news. I had to make her calm down, so I could understand what she was telling me. So this is what happened. That dirty ass police officer that I ran on had put a fake violation of probation warrant on me, so it could stop my bail, and it did just that. He was trying to buy time for the Feds to pick up my case. My girl said the bondsman was nice enough not to just take our money knowing it wouldn't do me no good. So now I'm going to have to sit until I go to court. Than we could straight out the lie this sucker ass cop put on me. They had me scheduled for a bond hearing that morning. But my girl said don't look for nothing to happen then. We have to see how far they set my next date, but it would be better to have my lawyer present at the hearing. So, she was going to call him as soon as his office opened at 8:00 AM. My time was up on the phone. The next time we talked was at my bond hearing. That's where the bombshell was dropped on me. My lawyer tried to explain to the judge that I wasn't on probation, but it didn't matter no more because the Feds had already put a hold on me. Meaning no matter what we did, I wasn't making bail or even getting out no other way. I was stuck like Chuck! My girl was in tears when she heard the judge say detain him into custody under Federal hold. I looked back at my girl, and even though she was crying to me she looked so beautiful. I guess because I never had nobody cry for me before in the courtroom. I didn't cry even though I wanted to. I wasn't going to let these white men see me break. And I had to be strong for my girl. But deep down I was feeling that Federal pressure. I never forgot that day, it was 6/6/06: The mark of the Beast – I went Fed! I was under a new kind of pressure!!

Federal Pressure! This was different from all the pressure I had ever been through! "How would I handle it?" The little money I had left couldn't help me beat the Feds. Money doesn't matter when the Feds want you. "What kind of time was I facing?" "Where will they send me?" This wasn't state, I could end up anywhere and I might never see my family again. [They weren't coming this far to visit me, how then would they visit when I am away.] "What about my girl? Would she ride with me if they gave me a lot of time?" Damn I let my daughter down again. How was I going to get out of this?! God help me!! The Feds got me!!!

*Federal Pressure* ....

**To be continued...**